PARTY RENEWAL IN AMERICA

AMERICAN POLITICAL PARTIES AND ELECTIONS

General Editor, Gerald M. Pomper

Copublished with the
Eagleton Institute of Politics,
Rutgers University

PARTY RENEWAL IN AMERICA

THEORY AND PRACTICE

Edited by

Gerald M. Pomper

PRAEGER

PRAEGER SPECIAL STUDIES • PRAEGER SCIENTIFIC

Library of Congress Cataloging in Publication Data

Main entry under title:

Party renewal in America.

    (American political parties and elections)
    Includes bibliographical references.
    1. Political parties--United States--Addresses,
essays, lectures. I. Pomper, Gerald M. II Series.
JK2261. P315   329'. 02   79-25184
ISBN 0-03-052991-3

Published in 1980 by Praeger Publishers
CBS Educational and Professional Publishing
A Division of CBS, Inc.
521 Fifth Avenue, New York, New York 10017 U.S.A.

© 1980 by Praeger Publishers

0123456789 145 987654321

Printed in the United States of America

To the party workers,
  the unsung and unnamed men
and women who do the work
of democracy.

PREFACE

*T*his volume is based on wishes and thoughts. The authors share the wish for a stronger political party system in the United States. We see parties as the best available means by which citizens can make democracy work. Parties, we believe, can organize choices for the electorate, frame issues for public discussion, and impose responsibility on government officials. While recognizing that parties—like all human institutions—fall short of the ideal, we still find them the most proven mechanisms for realizing the goals of a popular, representative form of government. One of our purposes in this book is to present the case for political parties to a broader public. The chapters by Pomper, Robinson, Crotty, and McWilliams deal with these arguments.

The thoughts in our work are based on some small indications that political parties are receiving new attention and new respect in the United States. For a long time, parties have been in decline, damaged by intended "reforms" that often worsened the political system, challenged by competition from advertisers and the mass media, and deserted by many erstwhile loyalists. Perhaps the wish is father to the thought, but we do see some signs of party renewal. The national Democratic and Republican organizations have undergone considerable modernization, although the forms of their change have been quite different. Longley, Casey, and Bibby elaborate these developments. In the states, where parties are based, there are other indications of party strength. Lawson, Marshall, and Mileur provide analysis of the movements in three important areas—California, Minnesota, and Massachusetts. Cronin then views the changing party system from the perspective of the presidency. In a final postscript, Burns summarizes the emerging trends toward the renewal of U.S. parties—and, with them, of U.S. democracy.

Our ultimate commitment is to truthful analysis, and, therefore, we cannot claim that the trend is clearly toward strengthened political parties. The analyses that follow recognize the dominant antiparty attitudes of Americans and their organizational weaknesses. Ultimately, we probably are left with our wishes and with our personal efforts to reconstruct the U.S. party system. These individual commitments, however, are only individual. There is no single ideology expressed in this volume, and the policy recommendations made in the various chapters do not necessarily express the opinion of the other authors.

Collectively, we do owe thanks to a number of individuals: the staff of the Center on Political Parties at the Eagleton Institute of Politics, Rutgers University; our individual typists, and particularly Cindy Schultz and Mary Wilk; and our editor at Praeger, Betsy Brown. The friends, spouses, lovers, and children who have helped us individually surely know we appreciate their support, even if we cannot list all of them.

CONTENTS

Page

PREFACE   vii

LIST OF TABLES   xii

Chapter

1   THE CONTRIBUTION OF POLITICAL PARTIES TO
     AMERICAN DEMOCRACY
     Gerald M. Pomper   1

     Notes   16

2   THE PLACE OF PARTY IN DEMOCRATIC IDEAS
     Donald A. Robinson   18

     Defining Characteristics of Democracy   20
     Homo Civicus and Apathy   21
     Applicability of Democratic Norms   23
     Place of Parties in Democratic Life   25
     Conclusion   27
     Notes   28

3   THE PHILOSOPHIES OF PARTY REFORM
     William J. Crotty   31

     Role of Theory in Reform   31
     The Nihilists (or "No-Party" Advocates)   32
     The Idealists   34
     Theoretical Issues in the Controversy over Political Parties 38
     Reform Movement of the 1970s   40
     Contribution of Reform to Party Theory   45
     Notes   48

4   PARTIES AS CIVIC ASSOCIATIONS
     Wilson Carey McWilliams   51

     Private Lives and Public Virtues   52

ix

The Parties in American Thought   55
Party Renewal and Civic Renewal   61
Notes   65

5   NATIONAL PARTY RENEWAL
Charles H. Longley   69

National Party Reform Commissions   71
National Party Law   73
National Party Elites   76
National Party Operations   79
The Theory of National Party Redefinition   82
Postscript   84
Notes   85

6   THE NATIONAL DEMOCRATIC PARTY
Carol F. Casey   87

Impetus for Reform   87
Delegate Selection Standards   89
Assessment of Delegate Selection Rules   99
Notes   100

7   PARTY RENEWAL IN THE NATIONAL REPUBLICAN
PARTY
John F. Bibby   102

Procedural Reform within the GOP   103
An Alternative Strategy of Party Revitalization:
    Programmatic Reform   107
Republican National Committee's Financial Resource Base   113
Conclusion   113
Notes   114

8   CALIFORNIA: THE UNCERTAINTIES OF REFORM
Kay Lawson   116

Progressive Reforms   117
Rebirth of Reform   122
Conclusion   134
Notes   136

9   MINNESOTA: THE PARTY CAUCUS–CONVENTION
SYSTEM
Thomas R. Marshall   139

Party Reform in Minnesota   140
Policy Making   142

Recruitment and Participation 146
Other Party Reforms 149
Sources of Support for Party Renewal 152
Practical Limits of Party Renewal 154
Notes 157

10   MASSACHUSETTS: THE DEMOCRATIC PARTY
     CHARTER MOVEMENT
     Jerome M. Mileur 159

Origins of the Charter Movement 159
The Draft Charter 163
The Politics of Passage 168
Conclusion 171
Addendum 173
Notes 174

11   THE PRESIDENCY AND THE PARTIES
     Thomas E. Cronin 176

Presidents as Party Leader? 177
Limits on Presidential Party Leadership 180
Presidents and Use of Party Appeal in Congress 183
Proposals to Increase Cohesion between President and
   Party 186
Prospects 189
Notes 192

12   PARTY RENEWAL: THE NEED FOR INTELLECTUAL
     LEADERSHIP
     James MacGregor Burns 194

INDEX 201

ABOUT THE EDITOR AND CONTRIBUTORS 205

LIST OF TABLES

Table   Page

5.1   Selected Demographic Characteristics of National
       Committee Members   77
9.1   Policy Discussion at Minnesota Precinct Caucus Meetings,
       1972 and 1974   143
9.2   Attendance at Minnesota Party Caucuses in Recent Years   147

PARTY RENEWAL IN AMERICA

1

THE CONTRIBUTION OF POLITICAL PARTIES TO AMERICAN DEMOCRACY

Gerald M. Pomper

*A*mericans do not like political parties.

This basic attitude can be traced in the intellectual history of the nation, in legislation, and in current public opinion and alleged "reforms." To the authors of this volume, who see political parties as vital agents in a functioning U.S. democracy, the depth of the antiparty sentiment is a challenge and a frustration.

We find antiparty attitudes expressed even in the most unlikely places. Annually, to celebrate Washington's birthday, the Senate of the United States engages in the ritual of hearing a reading of the first president's farewell address. This body of 100 politicians, every one elected as a partisan Democrat or Republican, attend a denunciation of parties as agents that "render alien to each other those who ought to be bound together by fraternal affection" and which "make the public administration the mirror of the ill-concerted and incongruous projects of faction, rather than the organ of consistent and wholesome plans digested by common councils, and modified by mutual interests."[1]

Although Washington's farewell warning was particularly directed against the rising challenge of the new Republican Party, that group's leaders shared many of his beliefs. James Madison had written similar sentiments in *The Federalist*, the basic exposition and defense of the Constitution. The central problem Madison addressed was "that our governments are too unstable, that the public good is disregarded in the conflicts of rival parties, and that measures are too often decided, not according to the rules of justice and the rights of the minor party, but by the superior force of an interested and overbearing majority." The virtue of the Constitution, he argued, was its ability "to break and control the violence of faction," that is, of groups and parties, "whether amounting to a majority or minority of the whole, who are united and actuated by some common impulse of passion, or of interest, adverse to the rights of other citizens, or to the permanent and aggregate interests of the community."[2]

Like many political theorists and politicians, Madison found it necessary to modify his principles when confronted with the realities of government. Unhappy with the administration of the government under Washington and Alexander Hamilton, he organized a national coalition, which brought Thomas Jefferson to the presidency. Yet Jefferson, too, although owing his triumph to party politics, would not accept its desirability. He sought not the continuance of partisanship but its dissolution. "We have called by different names brethren of the same principle. We are all Republicans; we are all Federalists," he urged in his first inaugural address.[3] In thus minimizing the differences of the past decade, he was being conciliatory toward his opponents, but he also hoped to eliminate them peacefully. Shortly after taking office, he clarified his meaning: "Nothing shall be spared on my part to obliterate the traces of party and consolidate the nation, if it can be done without abandonment of principle."[4]

After Jefferson, others also did their part "to obliterate the traces of party." Attempts to deal with U.S. parties through legislation and extralegal enactments have occurred in three major periods in U.S. history.[5] They are alike in basic characteristics. Each period has witnessed an attempt by would-be reformers to weaken the power of party officials, to reduce the hierarchical components of party organization, and to increase at least nominal participation within the parties. Most fundamentally, in each period, the philosophical basis of these reforms has been the replacement of organized political coalitions by the direct, unmediated intervention of the individual citizen.

These tendencies could only be partially seen in the first period of reform, 1820–40, when national nominating conventions and national mass parties replaced the congressional caucus. These changes broadened the nomination of the president beyond the capital and enabled state and local politicians and some party members to participate. Creating a national party structure and platform transformed the parties from elite cadres to elite organizers of an expanding electorate. Democracy was surely served, but at some cost to the cohesion and national perspective provided by the congressional caucus. With the new system, moreover, "whatever chances the nation might have had to develop a form of parliamentary or cabinet government were gone forever."[6] Parties lost some of their capability to build a ladder of advancement from Congress to the presidency. Instead, from Andrew Jackson to Jimmy Carter, the White House became more accessible to those antagonistic to the parties' legislative delegations.

It is not until the twentieth century, however, that the fullest attack on institutionalized political parties becomes evident. The second great period of party change came in the Progressive movement at the beginning of this century; the final era is our own, beginning in the mid-1960s. In these latter two periods, the challenge to parties has been open, obvious, and successful in most respects. Legislators, activists, and impersonal social forces have combined to weaken, circumvent, restrain, and degrade the formal party organizations.

Without disputing the desirability of any particular change, the total result can be seen as bringing us close to the full dissolution of the parties as effective political contestants. Let us briefly note some of the major results of these antiparty actions. Local and state nominations are now decided by direct primaries open to almost all voters, regardless of past loyalty, rather than negotiated within the parties. Presidential nominations are effectively determined in a series of state primaries and in the mass media and are only formally ratified in national conventions. Political financing is provided by the government or private interest groups directly to candidates, while party treasuries are empty. The very structure of the ballot encourages voting for persons of different parties, and elections are scheduled to reduce the likelihood of party trends across national, state, and local levels. Municipal officials are largely chosen on a nonpartisan basis, with parties prevented from using these positions as sources of training and future recruitment to higher offices. Most government workers are selected on the basis of anonymous examinations and then barred from political activity, while even the highest administrators are increasingly recruited from within the bureaucracy or professional associations rather than on the basis of political service. Thus, the parties have lost their former dominance in a number of functions: nominations, recruitment, electioneering, and government staffing.

The position evidenced in this legislation is present as well in public attitudes toward the parties. Even before the upheavals of the 1960s led to a general decline of trust in our institutions, Americans were skeptical about the worth of political parties. A majority believed, repeating the thought of Washington, that "our system of government would work a lot more efficiently if we could get rid of conflicts between the parties altogether," and nearly two-thirds complained that "the parties more often than not create conflicts where none really exists."[7]

More recently, political parties have received even less support. Once, only a quarter of the voters disclaimed loyalty to the major parties, but now, nearly two-fifths assert their independence. While seven out of ten voters once had something good to say about at least one party, now, a majority cannot find anything positive about either Republicans or Democrats.[8] The decline in attitudes toward the party system is equally stark. By 1974, the proportion of voters supporting the placement of party labels on ballots was down to a minority 38 percent, and parties had the least public confidence among major political institutions.[9]

In brief, then, Americans have denounced parties in theory, restricted them in legislation, almost eliminated them in reform, and scorned them in opinion polls. Nevertheless, we have continued to employ them, and even to cherish them, in practice. Americans—like other peoples—are often ambivalent. This is the nation, after all, which constitutionally abolished the use of intoxicating liquors and then vastly increased its consumption of alcohol. We resent as well our dependence on political parties but continue to imbibe in partisan politics. But—unlike the alcoholic—this dependence is not from weakness and not a debilitating illness. Our political parties are strengths in our governing processes and free the nation for constructive activity.

The American fondness for parties is evident throughout our history. Washington denounced narrow factionalism but became the instrument of the Federalists. Madison proceeded from his penetrating analysis of the evils of factions to the organization of the first popular-based party in the world. Jefferson was elected president through this organization and then created an effective executive-legislative bridge in the Republican congressional caucus. So it has gone for nearly 200 years. The great innovations in public policy have been dependent on organized political action through the political parties. Abraham Lincoln maintained the Union by mobilizing his new Republican Party in Congress and the border states. Franklin Roosevelt created the welfare state through enactment of a party program of social legislation. John Kennedy and Lyndon Johnson established a new agenda for the nation by their party leadership. Conversely, our most recent presidents have provided negative proofs of the importance of parties. Unable to mobilize their weakened factions, Richard Nixon resorted to corruption, while Jimmy Carter has floundered in frustration.

Citizens, too, show support for political parties despite their expressed reservations. Loyalty to parties has often been almost an article of religious faith, exemplified by the solid Republican patricians of Dutchess County, New York, who never voted for their good neighbor, Franklin Roosevelt, and by the Boston Irish clan, which was solidly Democratic except for the "family disgrace," the one Republican. Still today, when party loyalty is denigrated, more than three-fifths of the voters will assert their identification with the Democrats or Republicans. Even in the 1960s, over two-thirds agreed that "democracy works best where competition between parties is strong" and that "people who work for parties during political campaigns do our nation a great service"; there has been a regular increase since then in individual financial contributions to election campaigns.[10]

The work of parties has drawn praise as well as blame from scholars and practitioners. Martin Van Buren set the tone for a long tradition of party approbation: when "the principles of contending parties are supported with candor, fairness, and moderation, the very discord which is thus produced may in a government like ours, be conducive to the public good."[11] In the nineteenth century, the place of parties was honored in thought, and devotion to party was observed in practice. The most pointed defense was offered by George Washington Plunkitt, a Tammany ward leader at the beginning of this century. The nation depended on the parties, Plunkitt argued tersely:

> I ain't up on sillygisms, but I can give you some arguments that nobody can answer.
> First, this great and glorious country was built up by political parties; second, parties can't hold together if their workers don't get offices when they win; third, if the parties go to pieces, the government they built up must go to pieces, too; fourth, then there'll be hell to pay.[12]

Some defend political parties, then, and many Americans depend on them. These attitudes and this behavior should be seen not as defects but as necessary and desirable attributes of an effective large-scale republic. We often neglect these attributes because we are not always willing to accept a fully democratic system. In the coming years, however, we must either acknowledge the mutual reliance of our parties and our democracy—or lose both.

The benefits of political parties are threefold: to institutions, to voters, and to civil society. Institutionally, the chief benefit of political parties is captured in the political scientists' phrase "the aggregation of interests." Conflicting interests are evident in every society. Indeed, they can be found even in the family; one famous commentator suggested that an investigation of the origins of parties "would have to be carried back to the garden of Eden, where the first caucus was held by Eve and the serpent."[13] Madison found the causes of faction "sown in the nature of man" and listed their bases as including "a zeal for different opinions concerning religion, concerning government and many other points . . . an attachment to different leaders ambitiously contending for pre-eminence and power" and, most importantly, "the various and unequal distribution of property. Those who hold and those who are without property have ever formed distinct interests in society.[14]

Parties are the means by which these various interests can be reconciled and by which they can be compromised to provide at least partial satisfactions to all contenders. The aggregation of interests by the parties is evident throughout our politics; three brief examples can denote a large range of activities. First, consider the variety of ethnic groups in the United States, each group having legitimate claims to a share of power. Without unifying mechanisms, campaigns could become, as in nonpartisan elections, divisive controversies between Catholics and Protestants, blacks and whites, Irish and Italian. When they are functioning well, parites submerge these communal clashes in a joint search for electoral victory. Their means is the "balanced ticket," by which all groups receive some recognition in return for mutual ballot support. Anti-Catholic Democrats will still vote for a Catholic candidate so long as he or is she a Democrat, and some of the same whites who oppose school integration will vote for a black candidate for school superintendent running under their party label.

A second example of interest aggregation is the party platforms, often attacked as meaningless quadrennial rhetoric. Detailed examination of these documents shows, however, that they are surprisingly specific and frequently implemented.[15] They are important as means by which different interests establish a claim on the government while adjusting to the demands of other groups. In 1976, to illustrate this point, Republicans favoring a hard-line foreign policy could be reconciled to the candidacy of Gerald Ford by praise of Alexander Solzynitzhen; among Democrats, feminists could be enlisted in the Carter coalition by support of the Equal Rights Amendment.

Third, parties aggregate interests in their legislative decisions. Their cooperative behavior is exhibited even in the terms we use, such as *horsetrading, logrolling,* and *backscratching.* Urban representatives will vote for high farm price supports and will expect rural legislators in turn to approve public housing subsidies; national parks in the Rockies are traded for national seashores on the coasts.[16] This cooperation is inevitable and necessary in governing a continental nation. It becomes feasible, as well as somewhat coherent ideologically, when included in a total party program.

These three examples are deliberately chosen to illustrate the realities of parties in the United States. Balanced tickets, platform compromises, and legislative trading are not philosophical enterprises, and our parties are not intellectual societies. They are groupings of generally honorable but relatively ordinary people who are interested in power more than in principles. Like other men and women, they are typically self-interested, occasionally devious, and only rarely altruistic. The important point is not the motives of politicians but their institutional functions. In order to win office, politicians must heed expressed public demands. By aggregating these interests, parties do not, to be sure, guarantee that all interests will be heard—and even less that they will be heard at the same volume. However, they do provide a means by which some demands can be combined and made effective.

Aggregation of interests is particularly necessary, given the formal governmental structure of the United States. The Constitution has served us well, but only because we have not adhered to its provisions rigorously. A literal implementation of the original document would have given us two legislative chambers with only formal relations, an executive branch completely distinct in its base of authority, and a severe demarcation between the national and state governments. Amendment of the Constitution, in practice rather than by law, has enabled the parties to bridge its gaps through such integrative institutions as the national nominating conventions, the joint meetings of the president and congressional party leadership, the House and Senate party caucuses, the governors' conferences, and the intergovernmental political career.[17]

The more important benefits of parties, however, are not to institutions but to voters, our second category. These contributions depend on competition between the parties, that is, on a party system. Aggregation of interests and constitutional bridging, after all, are achieved by authoritarian parties, yet few advocate the Soviet Communist Party as a model for the United States. Because U.S. parties provide a choice, they enable the voters to exercise at least an indirect influence over the course of government.

Admittedly, that choice is limited and, often, clouded. It is difficult to find advocates of either free market capitalism or a socialized economy among major party candidates, while both Republicans and Democrats simultaneously urge an increase in social security benefits and restraints on governmental spending. Nevertheless, voters do see some significant difference between the parties. In 1976, for example, 70 percent of the nation found a conservative-liberal distinction between them: the Democrats were chosen as the more liberal party by a three to one margin.[18] What the voters saw reflected the reality of the parties. Democratic economic policy has been markedly different from that of the Republicans, their platforms and actions reflecting a definite concern with problems of unemployment, while Republicans have devoted considerably greater attention to inflation. Illustratively, in 1976, the Democratic platform spoke of unemployment 48 times, the Republicans only once.[19] Floor voting in Congress also shows a distinct party split, with northern Democrats supporting liberal policies three times more frequently than Republicans.[20]

More significantly, it is possible for the parties to promote popular influence over government even if there are not marked policy differences between them. This effect is achieved because one party can be held responsible for governmental action, so that it provides a convenient target for the electorate's praise and blame. Voters have too many pressing tasks, from making money to making love, to follow the arcane procedures of government and to understand all the issues and outcomes. Instead, they can rely on the convenience of party labels and simply vote for the "ins" when times are good and for the "outs" when dissatisfied. Many Americans follow this simple and not unreasonable rule to achieve a rough political justice. Democrats, therefore, suffered defeat when their leader, Lyndon Johnson, conducted an unpopular war in Vietnam, and Republicans were replaced when Nixon attempted to subvert the laws. "By virtue of the combination of the electorate's retrospective judgment and the custom of party accountability, the electorate can exert a prospective influence if not control," as Key argued: therefore, "governments must worry, not about the meaning of past elections, but about their fate at future elections."[21]

Worried about elections, parties are responsive. They respond particularly to demands voiced by large numbers of people. This characteristic has made parties the special agency of the poor and disadvantaged. Those who have wealth, education, and other privileges can often make their own way politically and, in any case, have less need for governmental aid. The poor have only one real advantage, their numbers, in the enduring contest, underlined by Madison, over "the various and unequal distribution of property." But numbers are also the most basic resource in a democratic system and the resource and most interest to the parties.

The close association between the interests of parties and those of the lower classes has been repeatedly exemplified. As Aaron Burr registered craftsmen to promote Jefferson's election, so radical Republicans after the Civil War forced the enrollment of emancipated slaves. In state politics, there is a definite association between the degree of party competition and the level of redistributive public policy.[22] On the municipal level, cities without partisan elections devote less attention to the problems of the poor such as low-income housing, social welfare service, urban redevelopment, and employment.[23]

The classic example of the service parties provide for the disadvantaged was the urban machine. Corrupt and inefficient, the machine also showed a genuine concern for its constituents. As one leader put it: "I think . . . that there's got to be in every ward somebody that any bloke can come to—no matter what's he's done—and get help. Help you understand; none of your law and your justice, but help."[24] The machine did meet the needs of its poor supporters, providing jobs; emergency aid; desired illegal services, such as gambling; entertainment; opportunities for social mobility; and intervention with the law. At the same time, it promoted the economic development of the cities and even engaged in some imaginative urban planning, as in the development of New York City's subway and parks systems.

Today, the urban machine has virtually disappeared, its functions assumed by nonpartisan bureaucracies and ombudsmen. Welfare needs are supplied better, surely, for food stamps are far more plentiful and regular than Christmas turkeys. But something also has been lost, for the machine did not provide charity. It supplied a service in exchange for votes. This implicit bargain was more dignified to the poor surely than the largesse of government. The welfare state is, necessarily, an impersonal organization; the machine was an expression of neighborly concern and of the interdependence of leaders and led. The party machine, therefore, helped to bring the poor into politics, first as objects and then as participants; the welfare state only considers the poor as "clients," not as equals. The machine was egalitarian in its basic attitudes. This nonelitist character of the machine is nicely described by Plunkitt's advice to the aspiring politician:

> Get a followin', if it's only one man, and then go to the district leader. . . .
> The leader won't laugh at your one-man followin'. He'll shake your hand
> warmly, offer to propose you for membership in his club, take you down
> to the corner for a drink and ask you to call again. But go to him and say:
> "I took first prize at college in Aristotle; I can recite all Shakespeare
> forwards and backwards" [and] he'll probably say: "I guess you are not to
> blame for your misfortune, but we have no use for you here."[25]

The machine illustrates the third kind of contribution made by parties, the promotion of a democratic life-style, a point further discussed by McWilliams (see Chapter 4). Parties are democratic in the most basic egalitarian sense, for in the voting booth, each person counts as one and only one. Parties seek votes and ultimately do not care if the hands that move the levers are black or white, male or female, or rich or poor. Parties, more than any other U.S. institution, accept our national premise, namely, that "all men are created equal."

A democratic life-style means widespread public participation in the affairs of the community. Competing parties promote participation, at least in general elections. It is hardly coincidental that voting rates are highest in those areas with the most vigorous two-party competition, that parties have spearheaded the successive extensions of the franchise, that electoral turnout was greatest in those periods of U.S. history when party loyalty was strongest, and that the contemporary decline in turnout closely parrallels the decline in party strength.

Yet, political parties are more than collections of voters. They are communities in themselves, which function to promote broader involvement in the larger community. They provide training, an awareness of others' needs and interests, and a personal understanding of democratic manners. Parties promote intimacy among their members, respect for the opinions of their constituents, and possible future leadership for the nation.

The communitarian aspect of party organizations is particularly notable in the selection of future leadership. Like members of other small groups, partisans get to learn one another's strengths and weaknesses in great depth. Party members watch each other, test each other, and gossip about each other. They learn through long and repeated experience whose word can be trusted, who will follow through on assignments, who is informed on public questions, and who disguises selfish interests in the cloak of the general interest. Relying on their personal experience, they are uniquely knowledgeable in the selection of public officials.

A democratic life-style involves more than participation in periodic elections. It also involves a commitment to public questions, an extension of the individual beyond his or her private concerns. Parties promote this maturation. Voters generally, and properly, are concerned with advancing their individual interests; party activists must take note of the interests of others. Voters act in isolation or in alliance with their close associates; campaigners must coordinate their activities with others in the common enterprise. Voters discharge their duty in a brief occasional act; partisans immerse themselves in the ongoing public world. For members of the parties, Tocqueville's description of the American is still accurate: "He takes a lesson in the form of government from governing. The great work of society is ever going on before his eyes and, as it were, under his hands."[26] Parties serve to make citizens out of voters.

By previous reckoning, parties are evaluated as immensely important to U.S. institutions, voters, and society: to recapitulate, they aggregate interests, as illustrated by ticket balancing, platform writing, and legislative trading; bridge the separation of governmental agencies; offer a choice to the electorate; enforce responsibility for policy on the governing party; respond to the needs of large groups, particularly the disadvantaged; provide welfare aid to the poor; stimulate participation; promote community life; foster a democratic life-style; and enlarge the political views of citizens. These merits surely account for the continued use we make of the parties. But if parties are that desirable, why do Americans have such unfavorable attitudes toward them? Why do we continue to reform them, even to the present point of almost eliminating them?

Certainly, one source of antipathy toward parties is a valid criticism of their faults. Their theoretical merits are often lost in their negative practices. Parties can degenerate from public agencies to private factions. Instead of pursuing a coalitional program, they may become instruments only for personal ambitions. Rather than offering the voters instruments for collective choice, they may obscure their policy objectives or serve the interests of the wealthy and the privileged. Rather than fostering community participation, they can become closed elites.

Political parties are based on private motives and therefore always present the possibility that these private interests will come to predominate over the public functions of parties. Party organizations are bureaucracies to some extent and, as in other bureaucracies, the interests of the organization may receive more emphasis than the needs of their clientele. The urban machine, even with its virtues, was also the fullest institutional expression of these defects of parties. It ignored fundamental social issues, dampened but left unsolved the grievances of the poor, concentrated political power in a few, usually corrupt, hands, and debased the quality of political discourse. These deficiencies were a major stimulus of the movement to reform parties.

There is also a deeper source of the antipathy toward parties. Unfavorable attitudes toward parties also derive from conflicts among American values, as well as from the inherent challenge that the very existence of parties presents to our most esteemed beliefs. We hold conflicting values, and parties emphasize the conflicts. We need parties, but we resent them, because they remind us of our confusions and inability to resolve some of the problems of our society. Mistaking effect for cause, we believe that by eliminating parties, we can remove the confusion and inability to resolve the problems. Let me briefly cite five illustrations.

One favored U.S. belief is individualism. Part of American mythology is captured by such figures as the rugged frontiersman, the lonely inventor, and the self-reliant Horatio Alger character, who overcomes problems by his or her own efforts. The political analogue of the rugged individualist is the independent voter, who studies all issues and then makes his or her own personal, rational decision. But parties are collective bodies. They exist in order to organize men and women to reach shared goals, and their existence underlines the incapacity of individuals to achieve their goals without mutual aid. In the individualistic ideology, political independence is the highest estate. To the parties, loyalists are the best citizens and independents are only fence-straddling "mugwumps," who have their mug on one side of the fence and the wump on the other.

A related U.S. value, and one increasingly evident in social and political life, is privatism. Automobiles are preferred over public transportation, detached homes over apartments, individually owned condominiums over cooperatives, personal television over motion picture theaters, individualistic psychological therapy over social movements, isolated recreation (such as running) over participatory team sports, and the nuclear family or the singles scene over the kin group. In politics, we find the substitution of the televised commercial for the public address, the selling of personalities for the discussion of issues, and the ideal of the private voting decision for that of partisan loyalty. However, parties are public, not private, bodies. Party politicians are gregarious people who love to mingle with others, talk, laugh, and physically touch one another. Private politics suggests an image of the lonely voter at home, pondering decisions; party politics suggests an image of a crowded three-ring circus.

Consensus is a third value that is highly esteemed in the United States. Programs are inevitably rationalized in terms of their contribution to the public good, and the general welfare and a commitment to these philosophical abstractions is particularly evident in the antiparty literature. Thus, Madison could defend the Constitution as insuring that "a coalition of a majority of the whole society could seldom take place on any other principle than those of justice and the general good."[27] The U.S. search for consensus is evident in ecumenical religion, mass culture, and even car styles. In politics, it is evidenced in bipartisan foreign policies, the reverence often paid to the presidential office, and the explicit disavowal of appeals to economic classes or other specific interests. But parties are by nature, even etymology, expressions of particular groups, efforts to win advantages for some interests even at the expense of others, as well as vehicles for personal ambition and selfishness. Parties are institutional expressions of conflict, recognitions that "the passions of men will not conform to the dictates or reason and justice without constraint," as Hamilton said, and that "ambition must be made to counteract ambition," as Madison agreed.[28] An emphasis on consensus presumes that disputes can be resolved—that the lion and the lamb can lie down together. By contrast, the development of parties presumes that coercion is at least implicit in political settlements and that the lamb had better watch its chops.

Parties even challenge the basic U.S. belief in equality. We assert that each man and woman is equal to every other, certainly in regard to politics. As Tocqueville has long made us aware, equality is the basic U.S. value, affecting all aspects of our lives, from commerce to dress. "Equality is their idol," he wrote; "Nothing can satisfy them without equality, and they would rather perish than lose it."[29]

Parties, too, share this value and aid considerably in its achievement. But in another sense discussed by Robinson in the next chapter, parties challenge the reality of equality. If citizens were truly equal in their knowledge, access, participation, and interests, parties would not be necessary. Parties exist because of a division of labor. They are specialized enterprises, providing information to less aware voters, evidencing greater political participation by their activists, and promoting the interests of some groups over others. We necessarily rely on the parties to structure our political communications, just as we necessarily rely on the telephone company to structure our voice communications. Yet, who loves Ma Bell?

Finally, parties challenge the U.S. ideal of a classless society. Public opinion polls inform us that most people place themselves in the amorphous category of the middle class; status differences are carefully disguised, so that it is difficult to tell a Cadillac from a Ford; unions and management lobby together to ease governmental regulation of their industries; and television creates a common mass culture, in which class differences are rarely noted—and never argued. The absence of class consciousness has been repeatedly underlined, occasioning satisfaction by liberals and despair by socialists. However, even our non-Marxian parties make us aware of the uncomfortable fact of status differences: their historical appeals are to the working class and the classical bourgeoisie, and their programs and legislative voting are most distinct on issues related to relative group advantages. To the limited extent we have been willing to acknowledge that politics involves economic conflict, the parties have embodied this consciousness.

One can—and I probably do—exaggerate the degree to which Americans hold fast to these values. There are other contrasting American commitments—to community, public involvement, competition, differentiation, and even class conflict.[30] The persistence of parties evidences these other beliefs, and parties themselves share in both sets of values. We are, ultimately, ambivalent, but the parties more fully embody one side of the internal quarrel of the American mind.

The conflict between parties and these sepcified values culminates in the dispute over direct democracy, exemplified in the Progressive Party legislation of California (see Chapter 8), and in such mechanisms as the direct primary, initiative, referendum, and recall. The advocates of direct democracy, expect intense individualistic activity to achieve the common good. No intermediate organizations, such as parties, are desirable, because such organizations will limit the equal power of autonomous individuals. No class movements are necessary, because the common good will harmonize the interests of all particular interests. Democarcy to the Progressives and their modern heirs is an organism that needs no care and feeding, in which, without any special mechanisms, "accountability is always to the composite citizen—individual unknown—always permanent, never changing, the necessitated result being that the public servant must serve the composite citizen who represents general welfare."[31]

The Progressive ideology has largely carried the day. After all, how can one argue against such cliches as, "Vote for the man (or woman) not the party," or, "There's no Democratic or Republican way to clean the streets"? Our schools spread the nonpartisan message, and parties are virtually absent from textbooks except as historical references.[32] Even candidates, sensing public sentiment, emphasize their personality over their political heritage, attack their opponents as "bosses," and avoid both party labels and the other members of their tickets.

In recent years, as already noted, social forces and alleged reforms in the spirit of the Progressive ideology have brought the parties to their present weakened state. These changes are neither accidental nor conspiratorial. They are, rather, the latest manifestations of those U.S. values hostile to parties. Individualism is evident in the revision of nominating procedures, especially in the Democratic Party (see the discussions of Crotty and Casey in Chapters 3 and 6, respectively.) The new rules of the party stimulate the choice of convention delegates by direct primaries rather than by party processes; they provide for proportional representation of the primary vote and thus restrict the building of coalitions; they give no assured representation in the highest party councils to its officials or those persons elected in its name; they minimize the states as political organizations; and they emphasize not party service in the choice of delegates but demographic characteristics of age, sex, and race. The basic unspoken premise of these changes is that the only important political relationship is that between the individual voter and the presidential nominee. The plebiscite among atomized individuals is replacing political organization.

Privatism, the complement of individualism, is also evident, particularly in campaigning, which is no longer conducted in public places, such as the streets or county fairs. Electoral messages are received in the isolation of television dens, and their meaning is not discussed among the voters, but only by strangers, the commentators of the press. Financing of elections through party committees has been replaced by contributions from wealthy individuals, anonymous checkoffs through the income tax system, or interest groups. Candidates emphasize their personalities or their activities in sports or entertainment rather than their political service. We no longer vote for persons who represent the historical heritage and identifiable program of a political party but for persons whose faces we see but souls we cannot touch.

We continue as well to disregard the issue of class in our politics. This neglect is most evident in our attempted reform of election finance. Watergate demonstrated the corruptibility of the existing electoral system, but in the process of responding to those evils, we created new dangers. Now, wealthy individuals are free to spend as much money as they want on their own campaigns or on the behalf of others. We now legally permit, indeed encourage, corporations to contribute to campaigns. In the last congressional campaign, specialized "political action committees" provided the majority of funding for congressional chairpersons, an average of $45,000 for each.[33] In total, some 2,000 groups spent $35 million advocating the special interests of corporations, as well as unions and other groups.[34] At the same time, contributions of individuals and spending by parties have been restricted considerably. At one time, we understood the danger of direct corporate involvement in elections and precisely labeled business contributions as *corrupt practices*. Today, we do no more than require that the contributions go through a separate political action committee rather than come directly from the corporate treasurer's office.

To be sure, corporations and other groups have interests that they should legitimately promote in elections. But only parties can aggregate these interests into a program that gives some recognition to a variety of demands. To be sure, candidates should make us aware of their personal qualifications, but only a team of partisan officials, sharing an historical record and some common responsibility, can readily be held to account by the electorate. To be sure, individual voters should exercise their best judgment in casting ballots, but only parties dependent on votes are likely to champion the cause of the disadvantaged and to promote a participatory, egalitarian life-style. If we value these qualities and if we value democracy, we must take action to renew our political party system.

We need a new period of reform, a time in which to develop a public policy toward politics itself and in which to center our efforts on the reconstruction of the political parties. This call has been made before, and usually futilely. A distinguished group of political scientists published a program for constructive party reform as long ago as 1950. They warned that the consequences of inaction would be incoherence in public policies, a dangerous enlargement of presidential power, public cynicism, and the growth of extremist movements.[35] Their recommendations for action were not heeded, but their predictions have proven accurate. We find ourselves unable as a nation to design a coherent policy to meet the energy shortage, to regulate the economy, or to control our foreign policy. We alternate between presidents who are too strong for our liberties or too weak for our security. We find fewer than a fifth of the voters expressing confidence in the three branches of the national government. We see loyalties attached not to known, accountable parties but to single-interest groups, such as antiabortionists, or single men, such as George Wallace.

There is still hope and time available. The need for stronger parties is becoming evident. As the chapters below will detail, the Democrats are developing a broadly participatory national party, and the Republicans are forging strong organizational links from the state to the federal level. State parties are being rebuilt by concerned citizens, who have written a new party charter in Massachusetts, organized open party caucuses in Minnesota, and increased local participation in California. Awareness of the problem is becoming apparent in the mass media, and there are nascent movements toward party rebuilding in Congress.

There are many steps to be taken, among which the three following institutional steps merit particular discussion. First, we need to revise the election finance laws, so that funds are provided to parties for their continuing organization, research, and training and so that campaign funds are channeled through the parties rather than independently to candidates. Second, we must reverse the trend toward presidential selection through a series of distracting, hyperbolic, and expensive primaries and enable the state party organizations more fully to exercise their experienced judgment in the choice of the chief executive. Third, we should encourage the trend to midterm party conventions and any other devices that will make the president more responsible to his colleagues in Congress and to the members of his party.

Neither these reforms nor any other will in themselves rebuild the parties. Ultimately, democracy depends more on an active citizenry than on institutions and leaders. It depends on widespread participation in those intermediate organizations and voluntary groups that stand between the individual and the overarching national state. Watergate should have made us aware again of the dangers of concentrated power, as American life should remind us daily of the need for more intimate communities. Party renewal is also a renewal of U.S. democracy. As Tocqueville warned, "There are no countries in which associations are more needed to prevent the despotism of faction or the arbitrary power of a prince than those which are democratically constituted."[36] We would do well to heed that warning.

NOTES

1. James Richardson, ed. *Messages and Papers of the Presidents* (Washington, D.C.: Government Printing Office, 1897), pp. 209–11.

2. James Madison, *The Federalist, No. 10* (New York: Modern Library, 1941), pp. 53–54.

3. George Biche Huszar, *Basic American Documents* (Ames, Iowa: Littlefield, Adams, 1953), p. 115.

4. Cited in Richard Hofstadter, *The Idea of a Party System* (Berkeley: University of California Press, 1970), p. 151.

5. Austin Ranney, *Curing the Mischiefs of Faction* (Berkeley: University of California Press, 1975), pp. 1–21.

6. Ibid., p. 15.

7. Jack Dennis, "Support for the Party System by the Mass Public," *American Political Science Review* 60 (September 1966): 605.

8. Norman Nie et al., *The Changing American Voter* (Cambridge, Mass.: Harvard University Press, 1976), p. 58.

9. Jack Dennis, "Trends in Public Support for the American Party System," *British Journal of Political Science* 5 (April 1975): 200–8.

10. Dennis, "Support for the Party System," p. 606, and Dennis, "Trends in Public Support," p. 211.

11. Martin Van Buren, *Autobiography*, p. 50, edited by Hofstadter, *The Idea of a Party System*, pp. 251–52.

12. William L. Riordan, *Plunkitt of Tammany Hall* (New York: Dutton, 1963), p. 13.

13. M. Ostrogorski, "The Rise and Fall of the Nominating Caucus, Legislative and Congressional," *American Historical Review* 5 (December 1899): 254.

14. *The Federalist, No. 10*, pp. 55–56.

15. Gerald Pomper, *Elections in America* (New York: Dodd Mead, 1968), pp. 149–203.

16. David Mayhew, *Party Loyalty Among Congressmen* (Cambridge, Mass.: Harvard University Press, 1966).

17. See Joseph Schlesinger, *Ambition in Politics* (Chicago: Rand McNally, 1966).

18. Data from the University of Michigan, Center for Political Studies, 1976 Election Study, variable 3194.

19. Edward Tuffe, *Political Control of the Economy* (Princeton, N.J.: Princeton University Press, 1978), pp. 76–77.

20. "Conservative Coalition Loses Strength," *Congressional Quarterly Weekly Report* 36 (December 18, 1978): 3442.

21. V. O. Key, Jr., *The Responsible Electorate* (Cambridge, Mass.: Harvard University Press, 1966). p. 76f.

22. Brain Fry and Richard Winters, "The Politics of Redistribution," *American Political Science Review* 64 (June 1970): 508–22.

23. Willis Hawley, *Nonpartisan Elections and the Case for Party Politics* (New York: Wiley, 1973), chap. 6.

24. *The Autobiography of Lincoln Steffens* (New York: Harcourt Brace, 1931), p. 618.

25. Riordan, *Plunkitt of Tammany Hall*, p. 10.

26. Alexis de Tocqueville, *Democracy in America* (1835), ed. Phillips Bradley (New York: Vintage, 1954), 1: 330.

27. James Madison, *The Federalist, No. 51* (New York: Modern Library, 1941), p. 341.

28. James Madison, *The Federalist, No. 15*, (New York: Modern Library, 1941), p. 92, and Madison, *The Federalist, No. 51*, p. 337.

29. Tocqueville, vol 1, p. 56.

30. See Wilson Carey McWilliams, *The Idea of Fraternity in America* (Berkeley: University of California Press, 1973).

31. Oregon Senator Brown, arguing for direct election of U.S. senators, in *Congressional Record*, 61st Cong., 3rd sess., 1911, 46, p. 2595–96.

32. See Sue Tolleson Rinehart, "The Mischief of Factions: Political Parties in School Textbooks" (Paper delivered at annual meeting of American Political Science Association Washington, D.C., September 1979).

33. New York *Times*, December 25, 1978, p. 1

34. *Congressional Quarterly Weekly Report* 27 (June 2, 1979): 1043.

35. American Political Science Association, Committee on Political Parties, "Toward a More Responsible Two-Party System," *American Political Science Review* 44 (September 1950): 91–96 (supp.).

36. Tocqueville, vol. 1, p. 202.

2

THE PLACE OF PARTY IN DEMOCRATIC IDEAS

Donald A. Robinson

*T*oday, everyone agrees that parties need to be "renewed" and "strengthened." Despite the broad consensus on this point, however, would-be reformers have not been able to agree on a program. The difficulty comes in specifying the problems and fitting remedies to them. To some observers, parties seem weak, ill-defined, and ineffective, their membership uncertain, their procedures muddy, and their control over their own acts indefinite. To another set of observers, the problem with parties is that they are boss-ridden, closed to participation by most citizens, unrepresentative of the population at large, and insincere in their supposed efforts at reform.

Almost everyone would level one or another, if not both, of these sets of criticisms at the parties. If parties are so universally deplored, why do people care about them? Parties attract serious attention, not just because they exist, and not only for their potential, but because they or something like them are widely seen as essential instruments of democracy.

But if this is the reason for concern about parties, it is also the source of confusion over reform measures. Parties are hard to reform because would-be reformers do not agree about the nature of democracy.

To see the relationship of ideas about party reform and ideas about democracy, let us begin by listing three of the leading issues on the agenda of party reform.

1. Party Membership.
Should there be criteria for party membership? Should there be marks of membership, such as dues, membership cards, and the right to vote at party meetings? Should there be explicit expectations of party members,

with disciplines assigned for failure to meet these obligations, or should there be open access to all party functions? Should the stress be placed on recruitment and affirmative action rather than discipline?

2. Party Program.

Should platforms be conceived as proposed contracts with the people, sufficiently detailed to serve as a standard for subsequent performance? Should machinery be created (watchdogs, reporting, follow-up conferences) to ensure that officeholders honor these commitments, or should party platforms be vaguely worded, indicating aspirations, but leaving officeholders with broad discretion?

3. Nominations.

Should nominations be made by conventions of party leaders, men and women who represent the muscle and machines and decentralized power of local organizations, or should they be made at primary elections, where all citizens, on a one-person–one-vote basis, have potentially equal influence?

There are other related issues of party reform the answers to which depend in part upon the answers given to these leading issues. For example, now that we seem to be committed to public financing, at least for presidential contests, should the money go to parties or directly to candidates? Presumably, if one favored stronger organization in answer to the questions above, one would probably favor the channeling of public financing to the parties.

The thesis of this chapter is that one's approach to these issues of party reform tends to reflect one's basic orientation toward democracy. Ideas about democracy are notoriously complex. However, it is possible for present purposes to distinguish between two contrasting clusters. Most persons interested in party reform tend to take the view that I will identify as *revisionist*. Others, perhaps less definite in their ideas, feel tugged by the appeal of a set of ideas that I will identify as *neoclassical*. I call this view *neoclassical*, for it is clearly an attempt to restate the classical democratic tradition in the face of the criticism of the revisionists.* Neoclassical ideas suffuse the political atmosphere in which party reforms are considered. It therefore behooves people interested in party reform to understand their bearing upon party life.

In the following pages, I will attempt to outline these two clusters of ideas about democracy. In general I shall treat the revisionists first, for their

---

*I considered using other terminology, such as *realistic* versus *romantic*, but as Reinhold Niebuhr once remarked, realism is not a distinctive outlook but a boast. In addition, those committed to the neoclassical outlook might regard the term *romantic* as perjorative. Similarly, revisionists take offense at the term *elitist*. See Robert Dahl, "Further Reflections on 'The Elitist Theory of Democracy'," *American Political Science Review* 60 (June 1966): 296–305.

approach is dominant in political science today and has considerable influence over the ideas of party reformers. Both are artificial constructs, in the sense that no single thinker holds all of the ideas in either set, and many thinkers hold ideas on both sides of the dichotomy.

By the term *revisionist*, I am referring to the work of Robert Dahl, Samuel Beer, James Q. Wilson, Austin Ranney, and, especially, Joseph Schumpeter.[1] It was Schumpeter who made the distinction between what he called the "classical" and "revised" theories of democracy.[2] I adopt a reversed form of his terminology here. However, I am sensitive to the criticism of his analysis by Pateman, who charges that Schumpeter's concept of the "classical" democratic tradition is a caricature of Rousseau, most basically in tying it to government by representatives.[3]

By the term *neoclassical*, I am referring to the work of C. B. Macpherson, Carole Pateman, Jack Walker, T. B. Bottomore, Henry Kariel, and Tom Hayden, among others. These writers are united in the attempt to restate the democratic vision in the context of large, industrial, urban nations.[4]

I will set forth the contrasting conceptions of democracy under five headings, beginning with the broadest matters of definition and proceeding toward a discussion of attitudes toward party as an instrument of democracy.

DEFINING CHARACTERISTICS OF DEMOCRACY

For the revisionists, rule by elites is inescapable. The "realism" of Vilfredo Pareto, Gaetano Mosca, and Robert Michels is taken as descriptive of the way the human community universally works.

However, the fact that minorities inevitably rule does not make all systems equally authoritarian or dictatorial. Everything depends on the elites' accountability. Winston Churchill and Franklin D. Roosevelt were not the same as Adolf Hitler and Joseph Stalin. The governing of New Haven is not the same as the governing of Minsk. The actual shaping of policy may inevitably be in the hands of elites, but this does not mean that power in society cannot be held accountable. In the words of Mannheim:

> It is sufficient for a democracy that the individual citizens, though prevented from taking a direct part in government all the time, have at least the possibility of making their aspirations felt as certain intervals. . . . [Although political power is always exercised by minorities,] it would be wrong to overestimate the stability of such elites in democratic society or their ability to wield power in arbitrary ways. In a democracy, the governed can always act to remove their leaders or to force them to make decisions in the interests of the many.[5]

For the revisionists, the question of the *viability* of democratic government is central. As Beer says:

> Two questions may be asked of modern democracy: how democratic is it? and, can it do the job? And what is the job? Democratic government, like any form of government, is an instrument for solving problems. It is a means by which a community defends itself, fosters its economic prosperity, and in other ways promotes what it conceives to be the general welfare.[6]

To achieve these ends, a democratic government must be both strong and stable. It must be capable of fashioning effective policies and durable enough to implement them.

For neoclassical democrats, on the other hand, the defining characteristic of democracy is a concern for human development. There is a defensive side to democracy: to reduce the danger of tyranny by insisting that no person be required to obey a law without having joined in its making.[7] Democrats also believe that participation of the populace improves the quality of government, by increasing the range of talent and perspectives from which policy and personnel are drawn. The central promise is that the quality of life will imporve as citizens gain a broader awareness of moral and social responsibility by participating in public life.[8]

Whereas for revisionists, the central question for democratic government is how to reconcile the demand for participation with the need for "coherent, effective" government, for neoclassical democrats, the central question is how to stimulate personal and communal development. About any structure or process of government, classical democrats ask whether it contributes to the development of public virtue. For them, to make the effectiveness of government the leading priority is to strip democracy of its elan and rob it of its cutting edge.

HOMO CIVICUS AND APATHY

For the revisionists, one's theory of democracy depends upon one's judgment of the political capacities and inclinations of common citizens. Are most people interested in making public policy for themselves, or do they believe that their interests will be better served if they have to make just one choice—between the aspirants for public office? Empirical evidence, as read by revisionists, admits of no doubt on this question. Most people have no opinions on most issues, and at least in the stable nations, they freely give their consent to a system that enables them to choose their leaders but not, normally, the policies of government.

From the revisionist perspective, "it is quite impossible for the government of a society to be in the hands of any but a few . . . there is government *for* the people; there is no government *by* the people."[9] Democracy is characterized not by general participation but by established procedures whereby governing elites may be challenged and replaced peacefully by processes in which "the people shall judge." Revisionists like to call attention to the fact that the demand for participation in the name of the people comes not for the people themselves but from the intelligentsia—"amateur democrats," Students for a Democratic Society, the McGovern-Fraser Commission, and the like. These prophets of participation are, in the eyes of the revisionists, mere counterelites.

Indeed, some revisionists, though not all, go so far as to suggest the need for positive limits on popular participation. Schumpeter, for example, says that democracy is not viable without popular self-control, that is, unless there is a popular disposition to let elites rule between elections without trying to interfere by pressure, demonstrations, and other expressions of demand.[10] Other revisionists note that tidal waves of popular engagement and political acitvity are often precursors of turmoil and a descent into tyranny.[11]

Neoclassical democrats, on the other hand, insist that the nature of political man must not be viewed statically. Human potential can be enhanced by participation in politics. By participating in politics, people gain in knowledge and understanding and develop capacities that are otherwise dormant. Those who regard apathy as an ineluctable fact are consenting to "the practical abandonment of . . . the distinctive moral function of democratic politics and government."[12] Where apathy exists, it ought to be viewed as an object of intense concern. Neoclassicists quote John Stuart Mill, who wrote that

> the most important point of excellence which any form of government can possess is to promote the virtue and intelligence of the people themselves. The first question in respect to any political institutions is how far they tend to foster in the members of the community, the various desirable qualities . . . moral, intellectual, and active.[13]

Any government that insures itself to widespread apathy is not only running the risk of allowing explosive situations to build but failing to provide opportunities for the development of moral virtue.

No one denies that most people in the United States today are politically inactive, but whereas revisionists trace this inertia to matters of temperament and aptitude, neoclassicists ascribe it to social and economic inequality and class division.[14] If apathy arises from these fundamental causes, can it be overcome? Are we not confronted by a vicious circle, in which class divisions cause apathy and apathy undermines the determination to change the conditions that give rise to class divisions? Neoclassical democrats tend to be guardedly hopeful. Pateman concludes a chapter on workers' self-management in Yugoslavia by saying that it "gives us no good reason to suppose that the democratisation of industrial authority structures is impossible, difficult and complicated though it may be." She adds:

> The claim of the participatory theory of democracy that the necessary condition for the establishment of a democratic polity is a participatory society, is not a completely unrealistic one; whether or not the ideal of the earlier "classical" theorists of participatory democracy can be realised remains very much an open and live question.[15]

Other theorists take encouragement from the rise of egalitarian movements between 1968–74, from experiments in workers' control of industry, from the rise of neighborhood associations, and from polls that reveal growing opposition to social inequality. Macpherson, for example, suggests that it may be possible to overcome class divisions incrementally and peacefully.[16]

Above all, neoclassical democrats insist upon broad participation in politics because they believe that people are, by nature, political animals and that all persons are entitled to fulfill this nature. Thus, all regimes are to be judged by the democratic canon: Do they encourage participation, and do they achieve it? No regime is acceptable that does not answer both these questions in the affirmative, no matter what its other achievements may be.

Bottomore adds another important emphasis, namely, that democracy should be conceived of as a *quest*, that social arrangements should be regarded as experiments and judged for their contribution to the process of moving toward the democratic ideal. "It would not have occurred to most of the democratic thinkers of the nineteenth century," he writes, "to regard universal suffrage, competition between several political parties and representative government . . . as the ultimate point of democratic progress, beyond which it was impossible to venture." In preference to a "static" conception of democracy, in which elite rule is sanctioned by periodic elections, Bottomore calls for "the development and improvement of a democratic system of government . . . in which a large majority of citizens, if not all citizens, can take part in deciding those social issues which vitally affect their individual lives."[17]

APPLICABILITY OF DEMOCRATIC NORMS

Democratic theorists generally would agree that the exercise of political power by the system as a whole should reflect the popular consensus. However, one significant point of difference among them concerns the applicability of democratic norms to elements *within* the system.

As noted, revisionists reject the idea of government by the people for the system as a whole. Similarly, they deem it utopian and self-defeating to insist that all parts of the system be internally democratic. Inconsistency with reference to internal democracy is an eccentricity of the middle class intelligentsia. What is worse, a focus on internal structure diverts attention from the strategy needed to tap traditional sources of left-oriented politics, namely, the lower classes. According to E. E. Schattschneider, democracy should be sought not within parties but between them. A democratic party that aspires to internal democracy is at a serious disadvantage in competition with parties which gird for battle without such self-delusion.[18]

For neoclassicists, on the other hand, the democratic ideal is relevant at all stages of social choice. Bottomore cites the interdependence of social institutions—family, work, politics—as a fundamental idea of sociology, and one ignored by revisionists.[19] Norms learned and applied in one major sector are inevitably practiced in others. Certainly, there are institutions in society—hospitals, military units, and churches—where discipline and training are important. No one thinks that it should be up to the patient to devise a strategy for curing Hodgkin's disease. Nor would anyone develop military strategy by holding discussions among the troops. Yet, the contagion of democratic ideals is evident, even in such organizations as these. In the military, the dignity of the foot-soldier and such norms as racial integration are fostered. In the churches (and not only in the reformed tradition), theology and liturgical practices are considered the proper work of lay persons, as well as the clergy. Even in the field of medical care, patients are urged to seek a second opinion, malpractice suits are tried by lay juries, and books promoting amateur treatment, such as *Our Bodies, Ourselves*, win a following and even gain professional respect.

However, it is in the workplace that neoclassical theorists have been most insistent on democratic ideals. Pateman points out that we spend most of our time at work. It is a mistake, she argues, to confine democracy to politics and, even worse, to voting alone. People learn political attitudes and habits by inference from one sphere to the other. Those who are active at church or in clubs tend to join unions and to take part in public life generally. It is therefore crucial to encourage people to take an active role in shaping their workplaces.[20]

Thus, for the neoclassicist, wherever discretion is exercised, the democratic person needs to understand and partake of the process of decision making. No aspect of personal life, and certainly no aspect of public life, escapes from the searching demand of this norm.

PLACE OF PARTIES IN DEMOCRATIC LIFE

The function of parties, according to James Q. Wilson, is to convert irrational loyalties into electoral majorities. It is impossible, he argues, to persuade 51 percent of the electorate to agree on all important issues. But where parties function properly, it is unnecessary to do so. In fact, "the ignorance of voters is what makes party government possible."[21] Most voters have no informed opinion about most items on the public agenda and no illusions about their ignorance. What they *do* have are feelings of loyalty to a political party. By playing to these feelings and avoiding debate over issues, party leaders are able to construct a government, even though there are no popular majorities on major problems and certainly no stable majorities across a range of issues.

From the revisionists' perspective, the ignorance of common citizens presents old-fashioned democrats with an insoluble problem. Either they must educate the people to the point where they can all become potential policy makers, which is impossible, or they must abandon democracy. Revisionists evade this problem by speaking with approval of "conventional political parties" that "organize the electorate so that it is confronted with a choice between leaders rather than between policies."[22] Then, while the parties insulate elected leaders from the direct pressures of public opinion, government can pursue the public good. Note that the perspective here upon parties is from the leadership downward. Parties are instruments for mobilizing support for the government and its policies, as well as an alternative or "shadow" government.

Revisionists, to be sure, are not satisfied with the current state of political parties in the United States. The dispersion of power in the system "creates a strong tendency to incoherence and immobilism," according to Herring. Partly this stems from the formal structure of authority under the Constitution. But the basic problem is the absence of strong political parties. Lacking them, there is no coherence to public policy. Programs set up one year may be eliminated the next. Programs promised by a winning party are not enacted. Decisions in one sector conflict with those in another, though both are nomimally controlled by the same party. As Herring puts it:

> Democracy inclines toward chaos rather than toward order. . . . Since the "voice of the people" is a pleasant fancy and not a present fact, the impulse for positive political action must be deliberately imposed at some strategic point, if democracy is to succeed as a form of government.[23]

Beer agrees and adds, "In a time that requires the utmost in efficient, long-run performance from our instrument of government, it fails to provide the base for a 'sustained flow of political power'."[24]

Some tension is evident here within revisionist ranks. Beer and Herring want parties to weld the parts of the constitutional structure together and build support for coherent programs. It is difficult to see how this can be done unless parties take explicit stands on controversial questions, which Wilson says will rouse sleeping dogs and threaten party unity. Despite this tension, the two strains of revisionist opinion are united on the implicit assumption that policy making is an elite function. One side might have more tolerance for such practices as policy councils and midterm issue conferences than the other. But neither expects rank-and-file party members to propose solutions for complex problems.

From the neoclassical point of view, parties are judged as instruments for facilitating participation by the masses in regime making and policy formulation. Usually, the judgment is harsh. Macpherson, for example, argues that parties operate to blur inequalities and deflect the determination to correct them. Earlier democratic theorists (Jeremy Bentham and James Mill), says Macpherson, were concerned that the democratic franchise would lead to expropriation and chaos, as the Greeks had predicted. John Stuart Mill, who (according to Macpherson) shared this apprehension, devoted his attention to schemes for weighted voting and legislative commissions, to cope with the dangers of popular participation. Macpherson argues that the strength of the existing class system made such precautions unnecessary. The need to produce a majority in class-divided societies led parties to broaden their appeal, thus giving the resulting governments room to maneuver, enabling them to "compromise" class interests. The result is that parties contributed to a situation in which true democracy is not possible. Instead, there is immobilism—or rather, when the dominant class interests require action, it is taken, but without real popular engagement.[25]

This tendency of parties to suppress participation and control conflict has led classical democrats to wonder whether party politics is compatible with democracy. As one item in his list of proposals for "rehabilitating politics," Kariel cites the need to realign political parties along ideological lines. Bottomore suggests that if politics and administration were decentralized, parties might not be necessary. Walker suggests that political scientists, blinded by the revisionists' theories of democracy, have neglected the study of political movements, although movements, rather than parties, have been the primary engine of popular involvement in politics during the past decade.[26] Macpherson, in an interesting echo of Ostrogorski, argues that when society evolves beyond class and participatory democracy truly begins, parties will not be necessary, though they may be useful if they confine themselves to single issues.[27]

What these thinkers have in common is the conviction that parties, as presently constituted, are unfit for popular government. Some hold out hope that partisan realignment can correct the problem. Others prefer to build movements for the expression of popular sentiment. They all see the need for a radical departure from the practice of accommodation and compromise that has characterized the approach of U.S. parties to public problems.

CONCLUSION

The preceding pages have tried to distinguish between two contrasting perspectives on democratic politics. The existence of these contrasting outlooks helps to explain why it is difficult to strengthen political parties. It is simply not clear what it would mean to strengthen them, and thus there is no consensus on the need or value of doing that.

One approach—we have called it *revisionist*—regards political parties as an essential component of a viable democratic regime. To perform properly, parties need to have clearly defined membership, reasonably well-articulated hierarchies, and a will to win. They need to be open to new membership, and there is no reason why they ought not to confrom to modern norms regarding free access, publicized meetings, and other forms of accountability. However, they ought not to be unduly programmatic, and their decision-making processes should honor talent, loyalty, and length of service and should not be bound to quotas. Revisionists tend to be conservative, even reactionary, where party form and process are concerned, though often liberal in policy preference. Sometimes, they are accused of yearning nostalgically for a golden age of party, though they are usually reluctant to identify any particular period in the past as displaying the norm they have in mind for party life.

Those whom we have identified as *neoclassical* democrats are at least suspicious of, and often openly hostile to, parties as they are or ever were. To Michels, they reply that if the human psyche needs security and order, it also needs challenge and renewal. The latter needs account for the resistance to bureaucracy and the recurrent demand for popular participation, and they are felt not just by counterelites but by braod groups of the citizenry—even under present conditions, which tend unnecessarily to suppress the instinct for involvement.

The classical spirit manifests itself in neighborhood action groups, in movements for workplace control, and, occasionally, in reform clubs but not among ward committees or at party caucuses. It supports the substitution of primaries for conventions and the abolition of the electoral college. It is represented by such organizations as Common Cause, Public Citizen, and Hayden's movement for a new society.

Are these two perspectives on democracy ultimately incompatible? Is it possible for those who see parties as essential to democracy to hope that they can be reformed to meet the objections of neoclassical democrats without demonstrating that one has not understood either of the two outlooks outlined in these pages? Or to put the question another way, can national political parties or statewide political parties be reformed so as to encourage greatly increased participation without rendering them ineffective as combatants in the political wars or as agencies of decision making in a modern society?

I would argue that the renewal of political parties depends upon the capacity of reformers to take the argument of neoclassical democrats seriously. Unless the yearning of John Stuart Mill for human development replaces the stoic realism of Schumpeter, parties will not be able to tap the idealism of a democratic citizenry. Those who value political parties need a positive program; they need to discover practical ways to encourage participation in and through political parties. Parties must combine a concern for effectiveness and discipline with a commitment to openness and responsiveness to the people. The challenge to parties, based on the fundamental principle that people can and should be fully self-governing, cannot be ignored. If parties rest content with current levels of participation, and seek to justify them by the doctrines of revisionism, they will disengage themselves from the cutting edge of democratic thought and aspiration.

NOTES

1. See Robert Dahl, "On Removing Certain Impediments to Democracy in the United States," *Political Science Quarterly* 92 (Spring 1977): 1–20, especially pp. 7–8 and 11.

2. Joseph Schumpeter, *Capitalism, Socialism, and Democracy* (London: Allen and Unwin, 1943), pp. 250, 269.

3. Carole Patemen, *Participation and Democratic Theory* (Cambridge: Cambridge University Press, 1970), pp. 17–18.

4. Most neoclassicists trace their inspiration to Jean Jacques Rousseau. C. B. Macpherson, however, insists that the tradition of "liberal democracy" begins in the nineteenth century with Jeremy Bentham and James Mill. Earlier democratic theorists, he argues, including Rousseau and Jefferson, did not face up to the reality of class and are thus utopian, rather than liberal, democrats. See C. B. Macpherson, *The Life and Times of Liberal Democracy* (Oxford: Oxford University Press, 1977), pp. 9–22.

5. Karl Mannheim, *Essays on the Sociology of Culture*, p. 179, quoted by T. B. Bottomore in *Elites and Society* (London: Watts, 1964), p. 105–6.

6. Samuel H. Beer, "New Structures of Democracy: Britain and America," in *Democracy in Mid-Twentieth Century: Problems and Prospects*, ed. William N. Chambers and Robert H. Salisbury (St. Louis: Washington University Press, 1960), p. 55.

7. Or as Madison put it on August 7, 1787, at the Federal Convention, it is a "fundamental principle" of popular government "that men cannot be justly bound by laws in making of which they have no part." (Max Farrand, ed., *The Records of the Federal Convention of 1787* [New Haven, Conn.: Yale University Press, 1911, 1937], 2:204, n. 17). Macpherson, in an uncharac-

teristically flippant footnote (*The Life and Times of Liberal Democracy*, p. 15), rejects the suggestion that Madison is a "pre-nineteenth century liberal democrat." This is not the occasion to refute this argument, but anyone interested in doing so need only check Macpherson's citations of Madison for the language that completes the sentences from which Macpherson's quotations come.

8. For a full exposition of this argument, see Richard Sennett, *The Fall of Public Man* (New York: Random House, 1978).

9. Raymond Aron, "Social Structure and the Ruling Class," *British Journal of Sociology* 1 (March 1950): 10, quoted by Bottomore, *Elites and Society*, p. 120.

10. Cited by Bottomore, *Elites and Society*, pp. 112–13.

11. The evidence is summarized by Seymour Martin Lipset, *Political Man: The Social Bases of Politics* (Garden City, N.Y.: Doubleday, 1960), pp. 217–19. Lipset does not argue that high participation is bad for democracy and apathy therefore functional, as is sometimes contended, but rather that "a *sudden* increase in the size of the voting electorate probably reflects tension and serious governmental mal-functioning and also introduces as voters individuals whose social attitudes are unhealthy from the point of view of the requirements of the democratic system" (emphasis added).

12. Lane Davis, "The Cost of the New Realism," reprinted from *Western Political Quarterly* 17 (1964), in Henry Kariel, ed. *Frontiers of Democratic Theory* (New York: Random House, 1970), p. 214. For a critique of the idea of participation as an intrinsic good, see M. B. E. Smith, "The Value of Participation," in *Participation in Politics*, ed. J. Roland Pennock and John W. Chapman (New York: Lieber-Atherton, 1975), pp. 126–35.

13. John Stuart Mill, *Considerations on Representative Government* (New York: Harper and Brothers, 1862), pp. 39–40.

14. See Macpherson, *The Life and Times of Liberal Democracy*, pp. 85–88; see also Tom Hayden, "The Politics of 'The Movement'," in *The Radical Papers*, ed. Irving Howe (Garden City, N.Y.: Anchor, 1966), pp. 373–76.

15. Pateman, *Participation and Democratic Theory*, p. 102.

16. Macpherson, *Life and Times of Liberal Democracy*, pp. 98ff. compare Dahl, "On Removing Certain Impediments," where the tension between the commitment to democracy and the commitment to corporate property in the United States is seen as fundamental.

17. Bottomore, *Elites and Society*, pp. 110, 118.

18. James Q. Wilson, *The Amateur Democrat* (Chicago: University of Chicago Press, 1966), pp. 347–48, 353–54. Citing Robert McKenzie's study of *British Political Parties* (London: Heinemann, 1955), pp. 581–91, Wilson argues that "Discipline . . . is the enemy of intraparty democracy" (p. 349).

19. Bottomore, *Elites and Society*, p. 115.

20. Pateman, *Participation and Democratic Theory*, chap. 4; see also Bottomore, *Elites and Soceity*, pp. 115–20.

21. Wilson, *The Amateur Democrat*, p. 357.

22. Ibid., pp. 344–46. Wilson quotes Walter Lippmann on the danger that comes when "destructively wrong" public opinion imposes itself upon the judgments of "informed and responsible officials" (p. 345).

23. E. Pendleton Herring, in Chambers and Salisbury, eds., *Democracy in Mid-Twentieth Century*, p. 59.

24. Beer, "New Structures of Democracy," p. 59.

25. Macpherson, *Life and Times of Liberal Democracy*, pp. 64–69; compare Raymond Aron, in Kariel, ed., *Frontiers of Democratic Theory*, p. 129.

26. Kariel, ed., *Frontiers of Democratic Theory*, p. 97; Bottomore, *Elites and Society*, p. 111; and Jack Walker, "A Critique of the Elitist Theory of Democracy," *American Political Science Review* 60 (1966): 293–95.

27. Macpherson, *Life and Times of Liberal Democracy*, pp. 112–14. On M. I. Ostrogorski, see his *Democracy and the Organization of Political Parties* (New York: Macmillan, 1902), 2: 651–95, and *Democracy and the Party System in the United States: A Study in Extra-Constitutional Government* (New York: Macmillan, 1910), pp. 441–45. For exposition, see Austin Ranney, *The Doctrine of Responsible Party Government* (Urbana: University of Illinois Press, 1962), chap. 7, especially, p. 129.

3

THE PHILOSOPHIES OF PARTY REFORM

William J. Crotty

U.S. political parties began a critical assessment of their role and fortunes in the year following the election of 1968. The reevaluation of party operations that was undertaken brought convulsions to the party system before it ran its course. The impact was particularly severe on the Democratic Party, the focus of the discontent and the party that instituted the changes.[1] The Democratic Party and its reform and antireform wings are the principal subject of the discussion that follows.

This chapter is concerned with one dimension of the reform movement, namely, the relationship between the traditional emphases of party theory and the recent reform movement. The chapter will attempt to answer such questions as the following: What theory underlay reform? What "philosophy" of party representation motivated the reformers or helped justify their objectives? What fundamental beliefs as to the operations of a political party in a democratic society influenced those who sought change and those who fought so strenuously to resist it? In short, what contribution did party theory make to the reform movement?

ROLE OF THEORY IN REFORM

E. E. Schattschneider, in his classic work on political parties, *Party Government*, comments that political parties are "the orphans of political philosophy." The "overwhelming tendency of all philosophers," he contends, is "to ignore the subject altogether."[2] The point is well taken. Political theory, at any level, has not dealt adequately with political parties.[3]

Parties evolved to fill representational and linkage functions uniting the formal governing institutions with the mass of citizenry. Political parties, in democratic nations, are the handmaidens of popular sovereignty. Schattschneider is as forceful on this point as anyone. He contends that political parties are one of "the principal distinguishing marks of modern government." "Political parties created democracy and modern democracy is unthinkable save in terms of parties."[4]

Political parties would appear eminently worth nurturing, a singular contributor to any democratic society. It is reasonable to expect that they would also represent a significant component of any serious theory dealing with democratic government. Unfortunately, this is not the case. Most theorists who have written about political parties have shared a common concern with their potential hazards. The distinction between the two major schools of thought on the subject, which we refer to as the *nihilists* and the *idealists*, is that one would abolish the institution of parties and the other would attempt to perfect it.

THE NIHILISTS (OR "NO-PARTY" ADVOCATES)

The nihilists' view dominates the writings on political parties in the United States. The nihilists saw little good and much reason for concern in the advent of political parties. Their solution was (depending on the theorist) to abolish political parties entirely; to substitute other, more limited groups to fulfill their functions; or to "reform" the parties into impotence. Some have contended that the present-day reformers share one (the last) or all of these objectives.[5]

Distrust of political parties is a long-held and popular U.S. tradition (see Pomper's chapter above). The most famous writings against parties came from two of the nation's founders, Madison and Washington. Madison, writing in *The Federalist, No. 10*, cautioned about the emergence of political parties and attempted to devise ways to counter their negative impact. Washington, in his farewell address, was still more blunt.

Political parties survived such early critical assaults because they were absolutely essential to the democratic enterprise. Their major functions—in leadership selection, communicating views to elected officials, providing a management tool for unifying a fractured governing structure, and building durable policy coalitions behind programs—could not be duplicated by any other agency. Yet, the warnings of Washington, Madison, and others, as well as the political parties' frequent abuse of their powers, did make an impact that lingers to this day in public sentiment.[6]

Washington and Madison preferred a "no-party" system, as (apparently) do many Americans today. These founding fathers tended to confuse political parties with factionalism, strife, and personal self-aggrandizement, which they desperately wanted to avoid. A second school of critics, coming at a later date, acknowledged the value of party contributions but preferred some other, more limited agency to carry out their duties. Exemplifying this line of thinking was M. I. Ostrogorski.

Ostrogorski was a Russian aristocrat with a deep concern for the vitality of democratic government. His most influential work, published at the turn of the century, was a comparison of the organization and operation of political parties in Great Britain and the United States.[7] Ostrogorski's standards of acceptable democratic performance were high: he believed in the eighteenth-century philosophic ideal of a representative government based on the rational character of man. Nonetheless, and despite his utopian objectives, Ostrogorski was able to appreciate the services performed by the political parties for a democratic governing order. His solution to the tension created by the need for political parties as against their inefficient, corrupt, and self-serving operations was to call for the creation of "single-issue" associations. These would be groups of like-minded individuals who would bond together temporarily to advance a policy they mutually supported. In this manner, Ostrogorski hoped to preserve the representative contributions of political parties, while eliminating their worst features.

A third general grouping of antiparty theorists would include certain types of reformers. Reform is an old and cherished tradition in the United States. The search for order, decency, and efficiency in political and economic life has long fascinated Americans.[8] Historically, it has represented a fundamental concern of undiminished attractiveness for generations of activists. Often, reform has had an aggressively moralistic overtone. Reform movements have justified their efforts to restructure ongoing social institutions in broad ethical or philosophic terms. Such was the case with the Progressives, the most influential reform movement on the political parties.

The Progressives distrusted political parties. They attacked parties for the abuses of privilege and the exploitation of the public treasury they associated with the urban machines of the late nineteenth century. The historian John Allswang recounts the danger:

> The picture of the boss and the machine in the late nineteenth century remained pretty consistent. The machine politician was corrupt, immoral, and entirely self-serving. Moreover, his power derived from an alliance with the most untrustworthy and disreputable elements in the urban society, thus posing the threat not only of bad government but also of social danger. It was a contemporary evil requiring excision.[9]

The Progressives' remedies for the problems they encountered were innovative: civil service reform and the creation of a city manager, city council, or committee form of government, to introduce businesslike proficiency into the management of municipal politics; the initiative, referendum, and recall, to provide voters with a direct control over legislation and officeholders; the direct primary, registration, and public statutes regulating political party structures and performance, to undercut the boss and weaken (if not destroy) the parties' stranglehold on the political process.[10] The Progressives succeeded in getting much of what they wanted. But the consequences were different than expected. The parties adapted to the new forms, and while the Progressive movement waned in the post-1915 period, the parties prospered.

There may be a lesson here. The parties survived because they were needed. They fulfilled a vital role in the exercise of responsible power. Whatever their shortcomings, their existence, at least at this stage in U.S. history, was crucial to the very operation of the government. Efforts to immobilize or destroy them proceeded on a misinterpretation of their functional significance in the society.

The nihilist critics of U.S. political parties shared certain characteristics: a distrust of parties, an uneasiness with their manner of operation, and a desire to weaken, replace, or destroy them. The next school of thought sought quite different ends. Their aim was to change the operations of parties to conform to an idealized model of democratic representation. Their objectives were as extreme in their own regard and as unrealistic as those of the nihilists.

THE IDEALISTS

One of the most seductive visions to the student of political parties is the myth of the perfect party: cohesive, policy oriented, representative, and disciplined. The definition of the terms might differ, but the end result would be a party-directed government that offered clear, deliverable policy choices to its electors; that controlled its representatives once in office to the extent that the party could deliver on its campaign promises; and that stood or fell on the quality of its performance in enacting its pledges. The model for this ideal form was based on a misconception of the English party system, always held to be more disciplined, responsive, and, in a policy sense, accountable to its constituents than the U.S. parties.[11] Practitioners and political scientists from Woodrow Wilson and Henry Jones Ford to Stephen Bailey and Schattschneider, in one form or another, have all held forth this dream.[12]

The desirability of such a party system, much less its practicality, is highly questionable. It does not fit American needs or conform to the

American historical and political experience. It is true, as many have argued, and as Janda has shown, that U.S. parties have greater power decentralization and coalitional diversity than political parties in other democratic nations.[13] Parties are the end product of a political system's needs and its governing structures. U.S. parties developed as local level ad hoc groups that combined into successively broader geographical and policy coalitions in an effort to win elective office. They are heterogenous in nature, undisciplined, and with loose (mainly psychological) ties of loyalty binding the membership.

European parties, by contrast, often were created from legislative nuclei and were based on clear-cut ideological postures. They are cohesive, respond to centralized direction, and offer voters meaningful policy alternatives. European political parties also provide their members with social and cultural services unheard of in the United States. By comparison, the activities of U.S. parties appear restricted, if not impoverished, and their approach to public policy parochial. Any comparison between the two types of parties has always worked to the disadvantage of the U.S. parties. It has encouraged party theorists to seek ways to enable the parties in the United States to confrom more with the types of democratic parties found in other nations.

The most influential expression of the idealist position was the report prepared by the Committee on Political Parties of the American Political Science Association (under Schattschneider's direction) in 1950.[14] It is worth recalling that this committee was composed of many of the leading political scienctists of the postwar period. Its work called upon the best the discipline had to offer, and its recommendations were widely debated in academic and political circles.[15] It is given credit for the Democratic Party's attempt to establish a national policy council, the Democratic Advisory Council, in the 1950s.

The Committee on Political Parties proceeded on the assumption that "popular government . . . requires political parties which provide the electorate with a proper range of choice between alternatives of action." To reach this objective, the party system would have to be "democratic, responsible and effective." The committee defined these ends as requiring "that the parties are able to bring forth programs to which they commit themselves and, second, that the parties possess sufficient internal cohesion to carry out these programs."[16] These were the objectives.

On the national level, to accomplish these goals, the committee recommended a smaller, biennial national convention; a national committee apportioned on the basis of relative party strength in the states; a 50-member council composed of national committee members, congressional representatives, state party officials, and the party's national candidates. The council was to interpret the platform, supervise the party organization, and screen presidential contenders. In regard to the state and national parties, the council would provide enlarged services, while enforcing discipline. Congressional parties would be reformed by giving greater power to the leadership and the party caucuses and making committee assignments dependent on party loyalty.[17]

The report drew a strom of criticism. Opponents argued that its authors misread the peculiar character and strength of the U.S. party system. The critics believed that the Committee on Political Parties underestimated the contributions of a coalitional party system that prized accommodation and adaptability. They felt that more ideological parties would be particularly inappropriate given the historical, geographical, and social roots of the U.S. parties and the diverse governing structures with which the parties must contend. The report's conclusions seemed incompatible with the pragmatic, New Deal pluralism that dominated the politics of the era.

Seen from the perspective of three decades, several things are apparent. The reform proposals, if intended to promote a more responsible party system, as they were, are illusionary. There is nothing inherent in them that would force more programmatic and ideologically responsive political parties. To be effective, they depend on the goodwill of the participants. They rest on the weak assumption that a superior coordination among party units, leaders, and followers would result in more policy-oriented parties.

There is nothing intrinsic to the mechanisms proposed that would deal with the fundamental weaknesses of a party system designed to embrace as many interests as possible in a large and heterogenous nation. In addition, the parties must contend with governing structures that are federal in design and which emphasize the separation, rather than the unification, of power. The American Political Science Association report does not adequately treat these problems. Any efforts intended to discipline members— for example, by denying them choice committee assignments in Congress— would backfire. The congressional member, then, as now, is more dependent on satisfying his or her constituency and its needs than he or she is on an amorphous organization, such as a national party structure. In most cases, the leaders of the legislative party are more dependent on him or her for his or her vote than he or she is on them for their goodwill.[18]

Overall, the proposals themselves lack theoretical cohesion. The Committee on Political Parties took a pragmatic approach to its subject (common to U.S. theorists writing on political parties). It made an accommodation to the realities of politics as found in the New Deal era. This led to an emphasis on piecemeal (but potentially achievable) middle-guage proposals. What is sacrificed in such an approach is the coherence and in-depth restructuring that would be needed to begin to realize the (more than likely still unattainable) goal of "responsible" parties.

The political parties have introduced, in one form or another, many of the features recommended in the American Political Science Association report. Congressional caucuses are more significant in House (especially) and Senate decision making; congressional committee chairpersonships and member placements do depend more on the support of party leaders and the vote of fellow party members; there are (in the Democratic Party) off-year conventions intended to upgrade the party platform; party structures, such as the national committee, national conventions, and presidential nominating procedures have been made more representative; staffs of party headquarters have been professionalized and can provide an impressive range of services (especially in the Republican Party) to candidates for office and to state and local parties;[19] political participation in party affairs has increased;[20] registration procedures have been eased; and campaign finance reform has been enacted. The latter may not be entirely satisfactory to the national parties, but it does provide them with more funding ($2 million to $3 million in election years for their national conventions) than they had otherwise.

Few, if any, would argue that these changes have produced a "responsible" party system. Many, in contrast, feel that they have weakened the existing system and could lead to its extinction.[21] Most believe that the parties are in a serious state of decline.[22] The 1940s and 1950s are now looked back to nostalgically by many proponents of a strong party system as a sort of golden age of party supremacy.

The recommendations in the American Political Science Association report resulted from a concern with the problems of the party system of the 1930s and 1940s. This becomes clear from a careful reading of the report and the documentation used to support its assessments of party practices and their implications. The report does not anticipate (and could not) the problems of the present era: the reliance on television and the media-oriented candidate-centered campaigns; the prominence of technologically sophisticated professional consultants in politics; the inflation of political costs; the irresponsible use of official power, from Vietnam to Watergate; the extreme disillusionment of the U.S. public; the drop-off in voting; the decline in party voting and the increasing independence of both voters and legislators; and the advent of corporate, trade, and ideological Political Action committees and their assumption of the role of principal funders of political campaigns. In short, the report did not foresee (and could not have) the forces within a changing nation that have combined to place the political parties in the position of an increasingly irrelevant and antiquated vestige of another age.

The report had its deficiencies, and these were considerable. Yet, and despite its shortcomings, it did not deserve the ferocity of the attacks it drew. It was more forward looking and displayed more of an intelligent grasp of the problems facing the New Deal party system than its critics allowed. A stubborn defense of the status quo, by itself, ill-served a party system entering a period of intensified change. What the report does symbolize is the constant quest for the improvement of the political and social order that has marked the U.S. experience with representative government. Whether the "ideal" of the responsible party school and a responsible party government, however, could fulfill the hopes of the American Political Science Association planners is, at best, moot. Nonetheless, and despite its faults, the report of the Committee on Political Parties may have been the most significant influence on the debate over the operation of the political parties that occurred between the Progressive period and the party reform movement of the 1970s.

THEORETICAL ISSUES IN THE CONTROVERSY OVER POLITICAL PARTIES

Two of the basic issues that crosscut the debate over the functioning of political parties in the United States, and hence the desirability (or lack of it) of reform, involve the nature of the party structure and the costs, in terms of electoral success, of the introduction of fundamental change. The controversies involve the centralization/decentralization of party power and the argument over party democracy versus party success.

Centralization versus Decentralization

Students of U.S. political parties are unanimous on one point: they agree that the structure of U.S. parties is highly decentralized. Schattschneider put the point explicitly and well: "Decentralization of power is by all odds the most important single characteristic of the American major party; more than anything else this trait distinguishes it from all others. Indeed, once this truth is understood, nearly everything about American parties is illuminated."[23] While the parties' organizational structures are complex, reflecting diverse sets of offices for which, and electoral requirements under which, they must contend at all levels, power is dispersed. If anything, it gravitates downward to the lowest electoral units. Key went so far as to suggest that parties were decentralized to the point that "in a sense, no nationwide party organization exists, though each party, to be sure, has its national organs."[24]

Surveys of state party operations by Jewell and Olson reveal the same extraordinary complexity of procedures, forced by circumstance and the diverse sets of state legislative statutes, and the same dispersion of power, cohesion, and control at the state as at the national level.[25] The most influential work on urban politics (by Eldersveld) classified the parties as "stratarchies." Power is dispersed among units at the varying levels of the party structure and is characterized by a "reciprocal deference structure." This development is the result of the need of the party to "cope with widely varying local milieus of opinion, tradition and social structure . . . [that] encourages the recognition and acceptance of local leadership, local strategy, [and] local power."[26]

A decentralized power structure within the political parties has policy implications. A decentralized party system works against coherent policy formulation and effective policy implementation. This, more than anything else, has been the rallying point for twentieth-century reformers. Many would contend that whatever the merit coherent policy stands have for parties, the decentralized party system cannot be changed. It responds to the social and political mix that characterizes U.S. life, which renders impossible any serious effort at national centralization of the parties or their policy-making procedures.

Party Democracy versus Party Success

Perhaps the most debated issue in the controversy (among party theorists) surrounding political parties is the role of the individual party member in decision making. (See Robinson's chapter, above, for a discussion of this issue in a broader context.) Most theorists believe that electoral success and a Democratic party operation are incompatible. Michels, in expounding his "iron law of oligarchy," emphasized the inequality in resources available to leaders as against followers and the tendency of an organization of any size to become oligarchical.[27] Studies of political party organizations, trade unions, and other mass associations have reaffirmed Michels's insights.[28] At present, the inevitability of oligarchy in broad-based organizations is accepted as a political fact of life.

There is another aspect of this debate. Most party theorists believe party democracy not only unlikely (or unattainable) but also undesirable. They equate intraparty democracy with a lack of coherent organizational direction and a failure to provide effective and determined leadership. The New Deal coalition was built on a pluralistic (many groups were in the coalition) but elitist (only a few of the top group leaders exercised power) party arrangement. The party system itself was basically closed to grass-roots influence. Party members were involved only to the extent of voting for or against the party's nominees. The representatives of the groups prominent in the New Deal coalition (organized labor, governors and state party leaders, big city bosses, and national party regulars) constituted an oligarchy within the Democratic Party. At the same time, the party remained effectively closed to rank-and-file influence; it continued to suffer from the power dispersion and structural inadequacies that have long characterized political parties in the United States. In effect, U.S. parties enjoyed the worst of several worlds. Yet, many look to this party system as a model. Party democracy is taken to mean, ipso facto, that a party cannot win electorally. Since winning elections is the raison d'etre of U.S. politics, the one function that explains the growth of parties, their role in society, and, in addition, their weaknesses, this represents a damning indictment of increased grass-roots participation.

A handful of party theoreticans believe intraparty democracy both possible and desirable. The Committee on Political Parties argued:

> Capacity for internal agreement, democratically arrived at, is a critical test for a party. It is a critical test because when there is no such capacity, there is no capacity for positive action, and hence the party becomes a hollow pretense. It is a test which can be met only if the party machinery affords the membership an opportunity to set the course of the party and to control those who speak for it. This test can be met fully only where the membership accepts responsibility for creative participation in shaping the party's program.[29]

Sentiments of this nature appear to exasperate most party theorists. For them, intraparty democracy is a luxury and one that would lead inexorably to the ruination of a political party in the competitive U.S. electoral environment. Intraparty democracy and electoral success, they would argue, are antithetical. Yet recent party reformers, to the dismay of the professionals, took a position similar to that of the Committee on Political Parties. The reformers believed that intraparty democracy was not only compatible with winning elective office but constituted a necessary precondition for any electoral success. Without party democracy, controlling political office would be rendered meaningless. "Political parties will survive only if they respond to the needs and concerns of their members," contended the McGovern-Fraser Commission, the bellwether of the reform movement. "We believe that popular control of the Democratic Party is necessary for its survival."[30]

REFORM MOVEMENT OF THE 1970s

Despite similarities in rhetoric and beliefs between theorists of an open party and the party reformers, the reform movement of the 1970s was remarkably atheoretical. It was not directly influenced by the debate over party theory or its concerns. Political scienctists did play a role in the reform movement—on both sides of the controversy—but their concerns were as political as those of the practicing politicans, namely, who benefited, who lost, and what forms would maximize the influence of the groups they wanted to dominate party affairs.

Reform developed out of pressures placed on the party system that it could neither cope with effectively nor ignore. Reform grew out of practical political concerns. It came because a large part of the Democratic Party's coalition believed the national party and its leaders to be out of touch and unresponsive to its, and the nation's, concerns. The pressure to do something fundamental had become extreme: the Vietnam War and the issues it raised, including the responsibility and accountability of those in power, had split the Democratic coalition. Violence had erupted in the streets and on college campuses. Cities burned. Those who protested were advised to take their pleas from the streets to the ballot boxes. Many did, only to find how antiquated party processes had become and the extent to which they could remain immune to grass-roots concerns. This—the unresponsiveness of the political parties in a time of great stress—was the specific impetus for reform.[31]

The insurgents did succeed in forcing an incumbent president from office in 1968. However, they did not win their party's nomination, and their influence on the party's platform on issues of vital national concern was restricted. In fact, by the time the national convention opened in Chicago, with Robert Kennedy's assassination and the unshakable lead in delegate votes held by the Johnson-Humphrey faction, it was clear to the insurgents (and everyone else) that they had no chance to capture the party's nomination. Yet, they believed that they represented a significant, if not dominant, division of the views among the party's rank and file.

The reformers had done well in head-to-head contests with the party regulars. Their strength of the grass-roots level, however, was not reflected in the national convention. Eugene McCarthy received 2.9 million votes in the Democratic primaries—38.7 percent of the total votes cast. Second was Robert Kennedy, with 2.3 million votes—30.6 percent of all votes cast. A distant eighth (behind even the withdrawn candidate Lyndon Johnson) was Hubert Humphrey, with 166,463 votes—2.2 percent of the total. Yet at the 1968 national convention, Humphrey received 67 percent of the delegates' votes, to easily win the presidential nomination. McCarthy, his closest competitor, could claim only 23 percent of the convention vote, and the insurgents' vote in toto amounted to only 28.5 percent of the convention vote. This minority share contrasted sharply with the 69.3 percent won by the insurgents (McCarthy and Kennedy combined) in the primaries.

Humphrey made few policy (or any other) concessions to the insurgents to gain the nomination. Furthermore, the insurgents had difficulty in nonprimary states in penetrating organizations controlled by party regulars. As a consequence of these experiences, the insurgents believed that party processes were closed and that they were not fairly represented at the national convention.

The inequities convinced the insurgents that reform of party processes was needed. They spent their time at the Chicago convention working for a resolution to establish a reform body to assess party priorities. Eventually, they were successful, and the reform era was inaugurated.

Once the reform bodies were established, their in-depth investigations revealed a party lax in organization; complacent at the top, while closed to significant influence from below; and abusive of the interests of its own rank and file. Once studied, presidential nominating procedures, for example, showed clearly why votes in a primary could not be translated into representation at national conventions and why party caucuses, party committees, and conventions, the procedures employed in nonprimary states to select national convention delegates, were not open to direct influence from the party's grass-roots activists.

The McGovern-Fraser Commission found considerable deficiencies in party procedures.[32] Some states lacked written rules; proxy voting was regularly abused; party meetings were often unannounced and manipulated; closed party elites dominated delegate selection; considerable fees were assessed on prospective delegates; discrimination on the basis of race, sex, and age was widespread; and the entire process was "untimely," beginning—and sometimes ending—long before popular preferences could be developed. (For further discussion, see Chapter 6.)

It is important to realize that problems of some magnitude were found in every state.[33] The party system had grown fat and lazy; it was unresponsive to (and perhaps unconcerned with) its grass-roots base. It cried out for reform, and the reformers were only too willing to oblige. Reform came because it was needed. This was the central lesson of the events leading to refrom and the motivating concern behind the reform movement.

The fundamental issue in the debate over reform dealt with the question of who would control the Democratic Party.[34] The uses the party apparatus would be put to was to be determined only after it was clear which group had become dominant in the power struggle (either the reformers or the party regulars). The debate over reform as a consequence had little to do with democratic theory, beyond a vague and unfocused feeling on the part of the proreform advocates that party procedures should be fair, open to all party members, and responsive to their wishes. As the dimensions of the reform initiatives became clear, the major issues in contention between the reformers and the party regulars revolved around ways to advance, or check, efforts to gain control of the party by one faction or the other. During the battles that ensued, a number of significant differences emerged that clearly separated the contending groups. These included affirmative action and the definition of a democrat. Two other issues were particularly relevant to the philosophy of party reform.

Nominations: Elite Representation by Party Regulars or Direct Representation of the Party's Grass-roots Membership

Party regulars favored the system in effect before 1972, which guaranteed them the dominant role in choosing the party's presidential nominee. Reformers rejected the closed system that had been encountered in 1968 and fought for open nominating processes which accurately reflected the party members' vote and policy views at all stages (from precinct meetings to national conventions). The reformers would not only open the party but, if successful, would reverse the power distribution over nominations. This is one area, involving the most important of party functions, in which power was centralized in the party regulars—the governors and mayors who led the state delegations and interest group leaders (such as the American Federation of Labor and Congress of Industrial Organizations' [AFL-CIO's] George Meany)—at the national convention. This issue, and the fights it spawned, such as the controversy over the proportional representation of a presidential candidate's strength in delegate selection, were crucial to the success of the reforms.

Defining the Purpose of a Political Party

The party regulars were clear on this point: the purpose of a political party was to win elections. This certainly was the time-honored assumption justifying U.S. parties. Anything that might divert the party's attention from this goal appeared to infuriate the regulars.

The reformers believed that a political party had to represent something more substantial, and, specifically, the policy views of its supporters, or winning office by itself was spurious. The reformers also felt that a strong and electorally successful political party was one that was directly responsive to the needs of its rank and file.

The argument over the feasibility of party democracy enters the debate at this point. The reformers felt that grass-roots party activists had to be given a direct and meaningful voice in party matters and that this was the way in which a strong, vital, and successful party organization was built.

Party regulars unequivocally rejected these contentions. They believed that the party professionals could best protect the interests of the rank and file and, in the process, win public office. They argued that the only time that the party's clientele could hold them accountable was in general elections. Such a strategy, of course, minimized the role of lower-level party supporters and left the national party as a closed corporation, virtually insensitive to change. The reformers would contend that this is exactly what happened in the 1960s and led to the drive for reform.

The argument between the contending sides spread to a number of other issues. The reformers were able to enact a party charter, bitterly opposed by the hardcore regulars, which formally expanded the functions and services of the national party.[35] Many reformers also wanted party membership to be acknowledged through some type of identification. A plan for a "card-carrying" party membership was not looked on favorably by regulars.

Overall, the reformers proposed to institutionalize the national party to a far greater extent than it ever had been before. It was their desire to engage the party in a range of full-time activities (beyond those connected with the immediate pursuit of elective office) that it had not been associated with previously. Party regulars strongly preferred the ad hoc electoral coalitions that could yield a loyal party vote but otherwise made few demands on their time or energy.

The reformers made their objectives, as well as the motivations underlying them, clear:

> If we are not an open party; if we do not represent the demands of change, then the danger is not that people will go to the Republican Party; it is that there will no longer be a way for people committed to orderly change to fulfill their needs and desires within our traditional political system. It is that they will turn to third and fourth party politics or the anti-politics of the street.[36]

The party regulars rejected each implicit assumption in the reform declaration. They opposed an "open party" as electorally sucidal; they believed the contemporary parties provided vehicles for orderly change; they did not think the party system sick; and they characterized the people who turned to the streets to express their displeasure with politics as those least concerned with saving the party system. They felt that more than likely, such dissidents would prefer gutting the system; indeed, the regulars suspected that too many of the reformers might fit this description.

With such views separating the protagonists and with the control of the dominant party in U.S. life, as well as its presidential nominating procedures, at stake, there was little likelihood of compromise. The reform spectacle was fought out to its bitter end. Eventually, the reformers carried the political battle, with enormous consequences for the practice of U.S. politics.

CONTRIBUTION OF REFORM TO PARTY THEORY

While party theory played no discernible role in party reform, on either side, the results of the reform initiatives might have something to contribute to theorizing about parties. At a minimum, they raise questions about some of the standard assumptions of the theorists writing on political parties. The contributions of reform to the theoretical debate over parties is just beginning to be understood.

First, the reformers assumed that the national party had the power to enforce their reforms; they contended that the national party could, with proper authority, implement what it decided upon—and most surprisingly, they managed to get the state and local parties, as well as the leadership of the national party, to believe them.

The reformers based their arguments on two sources. First was the little-known precedent established by the special Equal Rights Committee (1964–68), created by the 1964 National Convention, to eliminate discrimination against blacks in delegate composition. The committee had issued its report and sent its recommendations to the state parties to be implemented. They were presented as if they were mandatory, and in the 1968 National Convention's Credentials Committee, they were employed to judge the adequacy and representativeness of a state's delegation. The McGovern-Fraser and later reform commissions followed the same tack. The difference was that the vast majority of party regulars implicitly supported the Special Committee's standards. The reform guidelines were far more controversial and, in fact, split the party into factions. But the reformers did have this precedent on their side.

The reformers also assumed that the National Convention mandate creating the reform commissions gave them the power to enforce their rules. The national convention is the supreme governing body of the party, and this argument had merit. However, whether the National Convention intended any such interpretation is problematical.[37]

The party has become more centralized. This has resulted from a number of factors. The party regulars fought the reforms strenuously. They lost out politically at the 1972 National Convention, as well as legally, especially in the Supreme Court decision, *Cousins* v. *Wigoda* (1975), affirming the national party's perogatives in the area of presidential selection. When the antireform tide of the post-1972 period failed substantially to weaken the reforms, the state parties conceded the battle. They were willing to go along with almost anything the national party dictated. This attitude represents a dramatic reversal in outlook (and not necessarily a healthy one) from that of a decade earlier.

The consequences are many. The national party has been able to centralize its power in many areas, and there has been a new emphasis on national party concerns. This is true in all aspects of party activity, but its most telling impact could be on presidential nominations. With the present trend toward a centralization of authority and the subservience of state parties, any faction controlling the national party can undermine the independence and integrity of the nominating process. For example, the faction controlling the national committee could create a "reform" committee and dictate new rules of prcedure. The new rules would not have to be in line with any reform principles or even be politically wise. Nonetheless, most party units could be expected to accept them meekly. The Carter administration was quick to realize the potential of this new docility and, working through a new reform commission, enacted nominating rules particularly advantageous to the renomination of the incumbent president.[38] A constant restructuring of the system could be in the offing.

The trend toward the nationalization of both political parties extends not only to the areas directly concerned with the reforms, and to presidential nominations in particular, but also to such things as party finances, party law, staff services, and, within limits, the funding of campaigns and state organizations. The national party may be assuming a supremacy in areas which it has never exercised before.[39]

Third, the outcome of the reform battle has produced a situation that party theorists long thought incompatible: a highly centralized political organization *with* power dispersed among the rank and file. Party theorists have argued for one or the other: a democratic party structure and decision-making process *or* a highly structured, authoritarian, and, presumably, more electorally successful party organization. This is particularly true in the vital area of presidential nominations. It is a tribute to the ad hoc nature of the contemporary reform philosophy and the impact that unforeseen outside events had on the final product that both were incorporated within the postreform political party.

Fourth, reform has shown it is possible to centralize power in one area and have it remain decentralized in others, a possibility not seriously considered by party theorists. Rather than a unified, coherent party extending to all areas of party concern (the responsible party model) or a Michelian oligarchy carefully protecting its perogatives (the regular's model), the end product of the newly instituted reforms is a party with a great deal of centralized power over nominating rules and procedures for delegate selection at the national level. At the same time, local and state parties exercise much of the freedom they enjoyed in party organizational matters and operations prior to the reforms. The decentralization of structure and authority in nonnominating areas has been little changed. This arrangement continues despite the Democratic Party's efforts to restructure party operations through the adoption of the party charter. The impact of the charter on organizational arrangements and in increasing structural coherence has been limited. The state parties (with no noticeable help from the reforms) may be more vital and aggressive than we have been led to believe,[40] and the national party no more influential in their affairs now than in the prereform era. (The Republican Party case is quite different, however, see Bibby's analysis in Chapter 7.)

It may well be that a nationalization of both parties *in all areas* will only follow a shift in national needs (or governing structures—a possibility so remote as not to require extended attention). It may be a process that takes place over generations, receiving only spasmodic attention from party scholars. It appears that this is the case with the present party system: the nationalization has been progressing for over 100 years. Reform has simply helped to accelerate the process.

> Today the domination of the national party is nearly complete; there are no state parties which look after state issues and which are distinct from the parties and the policies that are of continental dimensions. In every step taken in ward or township, in every nomination made for local office, there is deference to the interests of the great national organization; local interests are nearly submerged.[41]

This was written in 1905. The process is more advanced today. It is the national issues, candidates, and loyalties that command the voters' attention. The organizational forms have not kept pace with the psychological and political realities.

Fifth, a responsible party (with emphasis on the cohesiveness and representativeness of national party structures) along the lines envisaged by generations of party theorists appears as far from realization today as it did a decade ago. Certainly, the Democratic Party charter and the reformulations of the National Committee and National Convention should have contributed to such ends. However, the national party continues to be oligarchic. The pattern is little changed from prereform days. The national committee is still essentially ineffective; it has no sense of grass-roots accountability, and it remains subservient to the president, when of the same party. The Carter administration's dominance of the Democratic National Committee has effectively made the point.[42] National conventions are little more amenable to influence from individual delegates than they were in the prereform period. Midterm conventions have been dominated by party regulors and have not been able seriously to revise the party platform. The reform movement has grafted an elaborate superstructure onto the national party apparatus, but one that has filed to result in a more representative and accountable party organization. In this area, the reform objectives remain unfulfilled. For theorists, and especially those of the responsible party persuasion, it may be time to go back to the drawing board.

If these trends continue, the old arguments over centralization versus decentralization and intraparty democracy versus electoral success may have as little relevance for understanding the contemporary party system as they did in motivating party reform.

NOTES

1. See William Crotty, *Decision for the Democrats: Reforming the Party Structure* (Baltimore: Johns Hopkins University Press, 1978), for an in-depth discussion of these developments.

2. E. E. Schattschneider, *Party Government* (New York: Holt, Rinehart and Winston, 1942), pp. 10, 4.

3. For diverse assessments and attempts, see Giovanni Sartori, *Parties and Party Systems*, 2 vols. (Cambridge: Cambridge University Press, 1976); Joseph A. Schlesinger, "Political Party Organization," in *Handbook of Organizations*, ed. James G. March (Chicago: Rand McNally, 1965), pp. 764–801; Kenneth Janda, *Comparative Political Parties: A Cross-National Survey* (New York: Free Press, 1980); William Crotty, "Political Parties Research," in *Approaches to the Study of Political Science*, ed. Michael Haas and Henry S. Kariel (San Francisco: Chandler, 1970), pp. 267–322; Austin Ranney, "The Concept of 'Party'," in *Political Research and Political Theory*, ed. Oliver Garceau (Cambridge, Mass.: Harvard University Press, 1968), pp. 143–62; and Maurice Duverger, *Political Parties* (New York: Wiley, 1954).

4. Schattschneider, *Party Government*, p. 1.

5. Austin Ranney, *Curing the Mischiefs of Faction* (Berkeley: University of California Press, 1975); Austin Ranney, "Changing the Rules of the Nominating Game," in *Choosing the President*, ed. James D. Barber (Englewood Cliffs, N.J.: Prentice-Hall, 1974), pp. 71–93; Austin Ranney, "The Democratic Party's Delegate Selection Reforms, 1968–1976," in *America in the Seventies: Problems, Policies, and Politics*, ed. Allan P. Sindler (Boston: Little, Brown, 1977), pp. 160–206; and Austin Ranney, "The Political Parties: Reform and Decline," in *The New American Political System*, ed. Anthony King (Washington, D.C.: American Enterprise Institute, 1978), pp. 213–47.

6. See Jack Dennis, "Changing Public Support for the American Party System," in *Paths to Political Reform*, ed. William Crotty (Lexington, Mass.: Heath, 1980), and Jack Dennis, "Trends in Public Support for the American Party System," *British Journal of Political Science* 5 (April 1975): 187–230.

7. M. I. Ostrogorski, *Democracy and the Organization of Political Parties* (New York: Macmillan, 1902).

8. See William Crotty, *Political Reform and the American Experiment* (New York: Crowell, 1977).

9. John M. Allswang, *Bosses, Machines, and Urban Voters* (Port Washington, N.Y.: Kennikat Press, 1977), p. 8.

10. Richard Hofstadter, *The Age of Reform* (New York: Knopf, 1955); Michael H. Ebner and Eugene M. Tobin, eds., *The Age of Urban Reform* (Port Washington, N.Y.: Kennikat Press, 1977); Crotty, *Political Reform*; and Simon Lazarus, *The Genteel Populists* (New York: McGraw-Hill, 1974).

11. David E. Butler, "American Myths about British Parties, *Virginia Quarterly Review* 31 (Winter 1955): 46–56.

12. Helpful in this regard is Austin Ranney, *The Doctrine of Responsible Party Government* (Urbana: University of Illinois Press, 1954), and Evron M. Kirkpatrick, "Toward a More

Responsible Two-Party System: Political Science, Policy Science, or Pseudo-Science?" *American Political Science Review* 65 (December 1971): 965–90.

13. Kenneth Janda, *Comparative Political Parties: A Cross-National Survey* (New York: Free Press, in press).

14. Report of the Committee on Political Parties of the American Political Science Association, *Toward A More Responsible Two-Party System* (New York: Rinehart, 1950).

15. Julius Turner, "Responsible Parties: A Dissent from the Floor," *American Political Science Review* 65 (March 1951): 143–52; William Goodman, "How Much Political Party Centralization Do We Want?" *Journal of Politics* 13 (November 1951): 536–61; Murray S. Stedman, Jr., and Herbert Sonthoff, "Party Responsibility—A Critical Inquiry," *Western Political Quarterly* 4 (September 1951): 454–68; Austin Ranney, "Toward A More Responsible Two-Party System: A Commentary," *American Political Science Review*, 65 (June 1951): 448–99; and Kirkpatrick, "Toward a More Responsible Two-Party System."

16. Report of the Committee on Political Parties of the American Political Science Association, *Toward a More Responsible Two-Party System*, pp. 1, 17–18.

17. Ibid., pp. 40–69.

18. See as examples of this argument Thomas E. Mann, *Unsafe At Any Margin* (Washington, D.C.: American Enterprise Institute, 1978); Morris P. Fiorina, *Congress: Keystone of the Washington Establishment* (New Haven, Conn.: Yale University Press, 1977); Richard F. Fenno, Jr., *Home Style: House Members in Their Districts* (Boston: Little, Brown, 1978); and William Crotty and Garry C. Jacobson, *Party Decline and Democratic Malaise (Boston: Little, Brown, 1980), pt. III.*

19. Charles Longley, "Party Nationalization in America," in Crotty, ed., *Paths to Political Reform*; and Charles H. Longley, Chapter 5, in this volume.

20. Richard L. Rubin, "Presidential Primaries: Continuities, Dimensions of Change, and Political Implications," in *The Party Symbol*, ed. W. Crotty (San Francisco: Freeman, 1980); and William Crotty, "Party Reform and Democratic Performance (Paper delivered at Conference on the Future of the American Political System, Philadelphia, Pennsylvania, 1979). A dissenting point of view can be found in Austin Ranney, *Participation in American Presidential Nominations, 1976* (Washington, D.C.: American Enterprise Institute, 1977).

21. Jeanne J. Kirkpatrick, *Dismantling the Parties: Reflections on Party Reform and Party Decomposition* (Washington, D.C.: American Enterprise Institute, 1978); and Ranney, "The Political Parties."

22. Everett Carll Ladd, Jr., *Where Have All the Voters Gone?* (New York: Norton, 1978).

23. Schattschneider, *Party Government*, p. 129.

24. V. O. Key, Jr., *Politics, Parties, and Pressure Groups*, 5th ed. (New York: Crowell, 1964), p. 315.

25. Malcolm E. Jewell and David M. Olson, *American State Political Parties and Elections* (Homewood, Ill.: Dorsey, 1978).

26. Samuel J. Eldersveld, *Political Parties* (Chicago: Rand McNally, 1964), p. 9.

27. Robert Michels, *Political Parties* (New York: Free Press, 1962); and Robert T. Golembiewski, William A. Welsh, and William J. Crotty, *A Methodological Primer for Political Scientists* (Chicago: Rand McNally, 1969).

28. For the conditions that make intraorganizational democracy possible, see S. M. Lipset, Martin Trow, and James Coleman, *Union Democracy* (Garden City, N.Y.: Doubleday Anchor, 1956).

29. Report of the Committee on Political Parties of the American Political Science Association, *Toward a More Responsible Two-Party System*, p. 66. See also Robert T. Nakamura and Denis G. Sullivan, "Party Democracy and Democratic Control," in *American Politics and Public Policy*, ed. Walter Dean Burnham and Martha W. Weinberg (Cambridge, Mass.: MIT Press, 1978), pp. 26–41.

30. Commission on Party Structure and Delegate Selection, *Mandate for Reform* (Washington, D.C.: Democratic National Committee, 1970), pp. 13, 49.

31. These events are recounted in Crotty, *Decision for the Democrats*, pp. 1–27.

32. Commission on Party Structure and Delegate Selection, *Mandate for Reform*, pp. 17–32. The Commission's actions are discussed in Crotty, *Decision for the Democrats*, pp. 68–103.

33. Crotty, *Decision for the Democrats*, pp. 125–47.

34. See Ranney, "The Democratic Party's Delegate Selection Reforms"; Ranney, "Changing the Rules"; Kenneth Janda, "Primrose Paths to Political Reform: 'Reforming' v. Strengthening American Parties," in Crotty, ed., *Paths to Political Reform*; Nakamura and Sullivan, "Party Democracy and Democratic Control"; and James W. Ceaser, *Presidential Selection: Theory and Development* (Princeton, N.J.: Princeton University Press, 1979), pp. 260–303.

35. Charles Longley, "Party Reform and Party Nationalization: The Case of the Democrats," in Crotty, ed., *The Party Symbol*; Crotty, *Political Reform and the American Experiment*, pp. 247–55; Crotty, *Decision for the Democrats*, pp. 240–50; and Denis G. Sullivan, Jeffrey L. Pressman, and F. Christopher Arterton, *Explorations in Convention Decision Making* (San Francisco: Freeman, 1976).

36. Commission on Party Structure and Delegate Selection, *Mandate for Reform*, p. 49.

37. Crotty, *Decision for the Democrats*, pp. 33–36.

38. Crotty, "Party Reform." See also Carol F. Casey, Chapter 6 in this volume.

39. Longley, "Party Nationalization in America," and Chapter 5 in this volume.

40. John Bibby and Cornelius Cotter, "The Impact of Reform on the National Party Organizations" (Paper delivered at the Annual Meeting of American Political Science Association, Washington, D.C. 1979).

41. Quoted in William Goodman, *The Two-Party System in the United States*, 3d ed. (New York: Van Nostrand, 1964), p. 629.

42. William Crotty, "The National Committees as Grassroots Vehicles of Representation," in Crotty, ed., *The Party Symbol*.

4

PARTIES AS CIVIC ASSOCIATIONS

Wilson Carey McWilliams

*I*n the Constitution of the United States, political parties are like a scandal in polite society: they are alluded to but never discussed.* The importance of parties in political life has led the federal and state governments to intervene increasingly in the affairs of the parties, regulating primaries and the selection of party officials. However the political parties grew up as private associations, outside the sphere of our formally public institutions.[1] In this sense, political parties began outside the law, and they have never become quite respectable.

Paradoxically, the private origins of political parties in the United States enhanced their understanding of public things. Public institutions in the United States use a language that speaks most often of private things, referring to individuals, their interests (conceived chiefly in terms of their private estates and power), and their rights (defined, for the most part, as immunities against public interference). Our public institutions reflect, if imperfectly, the "science of politics" on which the framers based the Constitution—the theory that human beings are by nature free, private, and self-preserving animals caught up in a struggle for the mastery of nature, warring with their fellows for scarce resources, and willing to "give up" some rights to the group only to escape that state of war and to gain more effective enjoyment of the rights they "retain." Human beings, in the "liberal tradition" that informs our constitutions, are political and public only by artifice and from necessity.[2]

---

*The twenty-fourth amendment alludes to parties, since it forbids poll taxes in primary elections, but parties are nowhere discussed explicitly.

By contrast, many "private" institutions—most notably, families, churches, and local communities—have often taught an older creed, which speaks more easily of the public as a whole, appealing to patriotism, duty, and the common good. Of course, these private bodies have been influenced increasingly by the liberalism and "modernism" of our public culture, and they articulate the more traditional view only infrequently, incoherently, and apologetically.[3] Nevertheless, the private order shaped the American character, in part, in terms of teaching that human beings are limited creatures, subject to the law of nature, born dependent, and—by nature—in need of nurturance and moral education. In the old phrase, we are by nature "political animals." Family, friends, and polity are essential to the development of human personality. "My self" is never separate from "my people"; I owe them my life and can rightly be asked to sacrifice it for the common good.

Rooted in the private order, political parties often voiced its doctrine. The famous question of Tammany's Tim Campbell, "What's the Constitution among friends?" amounts to an epigram summarizing the charge of traditional teachings against the public order and the framers' theories that shaped it.[4]

I will attempt to show the crucial role played by political parties in relating the private order to the public life of the United States, and correspondingly, the extent to which party politics in the United States depended on the private order for its vitality. I will argue that the increasing fragmentation of the private sphere is an important cause of the decline of political parties in the United States, and finally, I will maintain that genuine reform—for the country, as well as for the parties—requires the reconstruction of the private foundations of public life.

PRIVATE LIVES AND PUBLIC VIRTUES

When President Carter refers to a "crisis of confidence," he observes that Americans have too little trust in their political leaders to allow those leaders to govern effectively. He also argues that various "special interests" block needed legislation, and he urges public opinion to force Congress to act in the public interest. Carter's argument presumes that public spiritedness is now not strong enough to prevail, and though the president is too politic to say so, he implies that the American people are too preoccupied with private affairs and concerns. In other words, the public is generally disaffected and denies the government the resources of allegiance and dedication necessary to pursue the common good.

Contemporary problems—most visibly, the energy crisis—make us unusually aware of the need for public spirit. In fact, however, civic virtue is always in demand. Public spiritedness is never easy. My senses are always private, my own and no one else's. The more my reason and reflection tell me that I am like other human beings, that we are all parts of a whole or members of an interdependent political society, the more my senses and my feelings tend to insist on my uniqueness and my separateness. In reflection, Chesterton wrote, "Any man may be inside any men," but to look at others is to "leave the inside and draw . . . near the outside," emphasizing differences rather than similarities.[5]

This is to say the obvious: that public spirit is to some extent at odds with our feelings and sensations. We are, for example, notoriously unjust about our families. Parents value children disproportionately, and children see parents as larger than life. Plato saw no "solution" other than eliminating the private family altogether for his guardian class, and in regimes less ideal than The Republic, the family is a constant limit on our willingness to be public spirited. No citizen is perfect in his or her dedication to the common good, and any sort of civic spirit requires the discipline and governance of some of our most profound feelings and desires. Hence, the classical saying that those who would learn to command must first learn to obey.

The more our feelings and our private interests are at odds with public interests and policies, the more we will experience law and government as a kind of tyranny. The more law and government make us feel impotent, undignified, and confused, the more we will withdraw into private refuges to protect whatever dignity we can salvage—if we do not react furiously, seeking to hurt a regime that injures our self-esteem. The more we need such a regime, the more we will resent its injuries. Under such conditions, we may be forced to obey; we do not learn to do so.

The government of our private feelings, however, need not be a tyranny. Our emotions can be charmed out of their preoccupation with self and educated to be allies—if never entirely reliable ones—of reason and community. Until modern times, political philosophy argued in favor of the small states, because such states, keeping the polity within the emotional compass of the individual, reduced the distance between private feeling and public life and promoted civic virtue. Public spirit needs the shelter of limited space. In small communities, I can see, experience, and benefit from policies enacted for the common good. A bridge in Minnesota or a job-training program for the poor benefits me, but very indirectly; I may reason that such benefits exist, but I will not feel them.[6]

Similarly, small groups and communities help create trust, commitment, and allegiance. In the first place, the small community enhances our knowledge of one another. Small societies are personal: people know me, my leaders know who I am, and I, in turn, know them. The most frequent complaint against small communities, in fact, is that we are known too well. Ideally, such communities are stable because stability increases interpersonal knowledge. In a small but mobile community, like most suburbs, I know who you *appear* to be, but I do not know your past, and still less do I share it. I know you, in other words, only superficially and will trust you accordingly. What is even more important is that if I suspect that either you or I will move away soon, I am not likely to commit myself deeply to you or to the life of the community. It is a place where I *live*, not a part of what I *am*. Stability increases the feeling that I am with people who will not surprise me even if I do not like them and that we can pledge ourselves to one another without fear of being abandoned. Plato wrote: "Nothing is of more benefit to the *polis* than . . . mutual acquaintance; for where men conceal their ways from one another in darkness rather than light, no man will ever gain either his due honor or office or the justice which is befitting."[7]

The small community also makes me feel important. Its smallness increases my relative impact as an individual. In the great state, I am a statistic; what I say has only an insignificant effect on society as a whole. In small societies, I can participate in common affairs if I choose; in large societies, only a small percentage of citizens can participate effectively. There is an upper limit to the number of citizens who can play a full role in public deliberation. Even if we were willing to spend 24 hours a day dealing with public affairs, if it took 15 minutes to present one's views effectively, fewer than 100 of us could speak on any given day. In a community of 100, this is almost enough time for all of us; in a community of 1,000, either only 10 percent of us can speak or we will be able to speak only for a minute and half. In large states, most of us are silenced, and even those who talk are forced to speak in slogans.[8] Participation itself is not crucial—the important thing is the dignity that the possibility of participation reflects. In the small community, I can decide to listen and let others lead because I have the possibility of doing otherwise. In the large state, I will have no choice in the matter.

The case for the small polity is a strong one. In material resources, however, such societies were always relatively weak, and the advent of "modernization," that is, industrialization and commercialization, shattered the autonomy of local communities, tied their economic life to a national and international market, permitted easy migration, and introduced strangers and strange ideas into local life. Modernization and its attendant benefits rooted local communities and traditional peoples in massive, ill-comprehended, and threatening societies ruled by impersonal forces. It offered the individual freedom from the restraints of local community, but only because no individual mattered enough to be worth more than superficial attention. In the modern world, the large state became a necessity because only such states could hope to give people some control over the forces that shaped their lives. That necessity, however, does not create anything like public spirit or civic virtue.

In large states, disaffection—the retreat of emotion, trust, and commitment into private places—is the rule, not the exception. Madison and the Framers of the Constitution were content to have it so, provided that such private havens were numerous and, taken as parts of the whole, too weak to endanger society. In general, the framers were willing to rely on the appeals of material interest and power in foreign affairs to foster national allegiance, trusting that an admittedly diffuse "affection" would, in the long term, follow where interest led.[9]

But material advantage, while it may bribe us into complaisance, is counterproductive if the common good demands sacrifice, and "foreign danger" has its limits as a basis for national unity. Lacking an alternative, presidents term every major civic need the "equivalent of war"; however, few dangers really equal war in the sense of the immediate personal danger they inspire, and those that do—the Depression is the only salient example—do not do so for long. Even war, if the enemy is far away, does not rule our feelings.

If there was once a significant degree of commitment and loyalty to public institutions in the United States, that fact is more surprising than the "disaggregation" we seem to be experiencing today. Political parties, as "mediating strata," helped build the emotional and personal bonds between local communities and the republic as a whole. An examination of the traditional theory and role of political parties in the United States is essential to understanding their present and future.

THE PARTIES IN AMERICAN THOUGHT

It is a truism that the Framers of the Constitution disliked and distrusted political parties. Informed opinion, at the birth of the republic, saw parties as divisive forces that demagogically exaggerated conflict. Based on the English parties with which they were familiar, American leaders also associated political parties with cliquish corruption.[10] Eager to multiply competing factions so as to reduce the likelihood of a majority faction, the Framers and Madison could hardly admire an association whose purpose was the aggregation of majorities. The diversity of interests required to make up a majority in the United States might reduce a party to the level of a more or less trivial nuisance, but no positive claims could be made for it.

Jefferson was more ambivalent, but he, too, was no friend to the idea of party. Partisanship, he wrote in 1789, is "the last degeneration of a free and moral agent. . . . If I could not get to heaven but with a party, I would not go there at all." In 1798, Jefferson went as far as he would go in defense of the party: "In every free and deliberating society, there must, from the nature of man, be opposite parties. . . . Perhaps this party division is necessary to induce each to watch and relate to the people the proceedings of the other." That, however, was Jefferson in opposition; as Hofstadter points out, Jeffersonians in power pursued a "quest for unanimity."[11] Jefferson professed to be "no believer in the amalgamation of parties" because he saw parties as natural, rooted in temperament and biology, but he invoked this idea as much to deprecate his "sickly" opponents as to defend party.[12] Like Jefferson himself, the "first party system" he did so much to create accepted the idea of the party only hesitantly; neither he nor his followers created permanent, institutional parties in the modern sense.[13]

In his "ward system," however, Jefferson advanced an idea that was to be seminal in the development of American mass parties. Jefferson was concerned to synthesize local communities and the central regime, combining the warm if parochial patriotism of the former with the broader, more enlightened perspectives of the latter. The secret of free government, he suggested, is that citizens retain all those powers within their competence, delegating others

> by a synthetical process to higher and higher orders of functionaries. . . .
> The elementary republics of the wards, the county republics, the State republics and the republic of the Union, would form a gradation of authorities. . . . Where every man is a sharer in the direction of his ward-republic, or of some of the higher ones, and feels that he is a participator in the government of affairs, not merely at election one day in the year but every day; when there shall not be a man in the State who will not be a member of some one of its councils, great or small, he will let the heart be torn out of his body sooner than his power be wrested from him by a Caesar or a Bonaparte.[14]

Jefferson, of course, was speaking of transforming the government, not of organizing a political party, but it was the party that attempted to put his doctrine into effect.

Political parties in the United States had no great champion until Martin Van Buren. Van Buren's experience commands serious attention to his argument: he was a local party boss, a national party leader and elder statesman and, in 1848, he ran as a third-party candidate protesting his party's complicity with slavery. He had, in other words, played all the roles in the drama of party politics. Moreover, Van Buren's theory that political parties have an essential role in republican government of a large state has enduring validity on its own terms.

Staunch republican that he was, Van Buren recognized that elections can be shams. At least where mass publics are involved, nonpartisan elections work to the advantage of the well-to-do and the powerful, for they provide no organized alternatives and no basis, other than celebrity or prominence, on which the public could make a choice. The nonpartisanship of James Monroe's administration, praised as the "Era of Good Feeling" by defenders of the antiparty tradition, was the worst variety of nonpartisan regime, since Monroe purported to be a Republican but, in office, courted Federalists. Tacitly, if not consciously, Monroe was deceiving the public and, in the long term, was courting a general public disillusionment. *All nonpartisan systems encourage the belief that elections are a facade and that the "real" decisions are made somewhere else.* Undermining the legitimacy of the regime, they encourage citizens to abandon a "fraudulent" public life in favor of their private interests.[15]

Public choice demanded organized, visible alternatives, and Van Buren envisioned three modes of organizing a mass electorate, only one of which deserved the name *party*. In the first place, the electorate could be organized in what I will call *factions* on the basis of georgraphy, with factions speaking for particular sections or localities, or on the basis of interests, with factions speaking for classes, economic sectors, or trades. Second, the people could be grouped as the rival personal *followings* of political leaders. Finally, the electorate could be divided into *parties*.

Van Buren's meaning was subtle. He saw no essential difference between sectional factions and organized interests because both were essentially parochial, based on different varieties of private self-seeking. Factions, whether based on geography or special interests, could be easily fragmented into multipartite confusion, but that defect was not essential to Van Buren's argument. Even if a section or interest contrived to organize a majority, it would still be a faction because its constitutive principle would be private.[16] The Whigs, for example, were often condemned as a party of "interests" and "privilege," unconcerned with the moral unity of the people.

> The whig professes to cherish liberty, and he cherishes only his chartered franchises. . . . He applies the doctrine of divine right to legislative grants and spreads the mantle of superstition round contracts. He professes to adore freedom, and he pants for monopoly. Not that he is dishonest; he deceives himself; he is the dupe of his own selfishness, for covetousness is idolatry and covetousness is the only passion which is never conscious of its own existence.[17]

Discount the campaign rhetoric, and one is still left with the contention that a faction, even a potential majority, based simply on private interests is a danger to republican government. Such factions are essentially oligarchic or aristocratic, "feudal" in the worst sense, concerned with private privileges and immunities against the community as a whole.[18]

Similarly, Van Buren rejected personal followings, in part because they were ephemeral and because they encouraged demagoguery and "image" politics, but also because they were essentially monarchic, emphasizing person rather than law and hierarchy rather than civic equality. In the same spirit, George Bancroft set "the Tory principle" alongside Whiggery as the enemy of democracy.[19]

Forced to choose between democracy's two enemies, Van Buren might have leaned—as his Whig critics charged—to the monarchic side. Better a king who sees his realm as one property and who gives unity to the sovereign, Hobbes had argued, than a host of private factions, and I suspect that Van Buren agreed.[20] Certainly, he argued that a "tribunician executive" was needed to check the "interests" which tend to dominate the legislature. To control the executive, Van Buren relied on the party to train, filter, and select leaders. As Ceasar writes, "Party in this respect would be made 'prior' to leaders."[21]

Party, then, is the republican alternative, organizing the electorate on the basis of "principles," as opposed to the private concerns of factions, and governing its internal affairs collegially, as opposed to the hierarchy of followings. Van Buren used the term *party* judiciously: he meant an organization that self-consciously regards itself as a part of the public as a whole and which acknowledges higher political duties, regarding its own principles as an emphasis or priority—doubtless the right and correct one—within the common values that give a people its "unity of character." Party, then, is not only a form of organization but is a quality of spirit, a set of commitments, and a dedication to public life.[22]

Van Buren intended that parties should teach, as well as reflect, this sort of civic virtue. In an otherwise superb article, Ceasar has observed that the "principles" on which Van Buren hoped to base parties would be necessarily "broad," since Van Buren aimed at a truly national coalition. Ceasar goes on to conclude that Van Buren aimed to extend the "Madisonian system" of "competing factions and coalitions" into the election of presidents.[23] Here, Ceasar goes astray.

Van Buren was, a shrewd critic of the Framers, as well as a respectful admirer. The authors of the Constitution, Van Buren maintained, took too mechanistic and formal a view of government. "Theoretic" dangers led them to a fear of the majority which Van Buren regarded as misplaced in the United States. All governments, Van Buren held, rest on "opinion," and it is this opinion, not formal rules, which ultimately limits and sets the direction of government. It is important that Van Buren referred to *opinion* rather than *opinions*. Opinion, as Van Buren understood it, meant something like the term *doxa* in Greek antiquity: a "political culture," values, habits, and perceptions more fundamental than transient attitudes, rooted in the common language and experience of a people as a whole, shaping the very personalities of its citizens[24] (hence, Van Buren's assertion that the "truest service" one can offer one's country lies in "forming a right national opinion," akin to the *orthe doxa* of Plato's philosophy[25]).

Forming a right opinion is—to say the least—a formidable task. Fortunately, Van Buren did not think it necessary; a right opinion already existed in the United States. This opinion rendered pointless the Framers's fears of majority rule. Experience demonstrated, Van Buren contended, that American majorities could be trusted to govern with restraint, common morality, and civic responsibility.

Right opinion, however, is only the first step toward civic virtue; it needs to be educated and led. The small community was the natural homeland of democracy. The people can most easily control matters that are near at hand, Van Buren observed, and "popular justice" required decision by the "nearest tribunal." A large state, then, weakens the public's control and the quality of its judgment. The friends of republican government must attempt to keep the central government on as small a scale as possible and must defend the rights of states and localities. Nevertheless, republican government also requires the attempt to lead opinion out of the localities and prepare it for the governance of a large state.[26]

The political party would begin, like Jefferson's ward system, with the localities where popular judgment is sound and public control is possible. Following the logic of Jefferson's argument, local partisan groups were to choose their natural leaders. Natural leaders from several localities, united in a face-to-face society of their own, would select their natural leaders. Ideally, an ascending hierarchy of face-to-face societies, connected by relations of personal trust, would connect the locality and the central state. In one sense, the design of the party was a new departure in political life. In another, however, it appealed to an older order of things, and the traditionalism of the party recommended it to the private order. "Aristocracy," Tocqueville wrote, "had made a chain of all the members of the community, from the peasant to the king: democracy breaks that chain, and severs every link of it."[27] In the United States, political parties would attempt to reforge the chain, giving its metal a new, democratic casting.[28]

Van Buren was realistically aware that this hierarchy of allegiance was precarious, needing guileful maintenance. The small communities at the base of the chain were always tempted to fall back into purely private concerns. The fraternities of leaders that made up the chain were always in danger of fratricidal rivalries, on one hand, and, on the other hand, might become so intensely loyal as to develop their own exclusive parochiality, rejecting their obligations to the people below and to the larger republic above.[29] There was no way to avert those perils altogether, but at every level, the party would use all its resources—patronage, personal friendship, and public honor—to enlist the feelings of its members and to win and renew their allegiance.[30]

Van Buren prescribed broad principles as the basis for a party because, among other things, they were suited to his educational aim. Narrow principles, however desirable, would alienate citizens at the outset, reducing the ability of a party to create a public (and, of course, also increasing the chances of electoral defeat). Beginning with sound opinion, the party sought to persuade citizens that the division between the parties, defined by broad, *civic* principles, was the vital conflict in U.S. politics and that all other differences, for political purposes at least, were ephemeral. Parties sought to create civic identities, leading people to set aside, in public affairs, differences of religion, ethnicity, and class—except, of course, where those differences *paralleled*, rather than intersected, the lines of partisan division.[31]

The rhetoric of parties urged their followers to set aside lesser differences in order to defeat the greater enemy. In this, as in many things, party politics remains unchanged. Given the ancient and present animosities that divide groups in the United States, some greater fear is probably necessary to dispel hostility. But to define a common enemy presumes some common standard by which we can identify enemies and judge which are greater. Implicitly, a common enemy defines a common good. Baptists and Deists were at loggerheads theologically, but both detested the established churches, and the "wall of separation between church and state" defined the common denominator of their political creed.[32]

The political party gave Americans a new political credo: "Everything for *THE CAUSE*, nothing for men."[33] Parties, in other words, rejected "government by men." The party, as an institution, led voters a long step away from merely personal allegiance toward loyalty to the republic. But at the same time, "the cause" was something warmer and more more personal than the "government of laws" contrived by the Framers's "science of politics."[34]

Over time, American political parties did create civic allegiances. Partisan allegiance, for example, checked and sometimes overrode sectional loyalties in the years before the Civil War. Given the forces making for sectional conflict, it is not surprising that party feeling was ultimately unable to prevent war. It is more notable that party leaders tried, stubbornly and with some measure of success, to find a "national solution" and that they almost certainly delayed the advent of the war for many years.[35]

The urban machine often sought to connect various ethnic "tribes" to the larger polity; sometimes, the machines even helped to create local communities. For immigrants and urban newcomers, especially, the party provided jobs and social services (though rather less frequently than the machines' admirers imagine), opportunities for friendship and social life, and perhaps most important, a "master cue" to an otherwise baffling and alien polity. The machine did its business, as George Washington Plunkitt boasted, surrounded by the symbols and rhetoric of patriotism, and if the machine's orators ran to copybook maxims, they did inculcate loyalty to the republic. "This great and glorious country," Plunkitt declaimed, "was built up by the political parties." In considerable measure, he was right.[36]

Van Buren's theory presumed that the parties would teach republican virtue. That Plunkitt was no Coriolanus would neither have surprised nor disappointed Van Buren. He recognized that the teaching of a party would, of necessity, seem tawdry, diffuse, and compromised with private interest when compared with the standard of civic virtue established by classical political philosophy. That more exacting ideal, however, was possible only in small states. Van Buren aimed to teach and preserve that form of republican virtue suited to a large state and specifically suited to the United States. Van Buren weighed political life in ancient scales, even if the United States fell far short of their highest measure.

PARTY RENEWAL AND CIVIC RENEWAL

Whatever their virtues in the past, parties and party allegiance today seem to be in decay, and their role in U.S. politics has radically decreased.[37]

Of course, the established parties are to some extent outdated. It is nearly 40 years, after all, since the end of the Great Depression, the cataclysm that still defines the major lines of partisan division. The Jeffersonian and Jacksonian party systems did not last so long, and 40 years after the Civil War, the party system was beginning to experience the ferment of Progressivism.

There is abundant evidence, however, that the contemporary decline of the political party is part of a general political decay. Americans live lives that are more and more specialized, live in towns and neighborhoods that are less and less stable, live in families that are more and more likely to break up or—increasingly—in casual liaisons, and live in private havens that are more and more penetrated by mass media and mass culture and by the now thoroughly international economy. The private order is increasingly fragmented, and people are more and more alone in the face of a more gigantic and confusing political world.[38]

A growing number of Americans are preoccupied with desperate efforts to protect and gratify the private self, a wounded and incomplete self that lacks the ability to make strong commitments to others or to trust them and which certainly fears to give political allegiance.

Evidently, this "culture of narcissism" is ruinous for political parties. The search for common civic identities, after all, is radically at odds with specialization, and parties depend on citizens with a sense of enough self-coherence to be able to make enduring commitments.[39] Political parties in the United States grew up presuming a "right opinion" in localities, and they continued to rely on the private order to form the personal foundations of political character. For a long time, in fact, American parties have taken those foundations pretty much for granted. They can no longer do so. Party identification has, increasingly, come to be an *individual* response, reflecting personal history rather than any connection to party life and activity.[40] Even in these terms, however, contemporary parties are troubled. Families, the last bastion of the private order, have traditionally conveyed party identification. Today, they seem to be losing the power to do so.[41] The basic assumptions of U.S. party politics no longer hold: the foundation of the house is washing away.

At least part of the malaise of the parties, however, derives from the theories of party that dominate political discussion. Both the reforming tradition and its most articulate critics see the party as a central, national institution reflecting essentially private interests and values. Both reject the idea of the party as a civic educator and its corollary, the integral relation of the party to the small communities in which political participation and civic education are possible. Both, consequently, misunderstand our political parties and blind us to the needs and resources of parties in the contemporary crisis.

Progressivism, from which the reform tradition derives, distrusted the party generally and sought to reduce it to a vehicle representing voters as *individuals*. The Progressive movement was hostile to any "distortion" of existing public sentiment by party leaders, but it also disliked "bloc" voting, even though such voting reflected public perceptions and feelings. Politics and party, in the Progressive view, should represent individual citizens, that is, their attitudes and their interests. Progressives hoped for public-spirited citizens, but they saw this "public spirit" as essentially a matter of private character, to be produced by personal education, "communication," or by "social reform." In the eyes of Progressives, all communities between the individual and the state were suspect because they exerted power over citizens, shaping their feelings and their alternatives. Valuable in many areas of life, Progressive theory has been a disaster when applied to political parties. For Progressives, the preferred form of politics was a mass election—a national primary or the initiative and referendum—in which the power of party is reduced to the vanishing point and in which localities are lumped together in indistinction. The reform tradition, consequently, must bear much of the responsibility for mass politics.[42]

Many political scientists have addressed these faults of the reform tradition. One of the ablest was E. E. Schattschneider, a warm and eloquent partisan of party government, who assailed the reformers's view of the political party. The party, Schattschneider argued, derived from caucuses, from the attempt of an organized minority to outweigh a disorganized and indifferent majority. Politics always involves a passive majority and an active minority.[43]

In his distaste for primaries, Schattschneider went on to argue that partisan voters are not "members" of a political party. The party has no control over the admission of such members. They pay no dues, and they take on no obligations.[44] Schattschneider drew the apparently logical conclusion that partisan voters have no right to control intraparty affairs. (Revealingly, he drew an analogy between party voters and baseball fans and, hence, between the party and a private business.) Partisan voters exert influence through their ability to reject a party's nominee: "The test is, does it bind? Not, how was it done?" A party is an association of "working professionals," and democracy is "not to be found *in* the parties but *between* them."[45]

Schattschneider's argument presents the party as a species of private property and voters as political consumers. Certainly, his position rejects any role for the party as a civic educator. His thesis contends that the public has an interest in the product but not in the process. Presuming that the two can be so separated, locality is superfluous. A mass centralized party can have its products "tested," as well as any number of local ones. In fact, competition between the parties—as Schattschneider knew—exists at the national level but is relatively rare at the local level.[46] To argue that democracy exists between the parties is to create an imperative for centralized parties, which inhabit the more competitive environment.

Interparty democracy, moreover, deals only with elections, and Americans see voting and party as different things. In the United States, unlike Great Britain, people often vote for "the other side" without changing their party.[47] For the most part, U.S. voters do not even *think* of changing their party. The vote is something ephemeral and transient; party is closer to personal identity.

Party, for Americans, seems to involve a stable alliance with some people, a shared stance in relation to the state and to the political past. Party, in this sense, presumes we know who we are *with*; it does not imply that we necessarily agree on what *for*.[48] Historically, the Democratic Party has attracted citizens who felt themselves outsiders in relation to Anglo-American culture, on one hand, the localists and traditionalists who adhered to a creed older than the liberal tradition, and on the other those social critics who found Lockean liberalism not modern enough.[49] There is a commonality implicit among these outsiders, but disagreement about policy is almost an inevitable by-product of the effort to discover it. Intraparty conflict is likely to be particularly intense because the party is a kind of political family where feelings run high (and no arguments, as we all know, are more intense than political arguments within families).

People do change parties, of course, but people can also change nationalities. A party's hold is less powerful than that of nationality, but in both cases, people feel that to change is to lose a part of themselves. (To judge from the statistics, we take party identification more seriously than marriage: we leave it less frequently, and we stay unattached unless we feel ready for something like a lifetime commitment.)

The relative stability of party identification indicates that leaders and followers are part of a political community: theirs is a political relationship between rulers and ruled. The terms of this relationship will depend on authority. The machines, and party leaders generally, profited from the deference of traditionalistic peoples; similarly, at times of intense party competition, voters may be disposed to allow their leaders greater discretion.[50] But even when authority is most autocratic, voters are "insiders" and must be treated as such. Schattschneider is wrong: partisans *are* members, just as in *The Republic*, where even the artisans are citizens.

The decline of authority generally in the society, and in the parties specifically, compels the parties to become more internally democratic.[51] (See Chapters 2 and 3.) Party organizations that resist such a demand obdurately simply lose the allegiance of their partisans. The "democratization" of the parties, however, does *not* require primary elections: mass elections are neither the only nor the most admirable form of democratic choice.[52] In fact, if parties wish to retain or regain the allegiance of voters, primary elections are out of the question. Primaries suggest an electorate dominated by the mass media, as well as campaigns that are costly and closed to the average citizen. The new "professionals," the media specialists who shape such campaigns, have no ties to particular publics (or even, for that matter, to particular parties); they are part of the mass with which they deal, faceless and unaccountable. In such campaigns, the electorate is passive, and individually, voters know that they are unimportant: the public may "choose," but its choice does not convey allegiance.

By contrast, open local caucuses leading toward state and national conventions have genuine possibilities for democracy, party loyalty, and public spirit. They may not increase participation, but they do increase the opportunity for it, and that may be contribution enough. A caucus system, in the great tradition of Jefferson's ward republics, provides a smaller setting, which permits deliberation, personal relationships, and, perhaps, the beginnings of a sort of political community. (See Chapter 9.)

Even so, parties will need to continue to respond—as, willy-nilly, they have been doing—to the demand that they become more issue oriented or ideological.[53] In part, this reflects greater education and concern for the "issues," but it also is a symptom of the decline of the affective bases of interpersonal trust. Traditionally, *ideology* meant an implicit doctrine embedded in the life and habits of a group.[54] In U.S. politics, it means an explicit doctrine that defines a group. In fact, ideological politics often involves an intense desire for friendship, community, and personal dignity.[55] Ideology is a kind of test, a more sophisticated loyalty oath, designed to tell me who is worthy of my trust, but the test always fails of its intended effect. Ideological parties provide no affective certainty: one learns quickly that cognitive agreements may mask great differences of personality, taste, and motive. In ideological groups, interpersonal distrust is the rule. The ideological partisan says, "I will trust no one who does not agree with me," which is a way of saying, "I will trust no one at all; I will not allow you to do as you think best; you must do as I think best." A common ideology often seems to promise public spirit and civic identity: in fact, such groups are all roof and no foundation.

Political parties grew up outside government and, to some extent, at odds with it. Today, they may need its support. In the United States traditional political parties presumed, with Van Buren, that Americans had a "right opinion," which was heavily influenced by the traditional and religious creed of the private order. They used the local communities and personal identities of the private order as the starting points from which to build support for public policies and programs. Contemporary parties must begin with opinions rather than opinion, and their resources of allegiance are waning. If they, and Americans generally, are wise, however, they will turn their resources to the support of any public policies that can help to reconstruct the local and private foundations of "right opinion" and democratic life.

NOTES

1. See the development in constitutional law from Newberry vs. U.S., 256 U.S. 232 (1921) and Grovey vs. Townsend, 295 U.S. 45 (1935) to Classic vs. U.S., 313 U.S. 299 (1941), Smith vs. Allwright, 321 U.S. 649 (1944) and Terry vs. Adams, 345 U.S. 506 (1953).

2. Louis Hartz, *The Liberal Tradition in America* (New York: Harcourt Brace, 1955).

3. On the impact of modernism, see Daniel Bell, *The Cultural Contradictions of Capitalism* (New York: Basic Books, 1976).

4. William Riordon, *Plunkitt of Tammany Hall* (New York: Dutton, 1963), p. 13. Democrats have more often been spokesmen for the private order, but there is no dearth of Republican examples: see Matthew Josephson, *The Politicos* (New York: Harcourt Brace, 1938).

5. G. K. Chesterton, *What I Saw in America* (New York: Da Capo, 1968), p. 1.

6. Alexis de Tocqueville, *Democracy in America* (New York: Schocken, 1961), 1: 52-99; Mancur Olson, *The Logic of Collective Action* (Cambridge, Mass.: Harvard University Press, 1965).

7. Plato, *Laws*, trans. R. G. Bury (Cambridge, Mass.: Harvard University Press, 1952), 1:361 (Book V, 738e); on the political impact of stability, see Robert Alford and Eugene

C. Lee, "Voting Turnout in American Cities," *American Political Science Review* 42 (1968): 796–813.

8. See Bertrand de Jouvenel, "The Chairman's Problem," *American Political Science Review* 40 (1961): 368–72.

9. See Wilson C. McWilliams, *The Idea of Fraternity in America* (Berkeley: University of California Press, 1973), pp. 185–93.

10. Richard Hofstadter, *The Idea of a Party System* (Berkeley and Los Angeles: University of California Press, 1969), pp. 1–73.

11. Ibid., pp. 115, 170–212; Thomas Jefferson, *Letters and Selected Writings of Thomas Jefferson*, ed. A. Koch and W. Peden (New York: Modern Library, 1944), p. 460.

12. Jefferson, *Letters and Selected Writings*, p. 715; Hofstadter, *Idea of a Party System*, p. 27.

13. Ronald P. Formisano, "Deferential-Participant Politics: The Early Republic's Political Culture, 1789–1840," *American Political Science Review* 68 (1974): 173–87.

14. Jefferson, *Letters and Selected Writings*, p. 661.

15. James Ceasar, "Political Parties and Presidential Ambition," *Journal of Politics* 40 (1978): 725, 728.

16. Robert V. Remini, *Martin Van Buren and the Making of the Democratic Party* (New York: Columbia University Press, 1959), p. 132, and George Bancroft, *Martin Van Buren* (New York: Harper and Bros., 1889), p. 122.

17. George Bancroft, *Oration Delivered before the Democracy of Springfield and Neighboring Towns, July 4, 1836* (Springfield, Mass.: George and Charles Merriam, 1836), p. 7 (see also p. 8).

18. George Bancroft, *History of the United States*, ed. Russel B. Nye, (Chicago: University of Chicago Press, 1966), p. 24.

19. Bancroft, *Oration*, p. 4; Ceasar, "Political Parties, p. 726; Remini, *Martin Van Buren*, p. 35.

20. Thomas Hobbes, *Leviathan*, chap. 19. Oxford: Blackwell, N.d., pp. 122–23.

21. Ceasar, "Political Parties," p. 727, Remini, *Martin Van Buren*, p. 8; Bancroft, *Martin Van Buren*, pp. 68–69.

22. For contemporary examples of the argument, see Sigmund Neumann, *Modern Political Parties* (Chicago: University of Chicago, 1956), p. 296, and V. O. Key, Jr., *Political Parties and Pressure Groups* (New York: Crowell, 1958), p. 242.

23. Ceasar, "Political Parties," p. 730.

24. Bancroft, *Martin Van Buren*, p. 93.

25. Ibid., pp. 110–11.

26. Ibid., pp. 115, 128.

27. De Tocqueville, *Democracy in America*, vol. 2, p. 120.

28. P. Cutright and P. H. Rossi, "Grass Roots Politicians and the Vote," *American Sociological Review* 23 (1958): 171–79; Jeremy Boissevain, "Patronage in Sicily," *Man* 1 (1966): 18–31; C. Wright Mills, *The Power Elite* (New York: Oxford University Press, 1956), pp. 298–324.

29. On the duality and danger of partisan fraternity, see Boissevain, "Patronage in Sicily"; Harold Ickes, *The Autobiography of a Curmudgeon* (New York: Reynal and Hitchcock, 1943), p. 133; and Lionel Pearson, *Popular Ethics in Ancient Greece* (Stanford, Calif.: Stanford University Press, 1962), pp. 136–61. Robert Sutherland, Cornell College, has pointed out to me the probable influence of Van Buren's theories, especially in this aspect, on Henry Adams' novel, *Democracy* (New York: Holt, 1880).

30. Among recent comments, see M. Margaret Conway and Frank Feigert, "Motivation, Incentive Systems and Political Party Organization," *American Political Science Review* 62

(1968): 1169–83, and Peter Gluck, "Incentives and the Maintenance of Political Styles in Different Locales," *Western Political Quarterly* 25 (1972): 753–60.

31. Remini, Martin Van Buren, p. 165.

32. Robert Kelley, *The Cultural Pattern in American Politics* (New York: Knopf, 1979), pp. 130–31, 266; Key, *Political Parties*, pp. 347, 360, 363.

33. Ronald P. Formisano, *The Birth of Mass Political Parties: Michigan, 1827–1861* (Princeton, N.J.: Princeton University Press, 1971), pp. 22, 57–58, 70, 87.

34. Perry Goldman, "Political Virtue in the Age of Jackson," *Political Science Quarterly* 87 (1972): 46–62.

35. Joel Silbey, *The Shrine of Party: Congressional Voting Behavior, 1841–1852* (Pittsburgh: University of Pittsburgh Press, 1967).

36. Riordon, *Plunkitt*, p. 13; James A. Farley, *Behind the Ballots* (New York: Harcourt Brace, 1938), p. 237; Roy Peel, *Political Clubs of New York City* (New York: Putnam, 1935), pp. 245–46, Robert Merton, *Social Theory and Social Structure* (Glencoe, Ill.: Free Press, 1957), pp. 71–82; and Dennis B. Hale, "James Michael Curley: Leadership and the Uses of Legend," in *Political Leadership*, ed. Dennis Bathory (New York: Longmans, 1978), pp. 131–46. The term *master cue* is taken from Frank J. Sorauf, *Party Politics in America* (Boston: Little, Brown, 1976), p. 15.

37. Gerald M. Pomper, "The Decline of Party in American Elections," *Political Science Quarterly* 92 (1977): 21–41.

38. The case has been made by many critics. For one example, see my essay, "American Pluralism: The Old Order Passeth," in *The Americans, 1976*, ed. Irving Kristol and Paul Weaver (Lexington, Mass.: Heath, 1976), pp. 293–320.

39. Otto Kirchheimer, "The Party in Mass Society," *World Politics* 10 (1958): 289–94.

40. Jack Dennis, "Support for the Party System by the Mass Public," *American Political Science Review* 60 (1966): 600–615, and P. E. Converse and G. Dupleix, "Politicization of the Electorate in France and the United States," *Public Opinion Quarterly* 26 (1962): 1–23.

41. M. Kent Jennings and Richard Niemi, "The Transmission of Political Values from Parent to Child," *American Political Science Review* 62 (1968): 169–84.

42. Richard Hofstadter, *The Age of Reform* (New York: Knopf, 1955).

43. E. E. Schattschneider, *Party Government* (New York: Holt, Rinehart and Winston, 1942), pp. 39–44, 58.

44. Clarence A. Berdahl, "Party Membership in the United States," *American Political Science Review* 36 (1942): 16–50, 241–62.

45. Schattschneider, *Party Government*, pp. 55, 56, 60, 64.

46. David Brady, "A Research Note on the Impact of Intraparty Competition on Congressional Voting in a Competitive Era," *American Political Science Review* 67 (1973): 153–56.

47. David Butler and Donald Stokes, *Political Change in Britain* (New York: St. Martin's, 1969), pp. 41–42.

48. John H. Schaar and Wilson C. McWilliams, "Uncle Sam Vanishes," *New University Thought* 1 (1961): 61–68.

49. Kelley, *Cultural Pattern*, and Formisano, *Birth of Mass Political Parties*, pp. 81–90, 93, 166, 179–82.

50. Key, *Political Parties*, p. 233; Sorauf, *Party Politics in America*, p. 107; and Schattschneider, *Party Government*, p. 61.

51. Leon Epstein, *Political Parties in Western Democracies* (New York: Praeger, 1967), p. 210.

52. Austin Ranney, "Changing the Rules of the Nominating Game," in *Choosing the President*, ed. James David Barber (Englewood Cliffs, N.J.: Prentice-Hall, 1973), pp. 73–74; see

also William J. Crotty, *Political Reform and the American Experiment* (New York: Crowell, 1977).

53. Robert S. Hirschfield, Bert Swenson, and Blanche Blank, "A Profile of Political Activists in Manhattan," *Western Political Quarterly* 15 (1962): 489–506, and Edward Constantini, "Intraparty Attitude Conflict: Democratic Leadership in California," *Western Political Quarterly* 16 (1963): 956–72.

54. Karl Mannheim, *Ideology and Utopia* (New York: Harcourt Brace, 1955).

55. James Q. Wilson, *The Amateur Democrat* (Chicago: University of Chicago Press, 1966), p. 165.

5

NATIONAL PARTY RENEWAL

Charles H. Longley

*T*he point of this chapter is to suggest that the conventional wisdom concerning the role of the national party in the United States is no longer accurate. We are traditionally informed that the national organization is "politics without power," little more than a legal contraption whose principal task is to convene and manage a presidential nominating convention.[1] Between conventions, the national party organization is generally thought to be moribund. At the very best, it has been regarded as an adjunct of the White House or as a vehicle for attacks by the out-of-power party on the president's program. It may not be clear where the real action is—state or local parties or maybe Congress—but the national party organization is clearly where the action is not. There may yet be some truth in this general perspective, but there is much that no longer holds.

That changes within national party organization might have occurred is probable given the general institutional changes in the United States in the past few decades. Not only has the role of the national government greatly expanded, but underlying this growth

> has been the development of a modern industrial society with a national economy, nationwide networks of transportation and communications, and an increasingly interdependent and urbanized population. With the developments, more and more problems have become national in scope and impact and have generated demands for national action.[2]

Two issues in particular can be cited as catalysts of party change: the civil rights movement and the war in Vietnam. They were national issues that permeated the fabric of the country and produced enormous strains on U.S. political institutions. They gave rise to the party reform movement within the Democratic Party and thereby spurred the emergence of the more prominent—and powerful—national party organization.

A problem that confronts students of U.S. politics is a lack of congruence among those who write about political parties. This situation arises because authors are concerned with different facets of parties. Some writers focus on the implications of party identification as a voting cue for the electorate. Other authors analyze the role of party among those who hold elective office. A third topic of inquiry is concerned with the party as a discrete political organization made up of professional activists.[3] In other words, a common term—*political party*—subsumes a variety of analytical foci, and the consequent picture is less than precise. The definitional problem has been particularly acute in studies of contemporary party change. Ranney, for example, notes that some writers are concerned with questions of mass participation, others with voting behavior, still others with the implications of reform for elite attitudes, and yet others with the voting records of party office holders.[4] From a student's perspective, it can all get terribly confusing.

The prospect of ambiguity in the present study is lessened but not totally eliminated. Although the focus here is on the national party, we cannot ignore that even this term also has several dimensions. Strictly speaking, ultimate party authority rests at the national convention level. Convention delegates thus constitute the national party. More generally, however, the national party may be thought of as the party's national committee (including executive officers) and its Washington-based permanent staff. National committee members are variously drawn from the states (including the District of Columbia and U.S. territorial subdivisions), and they elect the party's executive officers, who serve a four-year term. The National committee generally meets twice a year. The permanent staffs are employees of the national organization and, along with the committee, provide the party with ongoing management. Both parties, albeit in different fashion, have also established internal reform commissions, and they too constitute a segment of the national party organization.

What has emerged over the past decade is a set of activities that both independently and collectively has prompted a redefined role for the national party. Long ignored and regarded as a political wasteland, the national party organization can now lay claim to a growing electoral presence. While its role is by no means dominant, the contrast with its traditional characterization amidst America's decentralized and variegated party system is stark and significant.[5]

The way in which the national Democratic and Republican parties have become more prominent is evident in several fashions. Both parties have undertaken internal reform efforts, but with markedly different outcomes. Both parties have been engaged in litigation leading to similar constitutional holdings, but with dissimilar practical results. Both organizations have embarked upon various party building activities, but through different routes. Even when the activities are programmatically comparable, there is a difference in scale. That there is not complete symmetry between the two parties reflects, perhaps, the peculiar character of each institution as a political entity. Even so, a closer examination of both organizations will clearly indicate that each has been involved in the task of national party redefinition.

NATIONAL PARTY REFORM COMMISSIONS

An understanding of the effort to revise party rules, particularly those dealing with national convention delegate selection, is central to an understanding of national party revision. Although both the Democrats and GOP have had reform commissions, the impact of the former panels has been considerably more substantive.

Delegates to the 1968 Democratic National Convention mandated the establishment of a Commission on Party Structure and Delegate Selection. It was initially chaired by South Dakota Senator McGovern and then, upon his resignation to seek the Democratic presidential nomination, Minnesota Representative Donald Fraser. The McGovern-Fraser Commission conducted a state-by-state analysis of delegate selection rules.[6] In formulating its recommendations, the commission sought to provide for a delegate selection process that assured full, meaningful, and timely opportunities for participation. State parties, for example, were made responsible for efforts to enhance the prospects of women, youth, and racial minorities to be delegates. The practice of "closed state making" by party groups also was banned, and a 10 percent ceiling was imposed on state party selected delegates. That many of the 18 guidelines required a revision of practices traditionally engaged in by state and local parties virtually assured a confrontation between those advocating change and those to whom the reforms were anathema.

It may not be possible to single out all the motives of those who supported the McGovern-Fraser reforms, but it is clear that the proposals were unprecedented in U.S. political history. And while over 70 challenges were filed before the National Convention's Credentials Committee, the new rules were widely if not consistently implemented.[7] Successful application of the reforms constituted a vital step in expanding the role of the national party. The reforms were the product of a national party panel, whose existence was mandated by national convention delegates, implemented first by a national commission and then by a national convention committee (and ultimately upheld by a later set of national convention delegates whose authority was recognized by the nation's highest court). The point is not that the central party organization defined the rules so much as the fact that the national party *redefined* the rules. State and local party units, long accustomed to virtual autonomy in the delegate selection process, could continue to ignore national party rules, but only with the expectation that politically costly (as well as embarrassing) sanctions would in fact ensue.

Party reform within the Democratic Party was continued by action taken at the 1972 National Convention. At this time, the delegates approved establishment of a second intraparty reform panel. Barbara Mikulski (then a Baltimore city council member) was named to chair the group. The Mikulski Commission undertook a review of the McGovern-Fraser guidelines and eventually recommended 20 provisions to govern delegate selection in 1976. Some of these proposals revised the initial set of reforms; others were maintained intact.[8] But the Mikulski Commission also charted new venues when it moved to restrict delegate selection participation to "Democrats only" and sought to better assure that presidential preferences would be fairly reflected and that candidates could approve of delegates to insure their fidelity. Moreover, this time, state party compliance was more readily forthcoming; less than half as many challenges were filed in 1976 as in 1972.[9] That such was the case might be explained by a variety of circumstances.* However, it can also be suggested that the 1972 precedent that established national party primacy in regulating delegate selection virtually foreclosed state party resistance. Once again, then, a national party commission successfully redefined the rules of the game.

At the 1976 Democratic National Convention, delegates moved to recognize and expand an interim party task force dealing with primaries and presidential selection. The Commission on Presidential Nomination and Party Structure, headed by Michigan state chairperson Morley Winograd, thus found itself entrusted with the authority for recommending 1980 delegate selection rules. Its proposals dictated further refinement of delegate apportionment criteria and to eliminate vestiges of winner-take-all primaries. Additionally, the panel amended the procedure for candidate approval of delegates and moved to expand the number of convention delegates from the party's officeholders.

More importantly, the Winograd Commission constituted what political scientist F. Christopher Arterton has termed the *institutionalization* of

---

*That Carter was regarded as being the party's de facto nominee and a concern for party harmony en route to the 1976 campaign both served to lessen credentials conflict.

reform.[10] It is now the *expectation* that there will be a national party reform panel *every* four years. Since 1968, then, the traditional practice of according state and local party units considerable autonomy in conducting delegate selection has been eclipsed. The central party organization now defines, monitors, and interprets compliance with delegate selection rules. In 1972, the mayor of Chicago denied that the rules applied to him; he was not seated at the convention. In 1976, one major state party chairperson barely avoided censure before the Credentials Committee, and a second "had his ass put through a meat grinder" for failing to comply with the spirit of the rules.[11] Experiences such as these quickly become party lore. The desire to avoid similar experiences thus serves as an incentive for compliance and, coincidentally, as a recognition of national party power.

The Republican Party has not engaged in a substantively comparable reform process.[12] In 1968, National Convention delegates mandated a reform commission, the Delegates and Organizations (DO); in 1972, convention action led to a second panel, the "Rule 29 Committee." Both the DO and Rule 29 committees prompted changes in the Republican's delegate selection process, but these reforms did not impose on state and local party units a burden akin to that felt in Democratic circles. The national party moved to ensure procedural regularities, as evidenced, for example, in requirements for a publicized and open delegate selection process. But in more sensitive areas, such as affirmative action or fair reflection of presidential preference, the GOP national organization did not mandate change. The reasons for this are varied, but the tenor of Republican reform is aptly suggested by one national committeeperson's comment: "There simply is no such thing as a national Republican Party. It is simply a federation of states."[13] Saying this does not deny the national party a role in writing rules, but it does clearly define organizational boundaries. Hence, the question becomes not what the national party might impose but what the state parties will accept.

The extent to which the party reform effort has given rise to national party redefinition must thus be qualified. The Democratic experience has obviously promoted centralization, but the GOP has not adopted a similar motif. Even so, the delegate selection process in both parties has become a key and persistent agenda item. As a consequence, the role of the national party has taken on new and, in some instances, significant meaning.

NATIONAL PARTY LAW

The party reform movement also sparked a unique series of legal challenges. Both parties found themselves enmeshed in judicial proceedings that challenged the authority of the national organization to conduct internal party affairs. Three cases in particular highlight the issues and illustrate another facet of national party revision.

Implementation of the McGovern-Fraser guidelines produced several cases, but the most important in establishing the current role of law involved National Convention delegates from Cook County, Illinois.[14] In essence, the publicly elected delegates supported by Chicago Mayor Richard Daley were accused of being in violation of the McGovern-Fraser guidelines. They were then challenged by an alternative set of delegates before the 1972 Credentials Committee. In this forum, the "Daley delegates" were unseated, and the challengers were recognized as the legitimate representatives, pending final approval by the convention itself. Those adversely affected by the credentials ruling lauched two legal attacks. The deposed delegates initially sought to have their ouseter overturned by arguing in federal court that the Credentials Committee could not legally contravene the results of a primary election. Under expedited hearings, however, the U.S. Supreme Court declined to grant relief. Instead, the nation's highest court ruled that the Democratic national convention was the proper arena for resolution of credentials decisions.[15] In other words, the Supreme Court chose not to intervene in what it saw as an intramural partisan context—the fitness of delegates—and the convention subsequently seated the original challengers.

The unseated delegates also sought relief from the Illinois judiciary. Here, they successfully petitioned for an injunction to bar the newly recognized delegates from sitting at the convention. Failure to comply with the injunction would bring contempt of court charges. Upon returning from the convention, the anti-Daley delegates were cited for contempt, thereby precipitating a long legal battle. The manner in which the Illinois court cast the issue is instructive for understanding the emerging character of national–state party relationships. Consider what the Illinois court said: "[National party rules] in no way take precedence over the Illinois election code . . . the law of the State is supreme and party rules to the contrary are of no effect . . . [state interest] is superior to whatever other interests the party might wish to protect . . . [national party rules] could not force upon the people of Illinois . . . representatives contrary to their elective mandate."[16]

The issue, then, is clearly stated in terms of state law versus national party rule, with preference obviously given to the former. On appeal to the U.S. Supreme Court, the contempt conviction was reversed, and the Court's rationale is seen in the following passage from Cousins v. Wigoda:

[The question is whether or not] the interest of the state in protecting the effective right to participate in primaries is superior to other interests the party itself might work to protect. . . . Consideration of the special function of delegates to such a Convention militates persuasively against the conclusion that the asserted state interest constitutes a compelling state interest . . . [because] the states themselves have no constitutionally mandated role in the great task of selection of Presidential and Vice-Presidential candidates . . . [leaving delegate selection criteria up to each state would produce] an obviously intolerable result.[17]

Although the opinion was not unanimous, there can be little doubt concerning the implications of the holding: national party rule takes precedence over contrary state law. Such a holding forcefully expands the scope of national party authority. Equally important, the *Cousins* decision became the controlling opinion in similar situations—it constituted a landmark case in party law.

The *lack* of change in the GOP also spawned a legal challenge to the national party's authority. In this instance, the Republican formula for allocating convention delegates to states was contested. Under the existing plan, a uniform number of "bonus delegates" was awarded to states when certain Republican candidates for public office were successful. Because the number of bonus delegates was not tied to a popular base, the practical result of this plan could disproportionately increase the relative size of smaller state delegations.* Claiming that this formula was violative of the Fourteenth Amendent's equal protection clause and citing the "one-person, one-vote" legislative apportionment decisions, the Ripon Society brought suit. The case, in one form or another, spanned nearly five years. Although this self-styled group of "progressive Republicans" initially received a favorable ruling, the appellate court felt otherwise. In a unanimous opinion, the court ruled that the Fourteenth Amendment claims were here offset by the First Amendment guarantees of freedom of association.[18] This meant that the national party organization (absent constitutionally proscripted discrimination) was free to allocate delegates on whatever bases it desired. The judiciary, certainly, was not about to tell a party how best to pursue electoral success. A subsequent appeal for certiorari was rejected by the Supreme Court.

To conclude that ostensible reformers "won two and lost one" would be inappropriate—the relative merits of the decisions are not at issue here. However, to conclude that the national party organization "won three and lost none" would be appropriate. The federal judiciary adopted a position

---

*For example, a state delegation with 20 delegates could receive up to four additional delegates, for a 20 percent increase. Adding four bonus delegates to a 40-member delegation would produce a 10 percent gain. Hence, the uniform bonus rule could result in a disproportionate gain for smaller states, with consequent implications for the number of voters "represented" by each voter.

that firmly accords a superordinate role to national party rule and largely insulated the national party interpretation of that authority. The holdings do not, of course, preclude subsequent challenge. But as constitutional precedents, this body of law will probably deter the legal hegemony of the national party organization from being contested. Should such in fact prove to be the case, the evolution of party law obviously constitutes a redefinition of party rule.

NATIONAL PARTY ELITES

A further indicator of party change can be seen in the makeup of party leaders. The composition of the national party cadre, however, may well be a sketchy criterion. Recruitment to central party councils is an admixture of circumstance, involving opportunity as well as interest and resources. A consideration of national committee membership, nonetheless, affords some insight into the composition of one set of party elites and, relatedly, into national party redefinition.

In 1972, the Democratic Convention delegates voted to increase the size of the party's national committee and, also, to seek more extensive representation on the Democratic National Committee for selected party groups—particularly youth and racial minorities—traditionally underrepresented within the party hierarchy. Prior to this, each state elected one committeeman and committeewomen. The newly adopted formula provided that Democratic National Committee membership would be tied to population, with state delegations ranging in size from four to 18 with a total of approximately 360. Membership would also be guaranteed for representatives from intraparty associations (such as mayors and Young Democrats) and from Congress. Twenty-five additional "at large" seats would be available to "balance" representatives. Membership on the Republican National Committee remained fixed at three representatives per state: a national committeeman and committeewoman and the chairperson of the state party organization.

The data in Table 5.1 reflect the composition of national committee members over two time periods. It is evident that the Democratic mandate for reform led to demographic change, but the variations were not substantial. The percentage of younger members slightly increased, and the Democratic National Committee's nonwhite composition also went up. Other measures of elite character remained generally constant. (Other indicators that were examined included party entry level, party office holding, education, and religious preferences).[19] To make too little of these shifts would be as irresponsible as to make too much. The data do indicate that the Democratic national party organization reconstituted its personnel and that affirmative action guidelines had some impact. Moreover, by increasing the number of representatives from designated target groups, the national party organization becomes a potentially more viable forum for the articulation of a wider range of policy perspectives and, as well, provides the basis for a more diverse communcation infrastructure.

Membership on the Republican National Committee (seen also in Table 5.1) evidences no marked demographic alteration. The GOP retained its three person per state base and adopted no plan to broaden descriptively the party elite. This suggests, however tenuously, that in the absence of a national mandate, Republican National Committee membership will adhere to generally established patterns. Indeed, one attempt to increase the

TABLE 5.1:
Selected Demographic Characteristics
of National Committee Members[a]
(percent)

	Democrat		Republican	
	1970	1975	1968	1972
Age[b]				
29 or younger	0	2	0	0
30–39	12	18	7	9
40–49	37	37	44	39
50–59	26	31	30	32
60–69	17	10	16	16
70 or older	8	2	3	3
N	92	220	135	192
Race/Ethnicity				
White	92	81	100	100
Black	6	13	0	0
Hispanic	1	5	0	0
Other	1	1	0	0
N	102	323	153	153

[a] Members are elected to a four-year term at each national convention. Excluded from consideration were ex officio members, with the exception of Democratic state chairpersons.
[b] Based on available data.
Source: Who's Who in American Politics (New York: Bowker, 1968–1976) and data from Democratic and Republican National Committees.

diversity of the Republican National Committee through membership for selected party auxilliaries was rejected.*

Membership on party national committees remains dependent upon a variety of circumstances. Yet, the Democratic National Committee sought to change it's demographic composition and succeeded in this quest. That the reconstituted body has largely avoided detailed policy debate within its councils and concentrated instead on administrative questions should serve as a stark reminder of the constraints that yet mark this set of party elites.

Reference might also be made to another coterie of party elites: national convention delegates. As the rules that govern Democratic delegate selection have changed, so also has the character of the delegates. In contrast to their prereform counterparts, today's delegates include a greater percentage of nonwhite, younger, and women members,[20] reflecting the Democrat's commitment to affirmative action programs.† A related line of inquiry deals with the policy preferences of delegates as they too might be affected by changing national party rules. Indeed, one study of the 1972 delegates indicates that they were so removed from the party's mainstream that Republican delegates more nearly approximated the policy orientation of rank-and-file Democrats.[21] A study of the 1976 delegates also reflected a gap between party elites and masses along a range of issues.[22] Given these findings, some political scientists have expressed concern that redefining the rules has adversely affected the "representativeness" of party elites.[23]

The implicit assumption that there should be attitudinal congruence between the rank-and-file identifiers and the convention delegates should itself be carefully appraised. To expect such symmetry underestimates the fluidity of nominating politics, and the disproportionate success of a particular candidate in the preconvention nominating phase obviously bears implications for a subsequent survey of delegate attitudes. Delegate selection rules are but one variable in the electoral calculus. For our purposes, it is enough to note simply that the ultimate character of party elites *may* be affected by the rules of the game but the rules of the game *are* set by the national party. Candidates now recognize this, as do state and local party units, and it is this recognition that further affirms the redefinition of national parties.

---

*To accord full voting privileges on the national committee for such auxiliaries as the National Black Republican Council, Young Republicans, and the National Federation of Republican Women was thought "violative of the elective nature" of the Republican National Committee because such members were not elected by the state organizations. See "Commentary: Rule 29," *Ripon Forum* 11 (March 1975): 1.

†It is also the case that convention delegates are more highly educated and more wealthy in contrast with general population figures.

NATIONAL PARTY OPERATIONS

The traditional notion of national party organizations as interim housekeeping and convention-managing agencies was well grounded. Aside from the "out" party's national chairperson, who rode the banquet circuit and weighed in with occasional attacks on the incumbent, the national organization as a whole enjoyed little visibility.[24] The "in" party chairperson, who served at the pleasure of the president, performed as an organizational lightening rod and heat shield. Both committees operated in the context of presidential-level politics. Little attention was directed toward the committees as such because, as a rule, little was going on.

The limited role of the national organizations can also be understood by looking at party finances. In 1959, for example, the Democratic National Convention was estimated to have a total spendable income of about $750,000; a $3.5 million debt, following the 1960 presidential election, still amounted to $500,000 in 1963.[25] On the Republican side, a monthly deficit of between $16,000 to $20,000 was reported after Nixon's defeat and a lingering $225,000 debt in 1963. By the end of 1968, the Democratic National Committee was over $8 million in debt due to having absorbed the campaign debts of Robert Kennedy and Hubert Humphrey. Since that time, the deficit has been reduced to slightly more than $1 million, but the party's operations have obviously been hampered for more than a decade.[26] In early 1979, for example, the Washington, D.C., staff was reduced to a core of about 50 full-time employees.*

The election of Carter provided the party with a "star" fund-raising attraction, but the president has not as yet engaged in many party-sponsored events. While it is estimated that the Democratic National Committee will be out of debt by mid-1979, the lack of a solid financial basis continues to constrain the extent to which the national party organization can provide services and direct cash contributions to Democratic candidates for public office. Even so, the party undertook an extensive—and

---

*Financial exigencies can also spur innovation. The Democratic National Party sponsored four nationally broadcast telethons between 1972 and 1975, which netted nearly $6 million, 60 percent of which went to state party organizations. Recently, the Democratic National Committee provided an estimated $135,000 to congressional candidates in 1978, although most of this amount was in the form of services and not cash. A federal Elections Commission news release of January 24, 1979, indicates that *nonparty* political committees, on the other hand, contributed $32 million to federal candidates during the period January 1977 through November 27, 1978. Additionally, $241,000 was expended on behalf of federal candidates. These figures obviously indicate that national party organizations are less successful in generating revenues than nonparty committees and highlight but one difficulty surrounding national party redefinition.

costly—reform effort and, in doing this, financed the changing context of national party politics.

The Republican National Committee, by way of contrast, has made significant gains in the financial area. If anything, the evidence suggests that the party's national organization has been remarkably successful in generating revenues. In 1978, for example, the GOP netted nearly $10 million, and it projected a $1 million gain in 1979.[27] In further contrast to the Democrats, where donors ($100 or more) now account for about 75 percent of total revenues, the Republican National Committee reports that nearly two-thirds of its gross funding comes from 500,000 donors, with an average contribution of $22. The remainder of the party's money comes from "associates," who contribute between $1,000 and $10,000, and over 200 members of the "Eagle Club," who contribute a minimum of $10,000.

Republican National Committee finances can also be viewed in terms of disbursements, and it is here that the national party's role is assuming new dimensions. In 1977, to cite one illustration, the GOP spent more than $165,000 on state and local elections. But this effort merely presaged the 1978 effort. In an unprecedented move, the Republican National Committee allocated more than $2 million to its Local Election Campaigns Division, newly created in 1977. This arm of the national party oversaw direct cash contributions of nearly $1 million to state and local contests and an equal amount in the form of services, such as polling and media-related expenditures. What is vitally important is that the bulk of these disbursements went to nonincumbent candidates. In effect, the national party was heavily involved in an effort to recruit attractive candidates and, also, to subsidize their campaigns. About 40 percent of the elections were won by the Republicans candidates. It would be naive to suggest that the national funds made—or did not make—a difference; after all, 69 percent of the contests were lost. It would not be naive, however, to suggest that as a result of the Republican National Committee's effort, the national organization enjoys increased visibility on the state and local level and, perhaps, even some gratitude and respect.

The Republican National Committee has also sought to expand its ties with state party organizations. During 1977–78, the committee initiated a pilot program that put full-time field organizers to work for the state organization. It is not clear that this project met the committee's preliminary expectations, but the effort is noteworthy as further evidence of nationally sponsored attempts to build the party on all levels. Additionally, as of 1979, state parties can tie into the national party's computer facilities through telephone linkups. This resource will enable state parties to engage in more sophisticated direct main and fund-raising operations, as well as provide access to a wide range of electoral and demographic statistics. The Republican National Committee allocated 13 percent of its budget to "party development" in 1978. This was a significant departure from previous years and one that if maintained, portends much in the way of recasting the role of the Republican's national organization.

While unable to match its counterpart in revenues secured and services provided, the Democratic Party has engaged in another mode of national party building. At its 1972 National Convention, the delegates voted to establish a Party Charter Commission.* Two year's later, more than 2,000 delegates assembled in Kansas City to vote on the proposed charter.[28] Opposition to the charter was expressed by those who felt that the 1972 reforms had weakened the party and in no little way contributed to Nixon's reelection. In particular, it was feared that the charter would hasten a "Europeanization" of the Democratic Party. From this perspective, attempts to specify criteria for party membership, impose national standards of affirmative action, or provide for proportional representation in the delegate selection process could splinter the party into factions and render the party less electorally effective.

From another perspective, however, the charter was differently appraised:

> The party, it was hoped, could be made relevant to the closing decades of the twentieth century. In the process, a subtle shift of power would occur: more authority would gravitate to the national party while at the same time the procedures of both the state and, more specifically, the federal party would be domocratized. To the extent that an essentially lifeless and unresponsive organization could be made both more accountable to and representative of its grassroots membership, the reform would be a success.[29]

As finally adopted, the charter set forth a statement of principles, specificed procedures, created new party councils, and specified organizational relationships.[30] Especially novel was the charter's language, which provided for an optional policy conference to be held midway between presidential election years. This forum would enable party members to take part in the kind of party-sponsored issue debate previously restricted to national nominating conventions. But it was, wrote one observer, a charter marked by "tradeoffs between centralized guarantees of free access to party decision-making and a reaffirmed commitment to a federalized party

---

*In 1968, delegates to the National Convention had also mandated the establishment of a second-party commission to reform convention rules. This panel was headed by then-Representative James O'Hara of Michigan. A preliminary charter draft was jointly authored by members of the McGovern-Fraser and O'Hara commissions in the spring of 1972, but action on this document was deferred at the 1972 convention. The Party Charter Commission was chaired by Terry Sanford, former Democratic governor of North Carolina.

structure."[31] Even so, the Democrats became the first U.S. political party to adopt a written constitution, and in so doing, "signified a potentially evolving interest in developing a cohesive organizational style. A restructured and more democratically representative party could result in an organization more responsive to contemporary political and social concerns."[32]

In 1978, the party's second midterm convention was held, and it demonstrated that the president has many resources with which to deal with party activists. By all accounts, Carter's interests were well protected. Over 150 advisors were in attendance, and the procedural ground rules were designed to inhibit controversy. The important point, however, is that the conference forced the White House to recognize the existence of intraparty criticism and engage in a "realistic exchange of views."[33] The delegates also, dealt with other matters and voted to "divide National Convention delegate spots equally between men and women, and to eliminate all vestiges of winner-take-all systems from the nation's presidential primaries, thereby settling two fights that have raged in the party for more than a decade."[34]

While policy impact of the conference may not be of the magnitude desired by advocates of the charter, it is also evident that the original fears of the charter's opponents have not been realized. The midterm conventions have expanded the orbit of national party operations and provided an additional setting for activity by party supporters. That the option to hold an interim meeting has been exercised in each case to date also suggests that this assembly will be a regular feature, thereby fostering national party redefinition.

THE THEORY OF NATIONAL PARTY REDEFINITION

The argument presented here is straightforward. The Democratic and Republican national organizations, in different ways to be sure, have become more important political institutions over the course of the past decade. The theoretical interpretation of this change, however, is less easily drawn. But, as one writer notes, analysts generally agree that

> most of the Western world's political parties are one or the other of two basic types: *cadre parties*, which are content to have their decisions made and their activities conducted by small groups of highly involved, active, and persistent "party activists" (or "militants" or "workers"); and *mass parties*, which seek to enroll as many people as possible in their memberships and to make their decisions according to the expressed desires of the mass memberships.[35]

Not surprisingly, U.S. political parties have been traditionally characterized as cadre parties, emphasizing above all else the winning of public office.

Consider, however, various changes undertaken by the Democratic Party. The 1972 McGovern-Fraser reforms were specifically designed to facilitate mass participation in the delegate selection process. Many practices long employed to preclude meaningful and timely involvement in the nomination of the party's presidential candidate were banned. Moreover, state parties were required to ensure that women, youth, and racial minorities were "reasonably represented" among national convention delegations, and state parties were obliged to follow uniform national standards. In 1974, the party held its first midterm convention and ratified a party charter, the first such constitution for a U.S. political party. As did the U.S. Constitution, the charter compromised between factions, but analogously, the charter symbolized the nationalization of the Democratic Party.

The 1976 reforms constituted a refinement of the original changes and somewhat eased the strictures imposed on state parties. At the same time, the new rules continued the general thrust of the initial reforms. The party moved to assure that the delegate selection process would more fairly reflect the presidential preferences of participants, and the party sought as well to ensure that only Democrats would have a role in determining the party nominee. The Winograd Commission's recommendations tended to differ from those of the earlier reform panels, and doubtlessly reflected the short-term electoral interests of President Carter. The commission, in general, adopted proposals that made it more difficult for candidates to mount a challenge to an incumbent, thereby inhibiting—but now precluding—accountability. Delegates to the 1978 midterm convention, however, confirmed the party's commitment to the proportional reflection of candidate preference and even mandated that women and men equally share delegate seats at the 1980 National Convention.

What stands out from the Democratic Party's efforts since 1968 is the conception of a national party model predicated on the principles of broad-based popular participation and elite accountability. It would be an error to conclude that these objectives have been fully realized, but it would be even more of an error not to recognize that the party has moved (however fitfully) in the direction of a mass party model of organization.

The GOP, on the other hand, has sought organizational objectives not directly related to the mass party model. Although the party has adopted procedures which require that the delegate selection process be publicly advertised and free of unlawful discrimination, the Republican national organization remains a confederation of state parties. Representation on the national committee (and convention-related committees as well) is tied to a geographical rather than a popular base. Attempts to alter the voting membership of the national committee have been rejected, as have attempts to make state delegations to the national convention numerically proportional. State party organizations, in addition, enjoy considerable latitude in how they chose to implement nationally endorsed positive action programs. In contrast to Democratic requirements, uniform criteria by which such party-broadening activities might be assessed are conspicuously absent. Upholding a philosophical belief in decentralization of authority, the party's activists have checked carefully the power of the national organization.

At the same time, the Republican national organization has undertaken an unprecedented program of expanded services to state parties and to individuals seeking office on the subnational level. Many of these efforts have the additional benefit of increasing the prospect of intraparty integration, while coincidentally promoting the efficiency of party operations. The visibility of the national party, as well as its utility, is thereby enhanced.

What emerges, then, is a party model keyed to contesting elections above all else. Party strength is measured in terms of funds raised, candidates fielded, services rendered, votes garnered, and elections won. The definition—and conduct—of all party affairs, however, is retained by generally well-insulated party elites. In contrast to the mass party orientation of the Democratic Party, the GOP has opted to become a contemporary derivative of the classical cadre party model.

POSTSCRIPT

The current U.S. electoral system is itself in a state of flux. This condition is variously described but depicts a process of "party decomposition." Voters (those who still participate) are portrayed as less identified with, informed by, and supportive of the party as an institution. They are thought to respond to specific issues or their perception of a particular office seeker. Candidate organizations and professional campaign consultants employ sophisticated marketing techniques, which further erode—if not totally supplant—traditional party functions. Presidential selection, suggests one respected analyst, "has become, in substance if not in form, something closely approaching a no-party system."[36]

But as Pomper sets forth in his introductory chapter to this book, the case for party decomposition may be overstated. Indeed, the redefinition of national parties can be seen as an attempt by the parties to deal with changes in the electoral process. The national parties had become moribund; they were neither responsive nor resourceful. To maintain, as does one author, that "reform is wrecking the party system" is to miss the central point: the party system was wrecking itself.[37]

The national party organizations have undergone a transformation.

The Democratic Party responded to systemic changes by emphasizing the necessity for intraparty democracy as a precondition for electoral effectiveness. The Republican Party has chosen to strengthen its national organization through the provision of expanded services. That the two parties differ in the manifestation of their redefinition should not obscure what is in fact a remarkable transition from the era of "politics without power." In the absence of continued party redefinition, it can be argued that public policy will but reflect the objectives of self-styled "citizen action groups" or privately financed Political Action committees, neither of which can profess to be more publicly responsible than political parties—themselves fragile vehicles for democracy.

NOTES

1. See Cornelius P. Cotter and Bernard C. Hennessy, *Politics Without Power: The National Party Committees* (New York: Atherton Press, 1964).

2. Walter F. Murphy and Michael N. Danielson, *American Democracy* (New York: Holt, Rinehart and Winston, 1979), p. 128.

3. See Frank J. Sorauf, *Party Politics in America* (Boston: Little, Brown, 1976), pp. 9–11.

4. Austin Ranney, "The Political Parties: Reform and Decline," in *The New American Political System*, ed. Anthony King (Washington, D.C.: American Enterprise Institute, 1978), p. 215.

5. Some observers now speak of "party nationalization." See William J. Keefe, *Parties, Politics and Public Policy in America* (New York: Holt, Rinehart and Winston, 1976), p. 186, or Gerald Pomper et al., *The Election of 1976* (New York: McKay, 1977), p. 7. For a more extensive analysis, see Charles Longley, "Party Nationalization in America," in *Paths to Political Reform*, ed. William J. Crotty (Lexington, Mass.: Heath, 1979).

6. The commission's report was published as *Mandate for Reform* (Washington, D.C.: Democratic National Committee, 1970).

7. See Austin Ranney, *Curing the Mischiefs of Faction* (Berkeley: University of California Press, 1975), p. 184.

8. See the commission's report, *Democrats All* (Washington, D.C.: Democratic National Committee, 1973).

9. To lessen the prospects for conflict, a "Compliance Review Commission" (CRC) was mandated by the Mikulski Commission. The CRC reviewed delegate selection plans proposed by states; upon approval, nonimplementation of the plan was the only basis of challenge before the Credentials Committee. See Chalres Longley, "Party Reform and Party Organization: The Compliance Review Commission of the Democratic Party" (Paper delivered at 1977 Annual Meeting of the Northeastern Political Science Association, Mt. Airy, Pennsylvania, November 10–12, 1977). A detailed examination of the 1976 Credentials Committee can be found in Charles Longley, "Party Politics and Party Reform: Voting at the 1976 Democratic Credentials Committee" (Paper delivered at 1976 Annual Meeting of the American Political Science Association, Chicago, Illinois, September 2–5, 1976).

10. See F. Christopher Arterton, "Recent Rules Changes Within the National Democratic Party: Some Present and (Short-Term) Future Consequences" (paper delivered at 1978 Annual Meeting of the Social Science History Association, Columbus, Ohio, November 3–5, 1978).

11. Quoted in Longley, "Party Politics and Party Reform."

12. See the discussion by William J. Crotty in *Political Reform and the American*

Experiment (New York: Crowell, 1977), pp. 255–60. A second discussion of Republican reform is in Longley, "Party Nationalization in America."

13. Quoted in "Commentary: Rule 29," *Ripon Forum* 11 (March 1975): 2.

14. See William J. Crotty, "Anatomy of a Challenge: The Chicago Delegation to the National Convention," in *Cases in American Politics*, ed. Robert L. Peabody (New York: Praeger, 1976), pp. 111–58.

15. Keene et al. v. National Democratic Committee, consolidated with O'Brien et al. v. Brown, 409 U.S. 4–5 (1972).

16. Wigoda v. Cousins, 14 Ill. App., 3d 460, 302 N.E. 2d, 625–29.

17. 419 U.S. 477 (1975).

18. See the discussion of Ripon Society, Inc. v. National Republican Party in "Politics: The GOP," *Ripon Forum* 11 (October 1975): 1.

19. See Longley, "Party Nationalization in America."

20. Ranney, "The Political Parties," p. 232.

21. See Jeanne J. Kirkpatrick, *The Presidential Elites* (New York: Russell Sage Foundation and Twentieth Century Fund, 1976).

22. See Everett Carll Ladd, Jr., *Where Have All the Voters Gone?* (New York: Norton, 1978) in general and pp. 63–67 in particular.

23. For a general discussion of the meaning of representation, see H. F. Pitkin, *The Concept of Representation* (Berkeley: University of California Press, 1967). Kirkpatrick's *The New Presidential Elites* focuses on the topic in light of convention delegate characteristics.

24. See Cotter and Hennessy, *Politics Without Power*. Democratic National Chairperson Robert S. Strauss (1972–76) may be an exception to the general rule, but Strauss was head of the party during the particularly turbulent time following McGovern's defeat and the close-quartered combat between party reformers and regulars. As Chairperson, Strauss is widely credited with salving—if not healing—the wounds of 1972, thus making Carter's success even possible.

25. Cotter and Hennessy, *Politics Without Power*, p. 185, 174.

26. Ibid., p. 177, 174.

27. Data concerning Republican finances were provided by the Republican National Committee. I am particularly indebted for the assistance of David Ingerman of the Republican National Committee.

28. For a discussion of the 1974 convention, see Denis G. Sullivan, Jeffrey L. Pressman, and F. Christopher Arterton, *Explorations in Convention Decision Making* (San Francisco: Freeman, 1976).

29. Crotty, *Political Reform and the American Experiment*, p. 252.

30. For a detailed listing of the charter's provisions, see ibid., pp. 253–55.

31. David S. Broder, "Democrats Ready to Adopt Charter," Washington *Post* December 1, 1974, p. A-1.

32. William J. Crotty, "Party Reform and Democratic Performance" (Paper delivered at conference on "The Future of the American Political System: What Can Be Done to Make It More Democratic and Effective?," Center for the Study of Democratic Policy, University of Pennsylvania, Philadelphia, April 12–13, 1979), p. 31.

33. See TRB, "Memphis Blues," *The New Republic* 178 (December 23 and 30, 1978): 2.

34. Ken Bode, "Miniconvention," *The New Republic* 178 (December 23 and 30, 1978): 14.

35. Austin Ranney, "The Evolution of the Democratic Party's National Organization: Characteristics, Causes, and Consequences" (Paper delivered at a joint meeting of the Commission on Party Structure and Delegate Selection and the Commission on Rules, Washington, D.C., November 19, 1971), p. 5.

36. Austin Ranney, "The Political Parties," p. 213.

37. See Everett Carll Ladd, Jr., "'Reform' Is Wrecking the U.S. Party System," *Fortune* 96 (November 1977): 177–188.

6

THE NATIONAL DEMOCRATIC PARTY

Carol F. Casey

*T*he main impetus for renewal within the Democratic Party stemmed from two political issues that divided much of the country and many in the Democratic Party in the 1960s—the civil rights movement and the Vietnam War. The actions taken by the Democratic Party at its 1968 National Convention in response to the political pressures arising from these issues marked the beginning of the modern reform movement in the Democratic Party.

This chapter briefly reviews the actions of the 1968, 1972, and 1976 Democratic conventions and the reform commissions they established. We will then focus on the major issues confronting the party now in regard to delegate selection standards.

IMPETUS FOR REFORM

In 1964, the Mississippi Freedom Democratic Party filed a challenge against the all white regular Mississippi delegation, charging that it was not loyal to the national party and that the state party systematically excluded blacks from registering to vote and from participating in party meetings.[1] After emotionally charged hearings, the Credentials Committee approved a compromise resolution that (1) required the regular Mississippi delegation to sign declarations of support for the party's nominees; (2) directed that the Call to the 1968 convention require state parties to assure "that voters in the State, regardless of race, color, creed, or national origin, will have the opportunity to participate fully in Party affairs"; (3) directed the national chairperson to establish a special committee to aid state parties in meeting the antidiscrimination requirements; (4) seated two Mississippi Freedom Democratic Party delegates as convention delegates at large; and (5) designated other members of the Mississippi Freedom Democratic Party as honored guests of the convention.[2]

The Credentials Committee report, adopted by voice vote of the convention, was an important milestone for the civil rights movement, but the agreement was to have even greater historical significance due to its impact on the internal dynamics of the Democratic Party. For the first time, the national party established standards that state parties would have to observe in selecting delegates to national conventions. In the past, states had been free to use whatever procedures they wished in choosing delegates; no party authority at the national level had intervened in the selection process. After 1964, the states discovered that they no longer were fully autonomous. A doctrine of national party supremacy had been established, and the foundation had been laid for a major reform movement.

As a result of the 1964 convention's action, the Democratic National Committee established a special Equal Rights Committee. In July 1967, the committee unanimously adopted a resolution urging the 1968 convention to replace any delegation "not broadly representative of the Democrats of the State" with a rival, representative delegation.[3] This resolution was to form the basis for the seating of the Mississippi Freedom Democratic Party at the 1968 convention. The committee also adopted nondiscrimination standards, which state parties have been required to include in their party rules ever since 1969.

The other major force propelling the party toward reform was the antiwar presidential candidacy of Eugene McCarthy in 1968. Antiwar activists sought election as delegates to the Chicago convention. In state after state, the insurgents found a haphazard and informal delegate selection process, which frustrated their efforts. As the presidential primary season drew to a close, McCarthy strategists brought together a group of 1968 Convention Rules Committee members who formed the ad hoc Commission on the Democratic Selection of Presidential Nominees. That commission, chaired by then-Governor Harold Hughes of Iowa, undertook an independent study of the convention delegate selection process and concluded that "state systems for selecting delegates to the National Convention and the procedures of the Convention itself, display considerably less fidelity to basic democratic principles than a nation which claims to govern itself can safely tolerate.[4] The commission's report, *The Democratic Choice*, set forth five guidelines for reforming the delegate selection process—these would later form the basis for the report of the McGovern-Fraser Commission.

The Rules Committee of the 1968 convention—like the convention itself—was divided. In the majority report, the committee recommended the establishment of a study commission to evaluate the Hughes report.[5] A minority report specifically incorporated some of the commission's recommendations by requiring that delegates to the 1972 convention be selected by a process "in which all Democratic voters have had full and timely opportunity to participate," that "the unit rule not be used in any stage of the delegate selection process," and that the delegate selection process be "open to public participation within the calendar year of the convention."[6] The minority report was adopted by the convention by a vote of 1,350 to 1,206.[7] Complementary language contained in the majority report of the Credentials Committee, adopted by a voice vote of the convention, mandated the formation of a commission to aid state parties in meeting the 1972 requirements and to recommend "such improvements as can assure even broader citizen participation in the delegate selection process."[8]

DELEGATE SELECTION STANDARDS

Since 1968, three Democratic Party reform commissions have grappled with the problem of writing national party rules governing the selection of delegates to the national nominating conventions. These groups are popularly identified by their chairpersons, namely, the McGovern-Fraser Commission (1969–72), the Mikulski Commission (1973), and the Winograd Commission (1975–78).

Each of these commissions attempted to develop delegate selection rules that would strengthen the party be setting uniform standards of fairness to ensure the representation and participation of all Democrats in the presidential nominating process. But it was the McGovern-Fraser Commission that laid the foundation and whose original guidelines established the framework within which each subsequent commission operated.[9] Each of the delegate selection rules in effect for the 1980 national convention finds its roots in one of the guidelines originally adopted in 1969. This is not to say that the McGovern-Fraser Commission was prescient or that later commissions were unimaginative. Certain of the guidelines have been substantively modified in the last ten years. The changes have come partially as a result of the lessons of practical experience and partially because of shifting power bases within the party, leading competing interests to perceive—rightly or wrongly—certain rules as affecting their political fortunes. For example, in 1969, the AFL-CIO chose not to participate actively within the McGovern-Fraser Commission, perhaps believing that whatever rules were adopted would not be implemented. In

1973, when the AFL-CIO did choose to participate actively in the rule-making process, they found themselves in agreement with the liberal-reform wing on some questions.

Five major issues can be identified in the past decade of rules revision as being the major sources of controversy. These include the role of party and elected officials, the affirmative action/quota controversy, proportional representation of presidential candidate preferences, presidential candidate right of approval, and restricting participation to Democratic voters only.

The Role of Party and Elected Officials

Given the general political upheaval that characterized 1968—the decision of the party's incumbent president not to seek reelection, the channeling of antiwar sentiments into political activity that threatened the party's power structure and engendered a call for grass-roots participation, and the assassination of two national leaders—it is understandable that the McGovern-Fraser Commission concerned itself with such issues as "timeliness," clear designation of presidential preferences, and eliminating indirect methods of delegate selection. In its study of the 1968 presidential nominating campaign, the McGovern-Fraser Commission found that

> the day Eugene McCarthy announced his candidacy, nearly one-third of the delegates had in effect already been selected. And, by the time Lyndon Johnson announced his intention not to seek another term, the formal delegate selection process had begun in all but 12 of the states. By the time the issues and candidates that characterized the politics of 1968 had clearly emerged, therefore, it was impossible for rank-and-file Democrats to influence the selection of these delegates.[10]

Coupled with the 1968 convention's mandate, these findings led the commission to adopt guidelines which

- —prohibited ex-officio delegates (Guideline C-2)
- —required each step in the delegate selection process to begin in the calendar year of the Convention (Guideline C-4)
- —banned officials elected or appointed before the calendar year of the Convention from choosing nominating committees or proposing or endorsing a slate of delegates (Guideline C-4)
- —limited committee selection of National Convention delegates to 10% of the total delegation, and permitted that selection only when the committee was apportioned on a one-person, one-vote basis, elected in the calendar year of the Convention, and identified as to presidential preference or uncommitted status (Guideline C-5).[11]

Violations of these guidelines led to the unseating of Mayor Daley's Chicago delegates at the 1972 convention,[12] and sparked a controversy as yet unresolved within the party. The Mikulski Commission relaxed the stringent requirements of the guidelines by permitting 25 percent of a state's delegation to be selected by a state committee, allowing committees chosen two years prior to the convention to make that selection, and eliminating the requirement that committee members identify their presidential preference or uncommitted status. Essentially, the Mikulski Commission rule was a compromise between those who differed on the quota question and committee selection: the rules on committee selection were made more lenient, but the 25 percent at-large portion of a state's delegation was reserved for the purpose of ensuring adequate representation of women, blacks, and young people, if necessary, to balance a state's delegation, as well as for the inclusion of party and public officials. The Winograd Commission essentially retained the Mikulski Commission's requirements but added to a state's delegation an additional 10 percent of its total delegates to be reserved for party and elected officials. The Mikulski and Winograd Commission rules required that such at-large delegates reflect the division of presidential preferences of the previously elected delegates.

While the current rules on committee selection and party and elected officials generally have been accepted, these compromise rules do not come to grips with the fundamental issue of the role of party and elected officials in the presidential nominating process, a debate often characterized in the terms of representative versus participatory democracy (see Chapter 3). The McGovern-Fraser Commisssion was unequivocal on this point: no special role should be provided. If they chose to participate, it would have to be on the same basis and under the same rules governing any other Democrat.

Others have argued that party and public officials should have a special voice because they would be more concerned than the issue-oriented or candidate activists with choosing a candidate who could win the election, the ultimate goal of the party.[13] If one accepts those arguments, it seems logical that those officials should be exempt from the requirements of stating their presidential preference, gaining a presidential candidate's approval, and being allocated according to the presidential preferences of the elected delegates. If the party decides that it is in its best interest to include elected officials as national convention delegates, then it would make more sense to define which officials ought to be delegates and give them automatic delegate status than to give each state party an arbitrary 10 percent of its own delegates for that purpose. If elected officials are given special status at the national convention, then perhaps the party also could—and should—impose some specific obligations upon them, such as demonstrable support for the party's platform, thus introducing some measure of accountability to the party.

The Affirmative Action/Quota Controversy

By the time the McGovern-Fraser Commission met, the principle of nondiscrimination on the basis of race, color, creed, or national origin had been formally accepted within the Democratic Party. However, the commission went beyond this standard in its adoption of guidelines A-1 and A-2, which required state parties to overcome the effects of past discrimination by taking affirmative action to include minorities, women, and young people in the state's national convention delegation "in reasonable relationship to their presence in the population of the State."[14]

The commission's action was not without precedent. In early 1967, a subcommittee of the special Equal Rights Committee had proposed that convention seats be denied any delegation less than 10 percent black from a state with a black population of 20 percent or more.[15] Similarly, the 1968 Hughes Commission, building on the 1964 convention's antidiscrimination mandate, had urged the national party to impose an "affirmative obligation" on state parties to bring blacks and other minorities into "full and meaningful participation" in party affairs. The Hughes Commission maintained, moreover, that the burden of proof should be placed on a state party to demonstrate that it had not, in fact, discriminated during the delegate selection process if the percentage of minority people in its delegation was significantly lower than the minority percentage for the state as a whole.[16]

Throughout the debate on guidelines A-1 and A-2, concern was expressed that the adopted language imposed, or could be interpreted as imposing, a quota system for black, young, and female delegates. In an effort to clarify the commission's intent, Senator McGovern proposed, and the commission unanimously adopted, a footnote to guidelines A-1 and A-2, which stated, "It is the understanding of the Commission that this is not to be accomplished by the mandatory imposition of quotas."[17] The footnote, however, did not dispel the suspicions of some—and the hopes of others— that a quota system would be in effect for 1972.

In the implementation phase of the commission's work, state parties were reminded of their affirmative action obligations in a memorandum dated October 18, 1971, which included an outline for a model program. A second 1971 memorandum, signed by then-Democratic National Committee chairperson Lawrence F. O'Brien, warned state parties that in the case of a credentials challenge, underrepresentation of women, youth, and minorities on a delegation would be construed as prima facie evidence of discrimination. The burden of proof would then shift from the challengers to the state party.[18]

The fact that the commission neither intended nor tried to impose a quota system does not mean that one was not used in many states in 1972. On the one hand, presidential candidates—particularly in primary states where they had control over who could legally file as delegates pledged to their candidacies—were careful to balance their slates with appropriate numbers of women, blacks, and young people as insurance against credentials challenges that could cost them precious votes at the convention. On the other hand, the burden of proof in the case of a challenge rested on state parties rather than on the presidential candidates, so the state parties themselves had an interest in coming up with balanced delegations in order to avoid a challenge. Nonetheless, credentials challenges based wholly or in part on allegations of discrimination against, or underrepresentation of, women, minorities, and youth were filed against 20 states at the 1972 national convention.

The quota system was perhaps the most controversial issue before the Mikulski Commission. The Coalition for a Democratic Majority, opposed to many of the McGovern-Fraser Commission guidelines, characterized the quotas as "undemocratic and elitist," stating that "all the Party can properly do is actively provide assurances that the [delegate] contests will be open and fair, and take affirmative steps to encourage all groups to participate."[19] Other groups and individuals argued, however, that some guarantee of representation to previously underrepresented groups was still necessary until those groups could overcome the effects of past discrimination and have an equal opportunity for election. The Mikulski Commission worked out a compromise acceptable to opposing factions: (1) participation, rather than representation, was to be the specific goal of affirmative action programs; (2) the prohibition against the imposition of quotas was more emphatically stated, although equal division of delegate positions between men and women was expressly permitted; and (3) the composition of a delegation would no longer be prima facie evidence of discrimination nor would the burden of proof shift to the state party. In return, more explicit and stringent affirmative action requirements were placed on state parties. Each state had to establish an Affirmative Action Committee and develop an Affirmative Action Plan, subject to the approval of the national Compliance Review Commission, outlining the specific steps it would take to encourage full participation.[20]

Despite these requirements, however, fewer women, youth, and blacks were represented at the 1976 National Convention: women constituted 33 percent of the delegates in 1976, down from 40 percent in 1972; 11 percent of the delegates in 1976 were black, compared with 15 percent in 1972; and youth representation declined from 24 percent in 1972 to 15 percent in 1976.[21]

Although the Winograd Commission left the affirmative action requirements virtually unchanged, women will constitute 50 percent of the delegates to the 1980 National Convention because the Democratic National Committee, in the adoption of the Preliminary Call to the convention, provided for equal division between delegate men and delegate women.

Proportional Representation of Presidential Candidate Preference

Although requiring proportional representation of presidential candidate preferences might seem the next logical step for a party that had just abolished the unit rule, it was not one which the McGovern-Fraser Commission was prepared to take. One of its own consultants had argued in favor of the proposal, warning that

> if at such preliminary stages [for example, precinct and county conventions] successive majorities are allowed to prevail and to represent only themselves and if the representation of minorities is not carried forward through state-wide convention or other delegate selection processes to the National Convention, then it is quite possible, it is in some circumstances likely, that the final majority of delegates which prevails at the National Convention will represent a minority, not a majority of the Democratic voters in the Nation at large.[22]

However, strong opposition to a strict proportional requirement, led by Frederick Dutton, a persuasive and articulate defender of the California winner-take-all primary, resulted in a commission vote to urge, rather than require, state parties to provide fair representation of minority views. One manner of accomplishing that goal, the commission suggested, was by electing delegates from units no larger than a congressional district. In a different Guideline, the commission required convention states to elect at least 75 percent of their delegation at the congressional district or smaller unit level. In addition, the commission stated its intention of recommending that the 1972 convention adopt a requirement for representation of minority presidential preferences.[23]

Ironically, in the California credentials challenge at the 1972 convention, those who had originally favored the abolition of winner-take-all primaries (McGovern supporters), were put in the position of defending that system in order to protect their delegate votes.[24] Although the 1972 convention voted to seat the California delegation as elected—a decision consistent with the guidelines—it also adopted a resolution requiring that delegates to the 1976 convention be selected in a manner that "fairly reflects the division of preferences expressed by those who participate in the presidential nominating process."[25]

Faced with the task of implementing the convention's resolution, the

Mikulski Commission members formed an unusual alliance on this issue, with each side thinking that the adopted rule would work to its advantage. More than any other delegate selection rule, proportional representation was perceived as translating directly into delegate votes. As someone once facetiously suggested, "If we have more votes than they do, it's winner-take-all; if they have more votes than we do, then proportional representation will be required." The basic rule required that any presidential candidate (or "uncommitted" slate) receiving 15 percent or more of the votes be awarded a proportionate share of the delegates. However, the commission left a deliberate loophole: the requirement did not apply to states where delegates were elected directly on the primary ballot. This type of primary, as the members of the drafting committee well knew, usually results in winner-take-all at the congressional district level and was the type of primary system used in Illinois, New Jersey, New York, Ohio, and Pennsylvania—five of the eight states with the largest number of delegates at the 1976 convention.*

The adoption of the proportional representation rule was widely reported in the press as assuring a "brokered" convention in 1976 because no candidate could possibly win a first ballot victory.[26] Evidently, Carter failed to read the predictions, but the 1976 convention adopted a resolution banning future use of the loophole primary system.[27]

As the Winograd Commission learned, perceptions on the "fairness" of delegate selection rules may differ, depending upon whether or not one is running for the presidential nomination as an incumbent. Some commission members voiced support for rules that would diminish the chances of a challenger to the incumbent president. Called the "sliding window," the rule would have set high and rising thresholds for winning delegates at different times: 15 percent of the primary vote would be required from March 11 to April 8, 20 percent from April 8 to May 13, and 25 percent from May 13 to June 10. With the ban on the loophole primary in effect, the specter of a brokered convention again was raised, and the sliding window offered as a method of "consensus building."[28]

The Democratic National Committee rejected the sliding window, but replaced it with a far more complex rule, which would vary the threshold for winning delegates with the number elected in each district.[29] Those with Machiavellian minds could see how this proposal could easily benefit the front-runner, presumably the incumbent president. By manipulating either the size of the districts (making them smaller) or the number of delegates to be elected (allocating fewer per district), the threshold would be raised, to the disadvantage of challengers and minority factions. On the basis of the

---

*Texas later adopted a "loophole" primary for 1976.

1976 data, the effect would be a winner-take-all result in 38 percent of the districts, raising the threshold higher than in 1976 in 90 percent of the districts for 82 percent of the delegates elected in the primary states.[30] The rule finally adopted capped the threshold at 25 percent no matter how few delegates were to be selected. States not using primaries were given discretion to set their minimum percentage anywhere between 15 percent and 20 percent.[31]

The Mikulski and Winograd commissions expanded the McGovern-Fraser Commission's apportionment rule to require that all states—not just those with convention systems—elect at least 75 percent of their national convention delegations from units no larger than a congressional district. Given the fact that the original requirement was imposed as an indirect way of achieving a fair reflection of presidential preferences, it seems unnecessary in light of the more recent rules. Coupled with the requirement that the 1980 delegates be equally divided between men and women, the provision unduly complicates the delegate selection process. Unfortunately, the commissions have had a tendency to make their changes rule by rule, rather than taking a look at the broader picture and ensuring that the rules mesh in a logical manner.

Presidential Candidate Right of Approval

The only acknowledgment by the McGovern-Fraser Commission of any rights of a presidential candidate was the slate-making guideline. It required that "any slate presented in the name of a presidential candidate in a primary State be assembled with due consultation with the presidential candidate or his representative."[32] The interests of rank-and-file Democrats would have been better served if later commissions had left it at that, but out of a well-intentioned resolution adopted by the 1972 convention to address a legitimate problem came rules that have had a negative impact on the integrity of the delegate selection process.

In some states in 1972 where presidential primaries bound national convention delegations but where the actual delegates were selected in a separate process, Governor Wallace was denied the delegate votes to which he was legitimately entitled. In Tennessee, for example, Wallace won the presidential primary, and thus all 49 of the state's votes, yet only 33 of those votes were cast for him at the nominating convention because Wallace supporters were in the minority at the convention that selected the actual delegates. To remedy this situation, the national convention required that "any delegate mandated to vote for a presidential candidate be selected in a manner which assures that he or she is in fact a bona fide supporter of that candidate."[33] In adopting a rule to implement the convention's resolution, the Mikulski Commission gave presidential aspirants the right to approve delegate candidates identified with their candidacies. In this instance, the cure was much worse than the disease, for two reasons: it gave the representatives of presidential candidates the authority—which was exercised in 1976—to handpick national convention delegates through their use of the right of approval, and it set the precedent for shifting the focus of the delegate selection rules from assuring meaningful participation by rank-and-file Democrats to adopting rules that facilitated running national presidential campaigns.

Before proportional representation was mandatory, a legitimate reason existed for requiring a presidential candidate's approval of prospective delegates pledged to his candidacy. As Johnson learned the hard way in the 1968 New Hampshire primary, having more delegates pledged to one's candidacy than there are delegates to be elected will split the votes among those delegate-candidates. One's total vote may be higher than the total cast for an opponent, but the votes cast for individual delegates will be insufficient for their election. Now that proportional representation is in effect, the number of delegates to be won by a presidential candidate is determined only by the votes cast directly for that candidate and not by the number cast for the individual pledged delegates. The vote for delegate-candidates merely determines which persons will go to the convention to cast the formal ballot.

Sufficient safeguards currently exist and can be easily implemented to assure that elected delegates will be bona fide supporters of the presidential candidate they purport to prefer. For example, simultaneous nominating caucuses for each presidential candidate and uncommitted group, whether it be preprimary or in convention systems, make it unlikely that delegate-candidates can successfully masquerade as supporters of a presidential candidate they do not in reality support. Presidential candidate approval, on the other hand, prevents participants in a convention or voters in a primary from having a free choice in the selection of delegates that supposedly represent them—not the presidential candidate—at the national convention. While a delegate-candidate would have to indicate his or her presidential preference and be a bona fide supporter of that candidate, the persons selecting them legitimately have the right to take other factors into account.

Yet presidential candidate intervention in the delegate selection process does not end with their right of approval. The Winograd Commission went on to bind all national convention delegates on the first ballot to their stated presidential preference, unless released in writing, and further provided that

> delegates who seek to violate this rule may be replaced with an alternate of the same presidential preference by the presidential candidate or that candidate's authorized representative(s) at any time up to and including the presidential balloting at the National Convention.[34]

No reason was given in the Winograd Commission report for the inclusion of this sentence. It appears to unnecessarily confer upon presidential candidates dictatorial powers to "remedy" no perceived ill. The Winograd Commission failed to establish any ground rules explaining how a presidential candidate's representative would be able to know that a delegate was seeking to violate the rule. The door appears to have been left open for any number of abuses.

Restricting Participation to Democratic Voters

One major issue that has yet to be resolved satisfactorily by any of the commissions is that of restricting participation in the party's presidential nominating process to persons who are Democrats. While the McGovern-Fraser Commission soundly concluded that "a full opportunity for all Democrats to participate is diluted if members of other political parties are allowed to participate in the selection of delegates to the Democratic National Convention,"[35] it did not go on to set any party affiliation requirements for participants in the process.[35] The 1972 National Convention, however, felt it had remedied this omission by adopting a resolution stating that

> the call for the 1976 Democratic National Convention shall include provisions that assure that delegates . . . shall be selected through . . . processes in which adequate provision is made to restrict participation in such elections or processes to Democratic voters. Adequate provision includes laws which restrict participation to Democratic voters who have been registered as such at least 14 days in advance of such election . . . or, where appropriate, a system of party enrollment approved by the National Democratic party.[36]

The Mikulski Commission begged the question by simply requiring that state parties "take all feasible steps to restrict participation in the delegate selection process to Democratic voters only."[37] The Compliance Review Commission for the 1976 convention did not enforce a preprimary or precaucus Democratic registration or enrollment provision, and over time, the original intent of the convention resolution was redefined. According to the Winograd Commission report, the issue concerns only "banning open and crossover primaries," and a rule restricting participation in the delegate selection process to persons "who publicly declare their party preference and have that preference publicly recorded" was adopted.[38] The framers of the resolution intended—and the party itself should demand—more: actual registration or enrollment in the party in advance of the delegate selection process.

ASSESSMENT OF DELEGATE SELECTION RULES

Despite the objections to certain of the delegate selection rules discussed earlier, the rules as a whole have been beneficial for the Democratic Party and its members.

Perhaps the most important Guideline adopted by the McGovern-Fraser Commission, yet one often overlooked, was Guideline A-5, which required state parties "to adopt and make available readily accessible statewide party rules and statutes which prescribe the State's delegate selection process with sufficient details and clarity . . . [and] which provide for uniform times and dates of all meetings involved in the delegate selection process."[39] Today, in the age of required delegate selection plans and Compliance Review commissions, it is easy to forget that the McGovern-Fraser Commission had found that in at least 20 states, there were no—or inadequate—rules governing the delegate selection process. Meaningful participation necessitates being able to find out the times and dates of delegate selection meetings and the rules under which they will be conducted. Although uncontroversial and eminently logical, this Guideline may have been the most outstanding achievement of the commission because it ensured for all Democrats access to the rules of the game called *presidential nominating politics.*

Other guidelines, and the subsequent rules that grew out of them, set important procedural guarantees in such other areas as apportionment on a one-person or one-Democrat, one-vote basis; banning the unrestricted use of proxies; establishing quorum requirements; and prohibiting closed slate-making procedures.

Overall satisfaction with the rules, however, does not mean that Democrats who care about their party have reason to be complacent. Apart from an increasing orientation of the rules toward the convenience of presidential candidates rather than rank-and-file party members, as well as other issues identified earlier, the most serious problem presently facing the party is the proliferation of primaries. Since 1968, the number of primaries has doubled: in 1980 it is likely that 34 states will hold primaries, and some observers are predicting that a national presidential primary is not far in the future. The original mandate of the Winograd Commission raised false hopes that the party was ready to come to grips with this problem. A new Commission on the Role and Future of Presidential Primaries, concerned only with the issues directly related to the proliferation of primaries and on record as opposing a national presidential primary, ought to be appointed. The party should heed the warning recently given by a member of two of the delegate selection reform commissions:

If we force the national parties to perform their most important function in the hostile environment of a national direct primary, we may well reduce them to being no more than labels automatically awarded to the two winners of the national votes. What benefit of a national primary is worth that cost?[40]

NOTES

1. Brief submitted by the Mississippi Freedom Democratic Party. *Congressional Record*, vol. 110, part 16, 88th Congress, 2nd Session August 20, 1964, pp. 20742–53.

2. *Congressional Quarterly Weekly Report* 22, (August 28, 1964): 1990.

3. Warren Weaver, "Democrats Reject Convention Quotas," New York *Times*, July 13, 1967, p. 24.

4. Commission on the Democratic Selection of Presidential Nominees, *The Democratic Choice, Congressional Record*, 114, part 25, 90th Congress, 2nd session October 15, 1968, p. E9172.

5. *Proceedings of the [1968] Democratic National Convention* (Washington, D.C.: Democratic National Committee, 1968), p. 276.

6. Commission on Party Structure and Delegate Selection (McGovern-Fraser Commission), *Mandate for Reform* (Washington, D.C., Democratic National Committee, 1970), p. 53.

7. *Proceedings of the [1968] Democratic National Convention*, p. 309.

8. Commission on Party Structure and Delegate Selection, *Mandate for Reform*, p. 52.

9. For a comprehensive account of the McGovern-Fraser Commission's activities, see William J. Crotty, *Decision for the Democrats: Reforming the Party Structure* (Baltimore: Johns Hopkins Press, 1978).

10. Commission on Party Structure and Delegate Selection, *Mandate for Reform*, p. 30.

11. Ibid., pp. 46–48.

12. See William J. Crotty, "Anatomy of a Challenge: The Chicago Delegates to the Democratic National Convention," in *Cases in American Politics*, ed. Robert L. Peabody (New York: Praeger, 1976), pp. 111–58.

13. Jeanne J. Kirkpatrick, *Dismantling the Parties: Reflections on Party Reform and Party Decomposition* (Washington, D.C.: American Enterprise Institute, 1978).

14. Commission on Party Structure and Delegate Selection, *Mandate for Reform*, p. 39–40.

15. Warren Weaver, "Delegates Delay Rights Proposal," New York *Times*, March 8, 1967, p. 27.

16. Commission on the Democratic Selection of Presidential Nominees, *The Democratic Choice*, p. E9172.

17. Commission on Party Structure and Delegate Selection, *Mandate for Reform*, p. 40.

18. Crotty, *Decision for the Democrats*, p. 124.

19. The Coalition for a Democratic Majority, "Toward Fairness and Unity for '76" (Washington, D.C.: 1973), p. 3.

20. *Delegate Selection Rules for the 1976 Democratic National Convention* (Washington, D.C.: Democratic National Committee, 1975).

21. Martin Plissner, ed. *The 1976 CBS Democratic National Convention Handbook*, p. 1.

22. Alexander Bickel, "Fair Representation of Minority Political Views" (paper presented to Commission on Party Structure and Delegate Selection, October 20, 1969), p. 2.

23. Commission on Party Structure and Delegate Selection, *Mandate for Reform*, pp. 44–45.

24. For further information on the California challenge, see James Blumstein, "Party

Reform, the Winner-Take-All Primary, and the California Delegate Challenge: The Gold Rush Revisited," *Vanderbilt Law Review* 25 (October 1972): 975–1021.

25. *Proceedings of the 1972 Democratic National Convention.* (Washington, D.C.: Democratic National Committee).

26. See David S. Broder, "First-Ballot Victory Unlikely," Washington *Post*, (March 31, 1974), p. 1.

27. *The Official Preceedings of the [1976] Democratic National Convention* (Washington, D.C.: Democratic National Committee), p. 336.

28. Commission on Presidential Nomination and Party Structure (Winograd Commission), *Openness, Participation, and Party Building: Reforms for a Stronger Democratic Party* (Washington, D.C.: Democratic National Committee, February 1978), pp. 86–88.

29. Irie Nathanson, "The Democrats Rig the Primary Rules," *The Nation* 226 (June 10, 1978): 684–85.

30. Rhodes Cook, "Democrats Adopt New Rules for Picking Nominee in 1980," *Congressional Quarterly Weekly Report* 36 (June 17, 1978): 1571.

31. *Delegate Selection Rules for the 1980 Democratic National Convention* (Washington, D.C.: Democratic National Committee, June 1978), pp. 12–13.

32. Commission on Party Structure and Delegate Selection, *Mandate for Reform*, p. 48.

33. *By the People: The Report of the Rules Committee of the 1972 Democratic National Convention* (Washington, D.C.: Democratic National Committee, June 1972), sec. 8.

34. Commission on Presidential Nomination and Party Structure, *Openness, Participation and Party Building*, p. 84.

35. Commission on Party Structure and Delegate Selection, *Mandate for Reform*, p. 47.

36. *By the People*, sec. 9.

37. *Delegate Selection Rules for the 1976 Democratic National Convention.*

38. Commission on Presidential Nomination and Party Structure, *Openness, Participation and Party Building*, p. 68.

39. Commission on Party Structure and Delegate Selection, *Mandate for Reform*, p. 42.

40. Austin Ranney, *The Federalization of Presidential Primaries* (Washington, D.C.: American Enterprise Institute, 1978), p. 25.

7

PARTY RENEWAL IN THE NATIONAL REPUBLICAN PARTY

John F. Bibby

*O*ur understanding of political parties in the United States has been heavily influenced by the assumptions students of parties have perpetuated for at least three decades. Every sophomore taking American Government has been told that political parties are decentralized institutions, with only the most limited amount of integration between national, state, and local units. Frequently cited as prime examples of decentralization are the national committees.[1] A 1972 study of parties referred to them as "shadow committees" and "deadwood anachronisms."[2] The conventional wisdom regarding parties therefore contains the following assumptions: (1) national party committees are weak and lack influence with state and local party organizations;[3] (2) the activities and services of national committees are modest at best, and the committees "exist for the purpose of holding national conventions *every four years*";[4] and (3) national committees do not become involved in a meaningful way in state and local elections.[5] This conventional wisdom has been reinforced in recent years by a commonly accepted belief that political parties have become weakened both in terms of their hold on the electorate and organizational strength. A new text, aptly entitled *Parties in Crisis*, argues that parties "have increasingly seen their major campaign slip away" and poses the fundamental question about the future of parties in the United States; "Will the political parties cease to exist as a dominant part of the political landscape because they no longer have a job?"[6]

The preoccupations of political scientists have also had an impact on our understanding of the current state of the American parties. One of these preoccupations has been with the procedural rule changes governing national convention delegate selection within the Democratic Party since 1969. This interest has been quite natural because of the impact of these changes and the controversy they aroused.[7] One beneficial consequence of the attention given to Democratic procedural reform has been a reexamination of the conventional assumption that national committees are weak institutions. Political scientists are beginning to challenge this assumption because of the power now exercised by the Democratic National Committee over delegate selection in the states.[8]

There are, however, problems in this preoccupation with Democratic rule changes on the part of political parties students. First, it has caused observers to assume that the route to party reform and renewal is via procedural reform.[9] Second, it ignores an alternative method of party reform, which stresses strengthening the structural role of parties. Third, it fails to consider the changes taking place within the other major party, the Republican Party, and thereby leads to an unbalanced perception of the current condition of our parties and their likely future development.

This chapter seeks to provide a more balanced picture of the current state of U.S. parties and the trends in party organization by focusing upon the rebuilding strategy followed by the national Republican Party since 1976. The Republican National Committee's use of the alternative method of organizational reform to strengthen the party is given special attention. The GOP approach to procedural reform is also considered and compared to that of the Democratic Party. Finally, the accuracy of the conventional wisdom regarding political parties is assessed.

PROCEDURAL REFORM WITHIN THE GOP

A major difference between the national Democratic and Republican parties prior to 1969, when the Democrats began engaging in major rules revision, was the nature of the rules governing the respective national committees and conventions. The Republican National Committee and National Convention rules were a codified set of carefully worded and indexed party statutes that contained detailed statements on organization, operation, and powers of the national convention and the national committee. Any change in these rules required approval by the national convention, and the Republican National Committee normally conducted a review of proposed changes prior to the convention. By contrast, the Democratic rules were not well codified. They were a "kind of common law collection of resolutions adopted by previous conventions, decisions of previous convention chairmen, and customs and usage of the Convention."[10] Every four years, this "common law" was summarized in the *Democratic Manual*. Rule changes were easier to achieve within the Democratic Party because national convention approval was not required. Rather, rules changes could be approved by the Democratic National Committee.

The ad hoc character of national Democratic rules made them an obvious target for review and reform in the era of turmoil that characterized the party after the 1968 convention. Contending forces within the party became locked in an almost decade-long struggle over procedures of party governance. The most intense conflicts concerned the recommendations of the McGovern-Fraser Commission, which proposed a series of strict guidelines to govern the states in the selection of national convention delegates, including mandatory quotas to insure representation of minorities, women, and youth. Through adoption of the McGovern-Fraser guidelines, subsequent reform commission proposals, and the Democratic Charter in 1977, the Democratic Party achieved a highly codified set of rules and procedures. The powers these rule changes conferred on the national party to control presidential nominating processes are so sweeping that Ranney believes the Democratic National Committee and National Convention's legal authority is "at its highest peak since the 1820s."[11]

Although the GOP was not enveloped in turmoil following its 1968 and 1972 conventions, the Democratic concern about convention procedures had a spillover effect on the Republicans, which created two reform committees: The Committee on Delegates and Organization (DO Committee) appointed by the Republican National Committee chairperson in 1969 and the Rule 29 Committee, appointed in 1973.

The key difference between the McGovern-Fraser guidelines and the recommendations of the DO Committee was that the McGovern-Fraser guidelines called for a mandatory quota system and affirmative action program, whereas the DO Committee only recommended the election of greater numbers of minority delegates. Thus, whereas the Democrats moved in the early 1970s toward a nationalized set of procedures for delegate selection, the GOP retained the confederate legal structure of its party, with a states' rights approach to delegate selection procedures.

This pattern reasserted itself in the operations of the Rule 29 Committee appointed by Republican National Committee Chairman George Bush in 1973. Rule 29, which was adopted by the 1972 Republican Convention, called for the creation of a committee to review Republican rules pertaining to the convention and the Republican National Committee. Bush, who hoped that the committee would recommend a series of proposals to open up the party and broaden its base of support, appointed his close friend and former congressional colleague, William A. Steiger (Wisconsin) to serve as chairman.

From the moment its composition was announced at a 1973 Republican National Committee meeting, the Rule 29 Committee was embroiled in controversy. Entrenched forces within the party saw the committee as a potential threat to their position, and Steiger's reputation as a reformer reinforced their concern. The focal point of controversy was the committee's recommendation that state parties be required to file reports on their "positive [affirmative] action" programs with the Republican National Committee and that the Republican National Committee would be empowered to review and comment on these programs. No enforcement power comparable to that exercised by the Democratic National Committee was proposed. The March 1975 meeting of the Republican National Committee at which the Rule 29 Committee recommendations were considered was notable for the stridency of the debate, which was "reminiscent of Democratic meetings on the same subject, but extraordinary for Republicans."[12] The Rule 29 Committee's "positive action" plan was rejected by the Republican National Committee by a 75 to 74 vote amid warnings from some members that the plan was a "threat of party domination from Washington."[13] The Republican National Committee's states' rights approach to delegate selection was confirmed when the 1976 convention failed to adopt the Rule 29 Committee plan.

Because attention was focused on the volatile issue of "positive action" in delegate selection, the Rule 29 Committee's other recommendations, which were accepted by the Republican National Committee and the 1976 National Convention, have been largely ignored. These recommendations included the following: (1) the chairman and cochairman shall be full-time paid employees of the Republican National Committee; (2) there shall be eight vice chairmen, consisting of one man and woman elected from each of four regions; (3) the term of office of the Republican National Committee officers shall be two years (thereby giving the Republican National Committee formal power to pass judgment on its chairman and officers every two years); (4) the composition of the Executive Committee shall be specified (thereby limiting the appointing discretion of the chairman); (5) the Republican National Committee shall confirm the chairman's appointment of the General Counsel; (6) the powers of the Executive Committee shall be specified, and the chairman shall be required to call at least four meetings of the committee annually; (7) Republican National Committee approval of the budget shall be required; and (8) the chairman shall be required to send out in advance of Republican National Committee meetings on agenda, minutes, and the proposed budget.

It is generally believed that these limitations on the power of the chairman were adopted because of members' long simmering resentments against national chairmen designated by the Nixon White House without prior consultation with the committee. Many committee members resented what they perceived as the tendency of national chairmen to act as presidential agents rather than as Republican National Committee spokesmen.

The Rule 29 Committee had also recommended that broadly based reform committees continue to operate within the party on a continuing basis. The Republican National Committee rejected this proposal and gained 1976 convention approval of a revised Rule 29, which called for a continuing process of rules review by a subcommittee of the Republican National Committee. In the future, therefore, any rules reform activity would be under the control of the Republican National Committee, not noncommittee members. The Rules Review Committee, appointed by Chairman Bill Brock pursuant to the revised Rule 29, is not expected to recommend any significant rules changes to the 1980 convention.[14]

The GOP rules reform activities, while occurring simultaneously with those of the Democratic Party, have had different consequences. Although the Democratic rules changes have significantly strengthened the national Democratic Party organs, by giving those institutions control of the presidential nominating process, the GOP rejected proposals for national party control of delegate selection practices and has explicitly adopted rules that protect state delegate selection procedures.[15] Clearly, within the GOP, party reform and revitalization have not meant sweeping procedural changes.

The sharply contrasting patterns of rules development within the two parties in the late 1960s and early 1970s reflect the sharply contrasting conditions that existed within the respective parties. First, the stimulus for procedural reform in the Democratic Party came from an intense ideologically committed faction (the Democratic left), which believed that the rules had precluded them from winning the 1968 nomination for their candidate. By contrast, the intense ideological faction within the more ideologically homogeneous GOP, the conservatives, had not found the rules a barrier to party influence. The absence of strong intraparty ideological conflicts during the Nixon years also muted interest in major rule changes in the GOP.

Second, rule changes were more difficult to enact within the highly structured Republican national party than within the Democratic Party. Republican reform committees had to gain approval of their proposals through a succession of party units—the Republican National Committee, the Convention Rules Committee, and the national convention. By contrast, the dramatic changes recommended by the McGovern-Fraser Commission were achieved by merely having them approved by the Democratic National Committee.

Finally, it should be remembered that the condition of the pre-1968 Democratic and Republican rules was quite different. The GOP rules were well developed and codified, while the Democratic rules were less developed and more ad hoc in character. In addition, the GOP had already banned such practices as the unit rule, which so troubled Democratic reformers in 1968. The unstructured character of the Democratic rules not only permitted practices already banned by the GOP but also made the Democratic rules a more obvious reform target in a party engaged in a power struggle.

AN ALTERNATIVE STRATEGY OF PARTY REVITALIZATION: PROGRAMMATIC REFORM

A major thesis of this chapter is that the Republican National Committee, like its Democratic counterpart, has gained strength in the 1970s. It has not, however, achieved this status via procedural reform. Rather, the GOP's rebuilding strategy under Chairman Brock stresses organizational reform, *that is*, providing extensive services to state party committees and candidates.

When Brock was elected Republican National Committee chairman in January 1977, there were predictions of the imminent death of the party. It was at its lowest level of strength since 1936 and 1964, controlling only one-third the seats in Congress, 12 governorships, and four state legislatures.

Brock believed that the party's survival and revitalization depended on a rebuilding of its state and local base. He was particularly concerned that the GOP make gains at the legislative and gubernatorial levels in 1978 and 1980 in order to gain protection against hostile redistrictings after the 1980 census. The state legislative elections were also viewed as important by the chairman because he considered them the prime recruiting ground for future GOP congressmen, senators, and governors.

Brock was not the first Republican National Committee chairman to initiate a program of party building after an electoral defeat. Chairman Ray Bliss, the party professional from Ohio, had such a program after the disastrous 1964 election. Bliss's program stressed strengthening party organizations at the state and local levels through assistance from the Republican National Committee.[16] The scope of the Republican National Committee programs under Brock, however, goes well beyond any thing done in the 1960s. Brock's program is also different from Bliss's in terms of the extent to which the national committee has become involved in state party matters and in working directly with state-level Republican candidates.

Regional Political Directors

Under Brock's leadership, 13 to 15 Regional Political directors (RPDs) were appointed to work with state party organizations. Each RPD was responsible for from two to six states. The RPD was to assist state leaders in strengthening their respective organizations and to be a "point man" in terms of providing access to Republican National Committee services. For example, in 1978, each state party was encouraged to develop a state election plan to make certain that each state's resources were carefully targeted to achieve maximum electoral results.

In the 1978 elections, the reports of RPDs to the national chairperson and the national committee's director of the campaign division were extremely important in determining how national committee funds were allocated to gubernatorial and legislative candidates.

The Regional Political Directors not only had responsibility for national committee programs but also coordinated the work of the National Republican Congressional and Senatorial Committees in their regions. This coordination between the national committee and the normally autonomous congressional and senatorial committees is a post-1974 phenomenon. It reflects the efforts of the national chairman to integrate the work of the various campaign committees and the impact of the 1974 federal campaign finance law, which imposed reporting requirements and contribution limits on the congressional and senatorial committees.

Organizational Director Program

In 1977, Brock instituted an Organizational Director (OD) program, which by 1978 was operative in all 50 states, at an annual cost of $1 million. In an effort to encourage the states to engage in organizational development at the state and local levels, the national committee agreed to pay the salary of an OD in each state party headquarters. To participate in the OD program, the state parties had to meet the following conditions: (1) the person hired to be OD had to be approved by the national committee; (2) travel expenses of the OD were to be paid by the state party; and (3) the state party had to develop a plan for utilization of the OD.

Although there was some initial skepticism about this level of national committee involvement in state party affairs, the general reaction of state chairmen to the OD program was highly favorable. They gained an additional staff person, whose salary was not an encumbrance on their budgets. The program was extremely effective in developing goodwill between the national committee and the state organizations because it demonstrated that the national chairperson was serious about his announced desire to rebuild the party by assisting state leaders.

From the perspective of the national committee, however, the program was only a limited success. There was no effective way for the national committee to control the utilization of the ODs by the state committees. For example, many state organizations lacked sufficient funds to pay the travel expenses for the OD, and as a result, the OD stayed in headquarters and worked on fund-raising or headquarters administration. There was just no way of ensuring that the OD would be used for organizational develop-ment. It is estimated the program operated as the national committee had envisioned in about one-third of the states, worked moderately well in another third, and was not effective in the remaining third.

The OD program, in spite of its popularity with state chairmen, was not continued in 1979. The reasons for discontinuance, in addition to the problems of effectiveness, were mainly financial. It was extremely expensive ($1 million in 1978), and it tended to take money away from the high priority Local Elections Campaign Division (LECD).

Regional Finance Director Program

The Republican National Committee also introduced a program of technical assistance in the area of fund raising patterned after its Regional Political Director Program. The four Regional Finance directors were responsible for assisting state parties in developing a finance program that would put their fund raising on a continuing and sustained basis, as against programs designed to raise money for specific candidates. The Regional Finance directors were also charged with responsibility for making certain that each state party had a federal account that would enable it to make the maximum level of contributions to federal elections, as well as for assistance to the states in achieving compliance with the Federal Election Commission regulations.

Republican Party Data Processing Network

At the insistence of Brock, the Republican National Committee operates its own computer, which is available to state parties at a minimal charge. By mid-1979, ten states had joined the data processing program, which provides computer services—political accounting, word processing, correspondence systems, mailing list maintenance, a donor information system, and political targeting and survey processing. This program has enabled cooperating states to cut their computer costs while utilizing up-to-date computer services.

Task Force Program

One of the aims of the Republican National Committee as it worked with state leaders was to get each state to develop a campaign plan in 1978. The state campaign plan was a way of getting the state parties to set realistic election goals and then take the steps necessary to achieve those goals by focusing their activities and committing their resources to priority activities. To prod the states into developing these plans, the national committee held out the possibility of contributions of staff and funds to candidates in those states that had demonstrated they were making a wholehearted and well-organized effort to achieve their goals.

A task force of national committee senior staff members and an experienced Republican state chairman visited 12 states to provide on-site evaluations and advise on the campaign plans and headquarters operations. With the lure of national committee assistance in the background, this program showed that the Republican National Committee could effectively encourage state organizations to engage in national committee–recommended activities.

Local Elections Campaign Division

The Brock program of assistance to party organizations has been unprecedented in the history of American political parties. The Republican National Committee's involvement in state and local campaigns under his leadership, however, has been even more significant and unusual. He created a new unit, the Local Elections Campaign Division, to direct the national committee's effort to gain state legislative seats. The division was headed in 1978 by two experienced national committee staffers, who supervised the eastern and western regions, respectively. The eastern region had a staff of eight field coordinators and seven Washington-based support personnel; while the western regional director coordinated a staff of seven persons.

The program of the LECD involved a series of steps: district analysis, candidate recruitment, training and education of candidates and managers, and onsite assistance to candidates.

In conjunction with state party organizations, the LECD collected data on thousands of districts, developed district profiles, and helped state organizations identify target districts. The Republican National Committee staff also assisted in candidate recruitment. Cochairman Mary Crisp, for example, traveled thoughout New England, the Midwest, and her home state of Arizona, placing special emphasis on the recruitment of women candidates. This effort apparently had some impact, because 62 of the 63 new women legislators elected in 1978 were Republicans.

The LECD also engaged in an extensive program of political education for legislative candidates and their managers. From January to September 1978, the LECD sponsored 75 candidate seminars. In the eastern region alone, out of 4,100 legislative districts, the campaigns of approximately 2,700 candidates were represented at one of the LECD seminars. The seminars were cosponsored with the respective state party organizations, and therefore, the format of the seminars varied from state to state. In Wisconsin, a series of three seminars were held, in which candidates and their managers were given a series of assignments to complete for the next session. In New York, special emphasis was placed upon the use of video equipment to improve the speaking techniques of candidates.

The LECD placed its priority on those states where it was believed there was a reasonable chance to win control of a legislative chamber and thereby gain redistricting protection. In targeting individual legislative races for special assistance, the LECD relied heavily on the state party organizations to identify key races. Where targeting was handled by the LECD staff, it was always with the concurrence of the state party organizations.

The LECD allocated approximately $1 million in direct candidate cash grants in 1978. Virtually all of this money went to nonincumbent races. Approximately 40 percent of the contributions made by the LECD went to races where the Republican candidate was successful.

In the eastern region, 65 candidates in top priority districts received survey research assistance. The national committee staff helped these candidates develop survey questionnaires and then assisted in the training of volunteers to conduct telephone surveys. The LECD professional staff handled the coding and computer analysis of the surveys. In 45 of the 65 districts in the eastern region where surveys were conducted, the Republican candidate was elected.

In the fall of 1978, the LECD concentrated all of its staff resources on targeted districts around the country. The level and type of assistance provided varied depending upon the needs, resources, and circumstances of the particular candidate. Among the services provided were almost complete management of the campaign, preparation of direct mail pieces, planning and distribution of tabloids, development of campaign plans and budgets, and assistance with public appearances and advertising.

The Republican National Committee's 1978 investment of a major portion of its resources (the LECD cost $1.7 million in 1978) in legislative elections acted as a catalyst for state party involvement. With a staff of over 20 persons, the LECD was able to be in frequent and continuing contact with Republican leaders all over the country. These leaders were urged by the national committee staff to commit greater resources to legislative races. The availability of direct national committee contributions to candidates and the commitment of national committee staff resources to a state constituted an incentive for state chairpersons to demonstrate that a national committee investment in their states would pay dividends. As one GOP state chairman put it, "I figure that I should go along with Bill Brock and the National Committee as much as possible, because I want as much of their money as I can get for my state."

Republican National Committee and Gubernatorial Elections, 1978

Not only was the Republican National Committee heavily involved in legislative races in 1978 but it was also engaged in a major effort to support gubernatorial candidates. The vehicle for this effort was the Republican Governors Association (RGA), which had been created in 1963 at the urging of former Governor Robert Smylie of Idaho. Although Smylie had envisioned that the association would play a significant role in gubernatorial campaigns, the committee had never had sufficient resources to be a significant factor in elections.

In 1977, Brock and the Republican governors agreed that the RGA would play a major role in the 1978 gubernatorial elections. The national committee made a major financial commitment to this effort, and an experienced senior staff person was appointed RGA director of campaign services.

The RGA placed its primary emphasis on challenger campaigns, and the staff spent 80 percent of its time working with challengers in 1977–78. Contributions totaling $530,000 were made to 14 out of 15 races in which a Republican was seeking to replace a Democrat in 1978. Fifty-four percent of this money went to winning candidates. The size of contributions ranged from $700 in Georgia to $32,000 in New York.

Contributions were made directly to candidate organizations, and there was little interaction with state party organizations. The exceptions were in such states as Oregon and New Mexico, where the RGA paid for early public opinion surveys conducted under the auspices of the state party.

The RGA role in gubernatorial contests ranged from providing staff assistance to extensive involvement in campaign planning, selecting consultants, and providing technical assistance with special projects. For example, an experienced campaign manager was assigned to a midwestern state where, it was thought, an upset was in the making, and a specialist in telephone banks was assigned to another midwestern state when expert help was needed quickly;

In 1978, the GOP achieved a net gain of six governorships and 281 state legislative seats, winning control of ten additional legislative chambers. It is not possible to attribute either the gubernatorial or the state legislative gains primarily to the efforts of the Republican National Committee. This improvement in the party's condition at the state level did, however, occur simultaneously with an unprecedented involvement by a national party organization in state elections. Many state chairmen and candidates have therefore been lavish in their praise of the national committee for its assistance in 1978, believing that the committee's efforts were a critical factor in the elections. A veteran midwestern chairman has stated: "Bill Brock has changed the whole concept of the National Committee. The field people we had helping us were the best I have seen. They gave us staff, resources and money. In the last two years, we've had more help from the National Committee than in the whole time I've been around."

REPUBLICAN NATIONAL COMMITTEE'S
FINANCIAL RESOURCE BASE

Party-building programs of the Republican National Committee's magnitude have been possible only because the committee has developed a strong financial base. In 1978, the Republican National Committee had a budget of $9.73 million, the largest amount of money available to the national committee for a nonpresidential year in the party's history. Republican National Committee fund-raising operation has a great deal of stability because of its successful direct mail program. That program had 511,628 contributors in 1978, 87 percent of whom contributed less than $50.

The significance of adequate financial resources for building strong national parties capable of meaningful programmatic activity is illustrated by comparing the campaign role of the Democratic National Committee with that of the Republican National Committee during 1978. Whereas the Republican National Committee distributed $1 million in cash grants to state legislative candidates alone and the LECD spent $1.7 million, the total cash contributions of the Democratic National Committee to congressional, senatorial, and gubernatorial candidates in 1978 was $102,000. Interestingly, 1978 marked the first time in 12 years that the Democratic National Committee had made direct contributions to such candidates.

While the Republican National Committee financial resources have made it possible for the committee to engage in an extensive array of party-building activities, the fund-raising program has not been without its problems. National committee direct mail solicitations frequently compete with the fund-raising activities of state party organizations. The state chairman of Minnesota recently complained that his state's direct mail piece arrived at the homes of Minnesota Republicans at the same time as one from the national committee. In such circumstances of direct national committee–state party competition, state party organizations normally suffer.[17] The national committee party-building programs, however, are only viable to the extent they supplement the work of state party and candidate organizations.

CONCLUSION

The Republican National Committee has achieved increased power and an enlarged role in the political system by engaging in *organizational reform*—by performing or supplementing the organizational and campaign functions previously considered to be the domain of state and local party and candidate committees. The GOP has shunned rule changes that would significantly alter the confederate legal structure of the party, while the national committee has interjected itself into the organizational and campaign activities of the state parties. By contrast, the Democratic National Committee's increased power has been achieved via *procedural reform*—vesting legal authority over presidential nominating processes with the national committee. The two parties thus appear to be following two quite different paths toward greater party nationalization and integration.

While it would certainly be an exaggeration to suggest that political parties in the United States are no longer decentralized institutions, it is clear from the description of Republican National Committee activities since 1976 that the conventional wisdom of political science cited at the beginning of this chapter is in need of revision.

A word of caution is probably also in order concerning the widely accepted generalizations which assert that party organizations are becoming weaker and are on the verge of becoming obsolete. This type of sweeping generalization certainly does not apply to the post-1976 Republican National Committee. Indeed, the committee appears to be more influential than it has been at any time in the recent past. Rather than a general weakening of party organizations, it may be that what is taking place is a strengthening of the national organizations, as party functions previously performed at the state and local levels are transferred to a higher structural level.

It is, however, still too early to be certain whether or not the indications of party nationalization and integration cited in this chapter are part of a long-term trend. The viability of the Republican National Committee's organizational reforms is dependent on the party being able to sustain its present financial base. The ultimate test of the durability of Republican National Committee programs is likely to come when the GOP next regains the presidency and the Republican National Committee ceases to be the most important and inclusive Republican organization in the country. Recent presidents in both parties have tended to down play the role of their national committees and have preferred to concentrate partisan political power in the White House rather than in the more autonomous national committees.[18] In the case of the Republican Party, however, a pattern of extensive services to state parties and candidates has now been established, and it is doubtful that a Republican president would be in a position after 1980 to break the interdependent relationship of national and state GOP Organizations.

NOTES

1. See Cornelius P. Cotter and Bernard C. Hennessy, *Politics Without Power: The National Party Committees* (New York: Atherton Press, 1964.)

2. John S. Saloma and Frederick H. Sontag, *Political Parties* (New York: Vintage, 1972), p. 92.

3. V. O. Key, Jr., *Politics, Parties and Pressure Groups*, 5th ed. (New York: Crowell, 1964), p. 329.

4. Thomas R. Dye, *Politics in States and Communities*, 3d ed. (Englewood Cliffs, N. J.: Prentice-Hall 1977), p. 92. The most complete study of national committees states that the job of the committee is to survive. See Cotter and Hennessy, *Politics Without Power*, p. 8.

5. The leading parties and state politics texts contain no reference to national committee involvement in state and legislative elections. See, for example, Dye, *Politics in States and Communities*, pp. 92–161.

6. Ruth K. Scott and Ronald J. Hrebenar, *Parties in Crisis* (New York: Wiley, 1979), p. 1.

7. See Austin Ranney, *Curing the Mischiefs of Faction* (Berkeley: University of California Press, 1975); Jeanne J. Kirkpatrick, *Dismantling the Parties: Reflections on Party Reform and Party Decomposition* (Washington D.C.: American Enterprise Institute, 1978); William J. Crotty, "Party Reform and Political Stability" (paper delivered at "Political Parties in Modern Societies," a conference held at Northwestern University, Evanston, Illinois, September 21–22, 1978).

8. Austin Ranney, "The Political Parties: Reform and Decline," in *The New American Political System*, ed. Anthony King (Washington, D.C.: American Enterprise Institute, 1978), pp. 225–30.

9. See, for example, Charles Longley, "Party Reform and the Republican Party" (Paper delivered at Annual Meeting of the American Political Science Association, New York, August 31–September 3, 1978).

10. Austin Ranney and Willmore Kendall, *Democracy and the American Party System* (New York: Harcourt, Brace, 1956), p. 292.

11. Ranney, "The Political Parties," p. 230.

12. See the account by R. W. Apple, New York *Times*, March 6, 1975, p. 42.

13. Mississippi Republican Chairman Clarke Reed, quoted by R. W. Apple, New York *Times*, March 7, 1975, p. 11.

14. "No Major Changes Expected in GOP's Rules," *Congressional Quarterly Weekly Report* 37 (April 29, 1979): 777.

15. See Rules 31 and 32, *Rules Adopted by the 1976 Republican National Convention* (Kansas City, Mo., August 17, 1976).

16. For an account of Bliss's rebuilding program, see John F. Bibby and Robert J. Huckshorn, "Out-Party Strategy: Republican National Committee Rebuilding Politics, 1964–66," in *Republican Politics: The 1964 Campaign and Its Aftermath for the Party*, ed. Bernard Cosman and Robert J. Huckshorn (New York: Praeger, 1968), pp. 205–33.

17. Rhodes Cook, "Bill Brock Concentrates on the Grass Roots, but Conservatives Are Critical," *Congressional Quarterly Weekly Report* 37 (April 28, 1979): 778.

18. See, for example, David Broder, "A Neglected Democratic Party," Washington *Post*, June 14, 1978, p. A27.

8

CALIFORNIA: THE UNCERTAINTIES OF REFORM

Kay Lawson

*C*alifornia plays an interestingly ambiguous role in America's current passion for autocriticism. It has become a useful symbol for most of our supposed failings: loss of moral and religious certitudes, excessive and selfish consumption of energy, thoughtless narcissism, and cultural decline. Yet at the same time, and often on the same grounds, it serves as well as a symbol of many of our hopes and aspirations: freedom from outdated dogma, opportunity for individual accomplishment, the good life, the resurgence of creativity in an entirely modern setting—in short, "the future."

The same ambivalence is apparent in the national assessment of California politics. California, after all, gave the nation its most condemned president and intermittently threatens to place either a superannuated movie star or a boyish amateur of pop philosophy in the White House. Its political parties are so weak as to be almost nonexistent; it is the birthplace of campaigning by "hired guns"; and it has been run by special interests for so long that Californians have forgotten what is special about that. Yet, on the other hand, California receives high marks for the reforms it introduced in the Progressive era, which are credited with reducing political corruption, creating an efficient and honest state legislature, and opening up the political process to the people. Particularly admired is the introduction of the initiative, whereby legislation may be popularly generated, and which has most recently provided the means of translating the popular conviction that the costs of government had grown insupportable into statutory law limiting those costs definitively. It has a woman serving as chief justice of the state supreme court, and either women or blacks are mayors in four of its five major cities (Los Angeles, San Francisco, Oakland, and San Jose). California's government is progressive and clean, a lesson to us all.

Obviously, neither view of California's politics is entirely true—nor is either entirely untrue. The political realities of this large and volatile state necessarily escape the glib pronouncements of both detractors and admirers. California is complex and contradictory. Nowhere is this more apparent than in the analysis of its political parties, and of the efforts, past and present, to make them better.

Party reform may take, as others have frequently noted, one of two forms: it may be reform from outside, by legislative fiat or judicial interpretation, or reform from within, by the parties themselves.[1] As has also been noted more than once, party reform is often motivated by personal ambition as much if not more than by altruistic service to the public good.[2] Finally, however pure or impure the motives of reformers, the effects of reform have often proved surprising to those who supported, as well as those who opposed, the initial undertaking.[3] All three generalizations find ample illustration in the history of party reform in California.

This chapter will summarize that history, with an emphasis on the important reforms of the Progressive era, and then examine more intensively the current efforts to change the parties. In the process, we will consider not only the degree to which the preceding generalizations obtain but also the question of what it means to say that "parties are so weak as to be nearly nonexistent in California." Is this cliche true? If so, will it be true in the future? If significant change is forthcoming, what form will it take, and whose interests will it serve?

PROGRESSIVE REFORMS

The Setting for Reform

"Whereas, the organization and control of the Republican Party of the State of California have fallen into the hands of the political bureau of the Southern Pacific Company, which has usurped functions of right belonging to the Republican Party and its membership."[4]

Although two-party competition was stronger in California in the immediate post–Civil War era than in many other parts of the nation, by the election of 1898, the Republicans were firmly in control of the state government, and they were to maintain that control almost uninterruptedly over the half-century to follow. In the early years of this period of dominance, however, the Republicans were themselves under the control of the Southern Pacific Railroad: "The Republican party ran California and the Southern Pacific Railroad ran the Republican party."[5]

Parlaying national and local subsidies into political power, the railroad took over city and state government. Federal investigations by the Pacific Railway Commission, established by Congress in 1887 to determine the political usage of such monies, exposed the workings of the "Octopus," but early efforts to curb the railroad were unavailing.[6] A largely inoperative California Railroad Commission established in 1879 was no more effective after the federal investigation: in fact, by 1900, the railroad so successfully controlled the state legislature that the latter body made no appropriations for the work of the state commission for the next seven years: "The Commission could not conduct investigations of complaints or even print an annual report."[7] The political hegemony of the railroad, exercised via the Republican Party but apparent as well in the complaisance of the minority Democratic Party, had become so all-encompassing that many were persuaded that only the most drastic methods would serve to restore control to the people of California. Those who favored reform aligned themselves with the national Progressive movement; they had little difficulty in rallying followers and achieved a majority in the state legislature by 1908 and control of the governor's office (with the election of Hiram Johnson) in 1910. The reformers came into office with a detailed blueprint and went to work, rapidly and with near unanimity, to put their plans into effect. Although their reforms covered nearly every domain—from pensions for schoolteachers to suppression of racetrack gambling to energy conservation—we shall be concerned here only with those that proved relevant to the fortunes of the parties. By 1912, the following reforms had been adopted.

The Measures of Reform

Direct Primary

In 1909, the Progressive element in the legislature pushed through a bill calling for the direct primary. In 1911, the bill was amended to allow voters to state their preference for U.S. senator (still chosen by the legislature) and to provide for a presidential primary election. More seriously (for the parties), all partisan identification was removed from the ballot; henceforward, the parties were forbidden to make preprimary endorsements. The voters were to have no guidance from the parties; the parties were to wait quietly for the guidance of the voters.

Party Reorganization

California was the first state to regulate internal party organization, and in no state are the internal affairs of political parties more closely governed by statutory law than in California. The practice began as far back as 1866 with "An Act to Protect the Elections of Voluntary Political Associations, and to Punish Frauds Thereon." As the title of the bill suggests, early efforts were designed to make the parties more honest, not to destroy them. Indeed, an act of 1901 had the effect of strengthening the parties by mandating a system of local conventions for all counties and for the ten largest cities, as well as an elaborate system of primary elections for delegates to nominating conventions. The Progressives went much further, not only removing nominations from party control (see above) but removing control of the party from its own grass-roots organizations. In 1911, the legislature took over control of the parties for themselves and their defeated comrades; henceforward, the membership of state conventions would be all candidates for office on the party's tickets, plus any state senators whose terms still had two or more years to run. The members of the convention were, in turn, to select a state central committee, composed of three or more persons, from each congressional district. In 1913, the Progressives went a step further: county central committees, with no representation in the state organizations, were created to replace statutory conventions at the local level: "At a stroke, parties were almost totally decentralized. Local groups could continue to operate independently, but they were no longer authorized parts of the state party structure. The whole process of generating party policy and of selecting party slates through a statewide party association was abolished."[8]

Cross-filing

If forced to choose the Progressive reform most damaging to the health of the parties, one would have to select that inimitable (or, at any rate, never imitated) device, cross-filing. In 1913, the Progressives ruled that henceforward, candidates would be allowed to file for nomination in whatever and as many primaries as they wished. From 1913 to 1959, all that was required to file a "declaration of candidacy" was to pay a nominal filing fee and submit a petition signed by a small number of registered supporters of that party.[9] This meant that a candidate might well be the nominee of two or more parties on the November ballot, virtually assuring his or her election.

Non-partisan Elections

In one of their most openly antiparty moves, in 1913, the Progressives enacted a reform long dear to their hearts: they banned the participation of parties in county and municipal offices altogether. City and county government was declared to be simply a question of "housekeeping"; the issues of national politics (called forth by party labels on city ballots) were ruled out of place, and the machinations of party nominating procedures were labeled an unwarranted imposition on candidates at this level.[10]

Initiative, Referendum, and Recall

If being a Progressive meant anything, it meant fervent commitment to the idea that citizens must be able themselves to generate statutory law (the initiative), to demand that dubious laws enacted by their legislators be referred to them (the referendum), and to remove unsatisfactory representatives from office before the end of their terms (the recall). These three staples of "direct democracy" were adopted in 1911, and they have since played an important role in sapping the strength of parties in California.[11] Without the initiative and referendum, periods of high issue orientation might have seen citizen efforts to rebuild the parties as agencies to express their views; instead, the conditioned impulse is to take petitions to the street.

Results of Reform

The effects of the Progressive reforms on California's parties can be speedily summarized: parties became so weak as to be nearly nonexistent. County committees were now the only local organization. They had absolutely no structural ties to the state party, and they were forbidden to run candidates for local offices. The state party machinery was under the control of the legislators and was forbidden to make preprimary endorsements. Nonparty members could file for and win the party's nomination for any office, and the party could do nothing about it whatsoever. No longer an effective channel to elective office, the party lost control over appointive office as well; any patronage remaining after civil service reforms was more and more in the hands of elected officials, and consultation of party leadership before making such appointments became increasingly pro forma.[12] Given the parties' reputation as instruments of corruption and their own new rights to take direct action via the initiative, the referendum, and the recall, the people of California were well content.

In retrospect, however, it is clear that the Progressives did a much better job of emasculating parties than of preventing control of the political process by special interests. Southern Pacific's political heyday was over, and so was that of the parties it had controlled.* But the opportunities for

---

*In fact, it can be argued that the parties suffered far more than the railroads, which have been characterized as enjoying "continued and increased prosperity" throughout the Progressive era. In 1913, the Southern Pacific's own chief counsel and political manager suggested that the new regulations actually made life easier for the industry: "I think no railroad manager would agree to dispense with government regulation at the cost of returning to the old conditions" (Spencer C. Olin, Jr., *California's Prodigal Sons* [Berkeley: University of California Press, 1968], p. 171).

interest groups to manipulate governmental policy-making processes were in fact increased. Whether or not, as some have argued, the results were in fact intended by the more cynical of the Progressives, it is not an unfair assessment to say that "interest groups in California [came] close to replacing political parties as guides to the electorate in deciding state and local policy matters via the ballot."[13] Much less aided by, or dependent upon, party support than heretofore, the individual candidate was more and more likely to be both groomed and funded by private interests, and did not hesitate to show his or her gratitude appropriately once in office. Should the individual candidate's loyalty falter, he or she was certain to be reminded of the obligations incurred by a member of one of the nation's most aggressive corps of lobbyists (only partially curbed by new regulations imposed in 1959).[14]

Nor have the direct democracy measures provided the protection against such interests their progenitors had claimed for them. True, the ordinary voter has a part to play: he or she may be given the chance to sign the petition requesting such a measure be placed on the ballot, and will have the opportunity to vote for or against if it is so placed. However, the real battle is likely to be waged by conflicting organized interests: they are the ones with the funds to hire the armies of petition-bearers seeking the required number of signatures (which, based as it is on a percentage of voters in the previous election, has grown steadily higher with California's expanding population) and to wage the expensive advertising campaigns for or against the measures (campaigns whose simplism is often rivaled only by their obscurantism).[15] Their endorsements are often the only meaningful guide for a voter overwhelmed by so many issues, so many elective offices, and such frequent elections as is the Californian.* With rare exceptions, these procedures designed to supplant issue-oriented grass-roots party activism have proved a poor substitute in practice.

These, then, were the chief effects of that portion of Progressive reforms influencing parties, reforms "from outside," by legislative fiat. They give ample point to the twin truisms that party reform is often motivated, at least in part, by personal ambition and that the effects of reform are often surprising to those who undertook to effect them. California now appears to be entering a second period of party reform, this time "from within." Will the current reforms, if successfully enacted, prove equally guided by the motives of private opportunism and equally disappointing to their more disinterested proponents?

---

*California elects 11 state executive officers every four years, as well as superior court justices and county executive officers. In addition, numerous state and local propositions appear on the ballot. The average ballot asks the voter to make 50 separate decisions (John R. Owens, Edmond Costantini, and Louis F. Weschler, *California Politics and Parties* [London: Macmillan, 1970], p. 105).

REBIRTH OF REFORM

1920–70: Signs of Life in Coventry

As a separate party, the Progressives in California soon succumbed to the same forces that destroyed the national party: with much of its program adopted, the movement lost momentum; a world war brought other issues to the voters' attention; and the postwar "return to normalcy" blunted the passion for reform. However, crippled by the new rules, neither of the major parties could resume control. The 1920s brought a new era of Republican conservatism, but one in which individual Republicans, backed by powerful private interests, played a much more important role than the party organization. When the Depression gave the Democrats the chance to wage a strong counterattack, the party was unable to organize the effort effectively, and the opportunity was squandered on the exciting but hopelessly radical 1934 campaign of Upton Sinclair, whose "End Poverty in California" program and promises of a socialist utopia won the hearts of Democratic primary voters, unguided by what might have been more realistic party leadership. Lacking the cohesion of a strong organization in or out of Sacramento, the party was no more effective when Democrats did win the governor's office and the majority of seats in the state legislature in the late 1930s: little change was effected and the Democrats lost power in the next set of elections.[16]

During this period, the legislature ruled that county central committee chairpersons should be members of the state central committee, thereby reestablishing at least minimal links between the two levels of organization. At the same time, however, the parties lost almost all effective control over one of their key functions, namely, campaigning.[17] The first professional campaign management firm in the nation, Campaigns, Inc., was founded in California in 1933 by Clem Whitaker and Leone Baxter and quickly attracted imitators.[18] By this time, the decline of party had become a national phenomenon. A mobile population was breaking away from community ties, including those of party, either by moving from city to suburb or by making longer migrations in search of a vanishing economic security. Government social welfare programs and the spread of civil service further weakened the claims of party on citizen loyalty. These national trends were at their strongest in California, the last stop of so many uprooted Americans, and interacting as they did with the Progressive reforms, they ensured there would be no early resurgence of party. Professional hucksters homesteaded the fields of unattached voters, shifting the terms of their claims from election to election, and delivered the harvest to the powerful sponsors who financed their endeavors. Ambitious politicians formed private campaign organizations, accepted support from a wide range of interests, hired the professional firms as necessary and useful, and proudly declared themselves "above party," as they eagerly pursued the nominations and the voter support of both major parties.[19]

The consummate master of these techniques proved to be Earl Warren, California's governor from 1942 until elevated to the post of chief justice of the U.S. Supreme Court in 1953. Warren, who was a Republican, habitually minimized party, stressed "personal accountability," espoused and advanced the liberal policies of progressivism, and made a mockery of the Democrats' majority in voter registration (a majority achieved in the Depression era and never lost since, but very frequently *not* reflected in partisan choices at the polls)[20] by attracting a large share of the Democratic vote to his own candidacy.*

However, Warren's liberal policies sufficiently angered enough members of his own party to make the era following his "ascension" one of intense Republican factionalism, as different forces rallied around the various claimants to his abandoned crown.[21] Furthermore, it was during this period that national political developments were beginning to have an interesting effect on the Democrats in the state. Running for president in 1952, Adlai Stevenson had delivered a sermon that many of the state's Democrats found echoed in their hearts, and a new grass-roots commitment to the political process had begun to evolve. The abbreviated structures of party were inadequate to contain the fervor, and a new organization, the California Democratic Council (CDC), was formed in 1953.[22] The CDC was (and is) a statewide organization of clubs affiliated to, but independent of, the party. The decline of Republican strength that came with Warren's departure gave the new organization its opportunity to show what it could do on the level of the state. Some progress was made in the 1954 election, and by 1958, Democrats had regained control of the state with the election of Edmund G. Brown and other statewide officers.

The birth of the CDC was a first hint of party renewal, even though it took place outside the bonds of formal party organization. A second hint came in 1959, when cross-filing was abolished by the legislature. From then on, anyone seeking a party's nomination had to be a member of that party for at least three months prior to primary day and could not have been registered in any other party for the year previous to the time of filing.

However, neither the founding of the CDC nor the abolition of cross-filing meant the immediate resurgence of the parties—far from it. The CDC become discredited by what may now be seen less emotionally as politically premature antiwar sentiments during the time of the conflict in Vietnam. Its hitherto highly sought endorsement became political poison, and the

---

*In 1946, Warren won the nomination of both parties in the gubernatorial primary, the only candidate for that office ever to do so.

"radical" overtones the clubs gave the Democratic Party helped
Republicans—among them, the new governor, Ronald Reagan—to regain
political control. The Republicans' own voluntary associations were divided
along the lines of the factionalism left as the special legacy of the post-
Warren era, and were, in their different way, equally inadequate for the task
of party renewal. Nevertheless, by the end of the 1960s, one or two
important steps had been taken toward bringing the parties back to life.

The 1970s: One Step Forward, Two Steps Backward?

It is by no means clear whether the steps that have recently been taken
are the first signs of true party renaissance in California or merely futile
shots fired before beating a full retreat in face of the onslaught of single
issues, media blitzes, and free-wheeling populist initiatives, which also
characterize the present era. Although the first serious party reform
legislation in California since the Progressive era was enacted in 1979,
several developments, national and local, have further eroded the strength
of the parties. In order to assess the meaning of the recent reform
measures, we must first understand the political context in which they have
developed. Three changes in particular have characterized the 1970s: the
increasing importance of candidate organizations as opposed to party, the
limited return of partisanship to the California legislature, and a series of
developments that may be loosely linked together under the rubric of *a new
electorate*.

Candidate vs. Party

The national trend toward ever more personalized campaigning is
nowhere more in evidence than in California, where the transformation of
mere mortals into "stars" is one of the state's primary industries. The
tendency for candidates to form organizations independent of party has
become stronger than ever, and expenditures on campaign management
firms and the media have steadily mounted.[23] Of the 1974 gubernatorial
contest in California, it was said that "television dominated the candidate's
entire campaign effort. The purpose of the campaign became that of
attracting the media, rather than communicating with voters." In turn, the
increased use of television meant ever more emphasis on personality rather
than on substantive issues or commitment to a partisan program: "The
variety of appeals to bloc interests such as labor, women, teachers, etc., all
lost importance in contrast to the opportunity for one, single communication to all voters as television viewers. As a result, clarification of positions
important to these individual groups diminished."[24]

In such a situation, the parties found themselves with a yet more diminished role to play and received little appreciation for any efforts made. Organizing a corps of enthusiastic volunteers, one of the things a political party knows how to do best, began to seem "wasteful of time and money" and "inconsequential in comparison with television's audience." Candidates and their staffs complained of inadequate contributions and cooperation by party offices. Party officers complained of high-handed candidates who expected to "take over" and who failed to treat local party staff with tact and respect.[25] This split between party and candidate, common throughout the nation, has been exacerbated in California by the presidential aspirations of its two most recent governors. Their campaign efforts are seen by many in their own parties as reaching far beyond state office and interfering with state party priorities.

What candidates have wanted from the parties may be briefly stated: raise money for the candidate, register voters who will vote for the candidate, and get out the vote for the candidate. The proviso of the 1974 amendments to the Federal Election Campaign Act authorizing the parties to make independent expenditures on behalf of candidates has given some added significance to the first domain (considerably undercut by the 1976 U.S. Supreme Court ruling that spending limitations were unconstitutional except in publicly funded campaigns, that is, the presidential contest), but the same act's authorization of the proliferation of Political Action committees, for legal laundering of special interest funds has had the opposite effect.[26] One result of the Political Action Committee bonanza, which goes disproportionately into incumbents' coffers, has been to cool what had been the mounting enthusiasm of the California legislature for public financing (a step that would permit spending limitations on state campaigns and, thereby, make party expenditures on a candidate's behalf of greater import).[27]

The candidates' emphasis on raising funds to finance personalized media campaigns has not only made the parties' efforts on their behalf less significant but has also undercut the parties' efforts to raise money for themselves. A 1963 finding that in California, "unions, businesses, and individuals with interests they are anxious to advance are far more likely to give money directly to candidates, particularly incumbent candidates" is even more apposite today. [28] Various tactics, including the election by the Democrats of a new party chairperson best known for his munificent contributions to the party, keep the parties from going under altogether, but state party headquarters (especially Democratic) are sadly understaffed, and local offices are likely to be open only a few hours a week if that.[29]

Parties in the Legislature

As would be expected, party line voting has not been the norm in the

California legislature. Nevertheless, the past 15 to 20 years have seen a surprising, if limited, increase in partisanship. A quasi-successful effort by the Republican minority to block passage of the budget (which requires a two-thirds majority) in 1963 angered the Democratic speaker of the Assembly sufficiently to bring about changes in that chamber's rules which served to increase the role of party in important ways.[30] Since then, party caucuses are held much more frequently, especially in the Assembly and especially by the Democrats. Nevertheless, most issues in Sacramento do not divide along party lines, and partisanship is only one factor in committee assignments. With respect to the latter, seniority still plays an important role in Senate assignments, whereas loyalty to the speaker (who is still likely to be elected by a bipartisan coalition) is the key criterion in the Assembly.[31] The ties of party continue to mean remarkably little in executive-legislative relationships, California's governors having long preferred to build personal rather than partisan ties in the legislature.

A New Electorate

Californians have never been particularly apathetic participants in the political process. Their turnout in presidential primaries has been among the highest in the nation (in 1976, 65 percent of registered Democrats and 72 percent of registered Republicans cast votes in their parties' primaries),[32] and their voting rate in succeeding elections has usually been close to the national average. Furthermore, a 1976 legislative act made it possible to register to vote simply by completing a postcard form and mailing it to the county registrar, a step likely to improve voting rates in the future. But ease of voting and commitment have not been matched by a high correlation between identification and electoral choice. Since 1934, Democratic registrations have consistently outnumbered Republican (there has been a recent growth in the number of independent registrations, but of those identifying with a party, from 58 percent to 61 percent are likely to be Democrats).[33] Yet, Republicans controlled the state's top executive office for 26 of the 45 subsequent years, kept their majority in the state Senate until 1956, and regained control of the Assembly from 1942 to 1957. The voters have periodically sent a majority of Republicans to congressional offices and have given the Republican candidates their electoral votes in four of the past five presidential elections.[34]

This seeming inconsistency has usually been explained, at least in part, as resulting from the stronger financial backing, better organization, and wider press support of Republican candidates. In recent years, however, Republican disunity has diminished these resources, and Republican fortunes, particularly at the level of the state legislature (where, at present, there are only 30 Republicans in the 80-member Assembly and 14 in the 40-

member Senate) are in a serious disarray. This shift of California's feckless voters may be only partially caused by the aftereffects of Watergate. A more immediate cause may have been the tendency of Reagan to draw Republican energies to his own dramatic candidacies, causing a decline in the field work necessary to keep Republican strength in the legislature roughly at parity.[35] Since "there is no such thing as coattail voting in California," efforts made on behalf of Reagan have not paid off in other Republican victories.[36] Others suggest California's present Democratic governor has stolen all the Republican issue stances: fiscal conservatism, smaller government, and opposition to increased social welfare expenses. In any case, the Republican Party is at present in poor shape in California, and the state's businessmen have reached the point of recommending to each other that "maybe the thing to do is to find and encourage some moderate, free-enterprise Democrat to run. . . . That's better than trying to pour water up a hill and elect Republicans."[37]

A second, related change in California voting patterns has been the development of two-party competition throughout the state. For years, political map makers had confidently subdivided most of the state into solidly Democratic or solidly Republican, with the core of the former in the San Francisco Bay Area and that of the latter in Orange and San Diego counties. However, the number of safe seats has recently declined dramatically, for Democrats as well as for Republicans.[38] The result can only be heightened partisan activity, as the electoral battle sharpens in county after county.

The signs of ferment in California voting patterns have also been apparent outside the major parties. Minor parties (the American Independent Party, Peace and Freedom, and the Libertarian Party) have been attracting more and more attention, if a relatively small share of the vote, and there have been recent efforts to challenge California's unusually restrictive provisions for access to the ballot. Even more striking have been the uses made in recent years of the initiative process to propose and win changes in public policy contrary to the wishes of the majority of the state's elected representatives. The most remarkable examples of this new militancy in the use of the initiative have been the creation of the Fair Political Practices Commission in 1972 (recently deprived of several important functions by the State Supreme Court) and the passage of the Jarvis-Gann property-tax initiative in 1978, which mandated a 57 percent reduction in local property taxes and forced a Democratic governor to make an abrupt about-face on the issue. At present, the Campaign for Economic Democracy, led by Tom Hayden, former student activist and candidate for the Democratic nomination for the U.S. Senate, is mounting plans for an initiative to impose California's own windfall tax on oil companies and set up a state-owned refinery.

The duration and significance of this heightened volatility in a state never noted for its political predictability are impossible to gauge *in medias res*. Nevertheless, it is interesting that some commentators are hazarding such assessments as,

> California is in the midst of a populist movement not unlike the disenchantment and cynicism that gripped the state 100 years ago. . . . There is . . . great discontent with what is viewed as the unresponsiveness of the state Legislature and the seemingly omnipotent power of corporations. Perhaps the oil companies have taken the place of railroads as targets for popular distrust.[39]

Current Efforts at Reform: A New Day Dawning?

Candidates ever more independent of party, legislators slightly more likely to listen to party leadership, and an aroused citizenry shifting away from Republican candidates to Democrats they do not trust very much more, preferring the methods of direct democracy to ensure greater political and fiscal responsibility—Is this what it takes for a new era of party reform, this time reform generated from *within* the parties?

The answer appears to be yes, at least in California. The current situation there clearly offers suggestive stimuli to party leaders and activists alike. The leaders of both parties find themselves yet less powerful, as candidates become yet more independent of their services. Increasing partisanship in the legislature suggests new avenues for meaningful party action, but only if the elected representatives can themselves be held more responsible to the external party apparatus. Democratic party leaders (including those seated in the legislature) are eager for the means to attach the ever more independent and issue-oriented voters to their party; Republican party leaders would like to win at least some of them back to their own ranks. In such circumstances, internally conceived programs for party reform will not be rejected out of hand by party leadership. As for the activists, although they invest a certain share of their participatory energies in the parties, they function in the broader context of citizen discontent in California. They are not only unlikely to object to efforts to make parties more effective intermediaries between citizen and state but are likely to initiate such attempts on their own if the time appears ripe for positive response.

It is well and good to argue that the ingredients are suitable for internally generated reform, but as always, one must look to the pudding for proof: Is anything cooking in California? To answer the question properly, we must look first at the informal adaptations both parties have made to the shifting political tides and then consider the specific reforms each has adopted or proposed.

Informal Adaptations

In order to maximize its own strength as an organization and to attract as many supporters as possible from the agitated populace, each party has evolved a number of techniques. Both have worked to build stronger ties with the voluntary groups that surround them: the Democratic Party now "charters" all local clubs of Democratic activists (most but not all of which are CDC-affiliated as well), and the current and past Republican chairpersons are credited with developing stronger ties with the ultraconservative California Republican Assembly groups and the more moderate but relatively powerful Federation of Republican Women. Such groups frequently issue preprimary endorsements of candidates, a function the Progressives were careful to deny the parties themselves.[40]

In addition, both parties have set up issues committees at the state level, into which grass-roots resolutions on policy are funneled. Although most such resolutions are never heard of again, being in many cases the politically unrealistic pleas of particular interests or individuals, the committees do offer some semblance of a forum. More recently, the Democrats have made efforts to set up issues workshops at the base, although leaders in both parties find such tactics tricky to employ and would probably agree with the Republican county chairperson who said anything could be discussed so long as it was not "too controversial or too localized."

Another means of giving more importance to local party activities has been the technique of the "slate mailer" in local elections. Forbidden to run candidates in these nonpartisan races, in some counties, the parties nevertheless do issue endorsements, mailing out to their registered voters a list of the candidates they favor. In a few counties, one party or the other will have sufficient strength to issue such endorsements only if satisfied with the record of work for the party achieved by the candidate. In the present period of anti-Republicanism, local leaders of that party are careful not to impose endorsements where they may hurt, but they do use candidate development committees to encourage likely Republicans to run (unlabeled and unendorsed) for such offices.[41]

The parties have also worked to maximize their effectiveness by being "realistic" about the control of the legislature over their affairs and the independence of candidates, once chosen; such an attitude is particularly common among Republicans. According to one former Republican county chairperson, despite the ban on preprimary endorsements, the only time the party *can* be effective is during the 18 months prior to the June primaries or the summer presidential convention. During that time, *if* it has raised sufficient funds to be the "large and legal bagman," *if* it has a system for recruiting attractive candidates and funneling funds into their campaigns, and *if* it can coordinate the work of the county committees (the Republicans have a County Chairs Association to facilitate such coordination), ensuring a strong but selective voter registration drive and an efficient get-out-the-vote effort, *then* the party assumes importance to the candidates and has a role to play. Nevertheless, "if you're smart you'll be ready to take a back seat to the candidate and his management and work cooperatively with them" once the primaries are past.[42]

Such concessions, combined with the problems associated with the near total absence of patronage and the tendency of California voters to be frustratingly mobile, suggest that informal accommodations have brought only a very limited success in building stronger parties. We turn next to the efforts made by each party to effect significant change in the rules under which they must operate.

Democratic Reforms

In April 1979, the governor of California signed into law a bill significantly changing the internal structure of the Democratic Party (the parties are listed separately in the California Elections Code, and their structures may thus be altered by separate legislative actions). This legislative act established a new level of party organization at the base, the Assembly District Caucus. The chief function of the district caucus is to elect five delegates to the State Central Committee, for a total of 23.6 percent of the total membership of the committee. Each caucus is set up by an Assembly District Committee, to be composed originally of all members of the County Central Committee in the district. In addition, the County Central committees are themselves given the right to elect 21.4 percent of the members of the State Central Committee (the exact number per county depending on the number of registered Democrats in that county), and county chairpersons are no longer automatically delegates to the State Central Committee. Although the size of the State Central Committee is enlarged (from 1,345 to 1,695), the reform includes significant cuts in the number of members appointed by Democratic incumbents and unsuccessful Democratic candidates. The Code also requires that there be approximately equal numbers of men and women among the elected and appointed delegates.[43]

The change is, for California, a dramatic step in the direction of a more open and democratic party. Every registered Democrat residing in the district is entitled to vote at the caucus, and the bill stipulates that "every reasonable effort" must be made to publicize the meeting. Furthermore, the party has also revised its by-laws to establish permanent Assembly District committees, consisting of all members of the state and county committees resident in the district and "a representative resident in the district of each Democratic club or other chartered organization with members in the District."[44] The committee is responsible "for encouraging and developing the Party organization at the level of the precinct" and is expected to take on a reasonable share of the work of fund raising, voter registration, and getting out the vote.[45]

How has it proved possible to develop local structures and create new links between the base and State Central Committee for one of the parties in antiparty California? The question, when directed to party activists and leaders, elicits a variety of answers. Some credit the CDC for having laid the groundwork for grass-roots activism and trace the demand for change back to the activists' days of campaigning for Stevenson, then working in the antiwar and civil rights movements—and thereby both learning techniques for political change and developing dissatisfaction with the elite control of the party apparatus. Others think the now greatly weakened CDC played little part (although supportive) and believe the impetus came from inside the party, beginning with earlier and more radical plans for reform (which were finally diluted to the more widely acceptable bill that did pass). Electing reform-oriented Bert Coffey state chairperson of the party in 1977 obviously helped, as did the support of key legislators, such as Speaker Leo McCarthy, who wanted to be identified with "a good thing, especially if it should happen to succeed," according to some reformers. Other legislators, whose powers of appointment were being seriously curtailed, had to be persuaded that no serious harm would be done to their interests.

However, perhaps the single most significant spur to adoption of the reform bill came from outside California: in 1975, in the case of *Cousins* v. *Wigoda*, the U.S. Supreme Court ruled that the right of a political party to determine the makeup of its state delegations to the party's national convention was protected by the First Amendment from intrusion by the state legislature. (See Chapter 5.) In the fall of 1978, the legislative counsel of the California legislature drew upon this ruling, and various subsequent and related state court cases, in rendering his opinion that "if the provisions of the by-laws of the Democratic State Central Committee and the provisions of the Elections Code are in conflict with respect to the membership composition and the functions of the committee, the by-laws of the committee would control."[46] In short, the legislature was being advised that it had no constitutional right to determine the internal structures of the parties. The opinion has not been widely circulated, and indeed, the legislature simply voted approval of the bill rather than taking the more logical step of changing the Elections Code to omit all reference to internal party structures and procedures.[47]

Although the reform measure's way was thus cleared by the magic of judicial interpretation, it has its opponents within the party. Some opinions are mixed, such as those of the county chairperson, who appreciates the probable capability of the new structures to bring in more grass-roots people ("the closest California will ever get to precincts and wards") but worries that it will mean one more unit competing for operating funds and wonders what will happen in case of conflicts between the districts and the county.[48] A few legislators were much more strongly opposed. One of them referred to the new measure as "the most anti-democratic thing one can do . . . elitist, upper middle class, designed to thwart the will of the majority," and forced upon the rank and file by "Common Cause types, college professors, and party hacks." He asked angrily, "How many will go to those crazy caucuses?" which he characterized as "smoke-filled rooms—of a different sort, but that's all it is." In his own district, the first caucus had been "dominated by lesbians," and the whole show was being run by "those who cannot run for office but want to run political life without going through the crucible of campaigning." In his opinion, "Democracy can only take so much democracy," and he concluded that "California has had clean, efficient, honest government since Hiram Johnson with a few minor embarrassments here and there" and that it should be remembered that "you can reform yourself into a mess."[49]

Where will this party-generated reform take the Democrats of California? In general, it appears that the reform is having the effect of opening up the party, but that dramatic changes are not likely to be felt overnight. One of the nefarious "college professors" who helped steer the reform through the party and legislature sees signs in his county of increased activism and believes that if that participation can be kept interesting and exciting, further steps are possible, including giving grass-roots membership a real say in the election of party officers, in setting the party platform, and in selecting candidates.[50] The members of the reform-oriented Campaign for Economic Democracy are active participants in the new structures and are likely to become more so in the future.[51]

Given the legislative counsel's opinion, many of the proponents of reform expect the party to take the next step of making its own preprimary endorsements (rather than, as at present, abiding by state law and leaving such endorsements to the often conflicting extraparty voluntary organizations). At that point, the district organizations may be able to exercise real power over the composition of government. The first tests are expected to come when current incumbents decide not to run for reelection. In such a case, will the new local structure have the power to rally the voters to a nominee not necessarily blessed with the endorsement of the departing incumbent, thereby establishing more popular control over the nominating process? "The real battle in this state now," says one activist, "is not between the parties but between Democratic incumbents and nonincumbents."[52] They suggest that the district organizations may then be able to exercise real power over the composition of government. Others point out that incumbents will have little difficulty maintaining warm relationships with the district committees, rewarding supporters therein with the resources available to them, and suggest that "many of the same people will be elected to the State Committee who were previously appointed."[53] Still others soberly note that more democratic intraparty procedures are not synonymous with stronger parties: "It's not the Senate and the Assembly that caused the demise of party—it's television." But the last word may rest with the pressure group activist who pointed out that weak organizations are the easy ones to take over, after which they can sometimes be made into something.[54] The Democratic Party in California may have at last made itself worth "taking over." What that will lead to in this state in this era is anybody's guess.

Republican Reforms

The current Republican approach to party reform is quite different from that of the Democrats. A New Ways Committee set up in the early 1970s made a series of efforts to get more participation by the county committees and the various Republican volunteer groups in the election of members of the Central Committee, but it was not strongly backed even by those who might have benefited, and its efforts died for lack of support. A few years later, the number of appointees a failing candidate was entitled to make to the committee was decreased and that controlled by incumbents in the state legislature was increased. This change is candidly explained by party leaders as a means of stopping the threat of a take-over at the grass roots by the more conservative elements in the party. Supporters of Barry Goldwater and the John Birch Society had begun to stand as nominees wherever possible, even in the most hopelessly Democratic constituencies, seeking not election but the right to name appointees to the Central Committee—the "reform" put an end to that tactic. Another recent change has been to eliminate the three positions of "vice-chair," traditionally reserved for women,* substituting "regional chairs" open to men or women.[55]

There is, however, at present writing, a more serious effort underway to change Republican rules. Although the Democrats have changed to proportional representation in the selection of delegates to the national convention (that is, each candidate is allowed a number of delegates proportionate to his or her strength in the primary voting),† California

---

*Women have played and play an important role in both parties. The Democrats have gone so far as to abolish their separate women's organization, a good sign of successful integration. However, one Republican leader reported that most of his male peers resent younger, professional women, "almost bar them from membership," and prefer "older, nonprofessional housewife types."

†The Democrats currently have a bill before the State Senate that would make further minor modifications in their delegate selection procedure, with a view to bringing that procedure into full compliance with national party rules (Senate Bill no. 843).

Republicans still abide by the winner-take-all rule: whoever wins a plurality in the primary is assigned all 167 delegates. The effect of such a ruling had long been to keep all but the most confident candidates out of California Republican primaries: Why wage an expensive campaign with no chance of reward? However, once California followed Oregon's example and ruled that the secretary of state was obliged to list all known serious candidates for the nomination on the ballot regardless of whether or not they had filed, the situation changed. Now probable runner-up candidates were forced into a "no-win" situation: their poor showing would be national news, and they would have nothing at all to show for it.

Such a situation struck State Senator John Schmitz as very unfair, all the more so since he had become a strong supporter of U.S. Senator John Connally's quest for the presidency—and Connally was seen as unlikely to wrest Reagan's home state away from him in the 1980 primary. Schmitz accordingly proposed a bill to change the rules. Should it succeed, a candidate would have to win over 50 percent of the primary vote to be entitled to all the delegates; otherwise, the delegation is to be divided proportionately among the candidates.[56]

Response to the bill suggests that the question will be resolved on partisan rather than reform-oriented concerns. Schmitz was surprised at the extent of outrage expressed by Reagan supporters: "You'd think I'd gone to Hanoi and was broadcasting for the enemy."[57] Although he had the support of two of the three Republicans (he himself is one of them) on the Elections and Reapportionment Committee, he was unable to move the bill out of committee for the 1979 session and was persuaded to take the measure first to the next statewide meeting of Republicans.

The effects on internal party organization and on the relative strength of party versus the candidate of various systems for choosing presidential delegates are not clear-cut.[58] What does seem clear in California, however, is that such considerations are not playing an important part in the current Republican case. Here, if ever, there appears to be an unambiguous case of reform motivated—and resisted—by political ambition. The outcome is expected to be determined by one man's personal strength. However, even those who most resent Reagan's continuing hold on the California party do not appear eager to change internal party structures in such a way as to prevent concentrated personal control: "One of the reasons I'm a Republican is that I'm not enthusiastic about change for the sake of change" is a comment that seems to sum up Republican activism on this score.

CONCLUSION

The recent spate of efforts to reform and revitalize California's political parties seem as likely to be deflected by private ambition and unintended consequence as is usually the case with political reform. It is clear that the motives for reform have been partly those of ambition for the Democrats, as party professionals have struggled to regain some of the power usurped by the legislators, and will continue to be so in the future, as nonincumbents try to employ the new structures as organizational weapons for wresting control from incumbents. In the greatly weakened Republican Party, ambition appears to play an even stronger role at present. The eagerness to return to power has had the effect of making intraparty reform seem unimportant except in terms of how it will affect the chances for that renaissance. "The most important questions for the party," says one former party chairperson, "are: are you in or out of power, do you have money in the bank or not, and what kind of leadership do you have—all these are much more important than what kind of structure you have."[59] As noted, the prospects for the reform of party procedures envisioned by the Schmitz bill depend in large part on whether and how the supporters of one man will be able to block a change that would force them to share power with other contenders.

At the same time, the reform efforts in both parties may well prove to have results surprising to those who instigated them. The Democrats achieved their reform in large part by eliciting a quasi-judicial opinion that appears to have had the effect of annulling the shotgun marriage between legislators and parties performed under the ministry of progressivism, leaving the parties free to conduct their affairs as they wish. If the process of internal democratization goes forward, those who began it may well be surprised by the changes a liberated and expanded band of activists, tipped to the left by an influx of Hayden followers or to the right by a new wave of conservative migrants, may decide to impose on the party. Similarly, Republicans who are searching for the structural or procedural means to break Reagan's grip on the party may find they have delivered the party into hands they had not even realized were among those outstretched.[60]

Yet not all the surprises need take forms distressing to those whose intentions in working for reform were to increase the opportunities for popular participation in the political process. If the Democrats do continue to strengthen the powers of the base, it seems at least probable the Republicans will sooner or later find it appropriate to do the same. In the current era of popular discontent, strengthening the base—bringing in more activists and giving them a larger say in party matters—will necessarily mean channeling some of the renascent forces of populism *into* the parties rather than, as in the progressive era, *against* the parties. It is not inconceivable that one result of the reforms presently begun will be to open the California parties up to the demands of a more impatient and better-informed citizenry. It is not impossible that the parties could become important loci for the articulation and rational compromising of the interests of that aroused citizenry. One could even imagine the parties becoming, in effect, the voters' media—the citizens' way of letting those in office know both during and between elections what it is they have in mind. However, let us not end on an unduly fanciful note. For history tells us not only that reforms are often made for hidden purposes and to surprising effect. It tells us as well that if any state is likely to produce alternate fuels to keep the engines of personalistic politics humming cheerfully through the years to come, that state is California.

NOTES

1. Austin Ranney, *Curing the Mischiefs of Faction* (Berkeley: University of California Press, 1975), pp. 75–100.
2. Nelson Polsby and Aaron Wildavsky, *Presidential Elections*, 4th ed. (New York: Scribner's, 1976), pp. 213–15, 263. See also William Crotty, *Political Reform and the American Experiment* (New York: Crowell, 1977), pp. xi, 241, and Ranney, *Curing the Mischiefs*, pp. 1–21.
3. Crotty, *Political Reform*, pp. 277–79, and Ranney, *Curing the Mischiefs*, pp. 204–10.
4. Franklin Hichborn, *Story of the Session of the California Legislature of 1911* (San Francisco: Barry, 1911), p. xxviii. My assistant, Lynda McDonald, provided this and other useful references to the Progressive era reforms.
5. John R. Owens, Edmond Constantini, and Louis F. Weschler, *California Politics and Parties* (London: Macmillan, 1970), p. 33.
6. Ibid., pp. 31–32. *The Octopus: A Story of California* is a novel by Frank Norris based on the role of the Southern Pacific Railroad (Garden City, N.Y.: Doubleday, 1901).
7. Spencer C. Olin, Jr., *California's Prodigal Sons* (Berkeley: University of California Press, 1968), p. 15. According to George E. Mowry, "The main result . . . had been the creation of a new Southern Pacific literary bureau maintained at public expense (*The California Progressives* [Chicago: Quadrangle, 1951], p. 18).
8. Dean R. Cresap, *Party Politics in the Golden State* (Los Angeles: The Haynes Foundation, 1954), pp. 9–16.
9. Owens, Costantini, and Weschler, *California Politics*, p. 90.
10. Eugene C. Lee, *The Politics of Nonpartisanship* (Berkeley: University of California Press, 1960), p. 30.
11. Olin, *California's Prodigal Sons*, p. 6, and Winston W. Crouch, John C. Bollens, and Stanley Scott, *California Government and Politics*, 6th ed. (Englewood Cliffs, N.J.: Prentice-Hall, 1977), p. 120.
12. California scores in the lowest quartile when states are ranked by "patronage potential" according to Ronald E. Weber, "Competitive and Organizational Dimensions of American State Party Systems," paper prepared for annual meeting of the Northeastern Political Science Association, 1969, cited in Malcolm E. Jewell and David M. Olson, *American State Political Parties and Elections* (Homewood, Ill.: Dorsey Press, 1978), p. 80.
13. Crouch, Bollens, and Scott, *California Government*, p. 111.
14. Ibid., pp. 93–94.
15. Ibid., pp. 115–17. Note their comment: "The cost of circulating petitions by the use of professional petition firms usually has cost sponsors between $50,000 and $200,000 [circa

1977]—thereby limiting the use of the process to groups able to raise substantial funds" (p. 117).

16. Ibid., pp. 38–41.

17. Cresap, *Party Politics*, p. 17.

18. Dan Nimmo, *The Political Persuaders* (Englewood Cliffs, N.J.: Prentice-Hall, 1970), p. 36. See also Nancy Boyarsky, "The Image Makers," in *The Challenge of California*, ed. Eugene C. Lee and Larry L. Berg, 2d ed. (Boston: Little, Brown, 1976), pp. 134–38.

19. Nimmo, *Political Persuaders*, and Owens, Costantini, and Weschler, *California Politics*, pp. 157–60.

20. Owens, Costantini, and Weschler, *California Politics*, pp. 41–42.

21. Ibid., pp. 43–45.

22. The story of the California Democratic Council's early years is ably told in James Q. Wilson, *The Amateur Democrat* (Chicago: University of Chicago Press, 1962).

23. Bernard L. Hyink, Seyom Brown, and Ernest W. Thacker, *Politics and Government in California*, 9th ed. (New York: Crowell, 1975), pp. 98–102.

24. Mary Ellen Leary, *Phantom Politics: Campaigning in California* (Washington, D.C.: Public Affairs Press, 1977), p. 172–75.

25. Jewell and Olson, *American State Parties and Elections*, p. 185. Said one former state party chairperson who was interviewed for the purpose of this chapter, "They invite you to sit at the head table, but they never ask you to speak."

26. Bruce F. Freed, "Political Money and Campaign Finance Reform, 1971–1976," in *Parties and Elections in an Anti-Party Age*, ed. Jeff Fishel (Bloomington: Indiana University Press, 1978), pp. 252–53. See also Tony Quinn, "Political Action Committees—The New Campaign Bankrollers," *California Journal* 10 (March 1979): 96–98.

27. Tony Quinn, "Why the State Hasn't Bought Public Financing of Elections," in *California Government and Politics Annual 1978–79*, ed. Gary L. Wilhelm, Thomas R. Hoeber, and Ed Salzman (Sacramento: California Journal Press, 1978), pp. 68–69.

28. Wilson, *Amateur Democrat*, p. 108.

29. Democratic state party chairperson Richard O'Neill describes politics as being "like playing at the crap tables or being a big bettor on football games" but has a reputation for fund raising that goes well beyond deployment of his private fortune. See Larry Peterson, "The Political Resurrection of Chairman Richard O'Neill," *California Journal* 10 (May 1979): 177–79.

30. Joel M. Fisher, Charles M. Price, and Charles G. Bell, *The Legislative Process in California* (Washington, D.C.: American Political Science Association, 1973), pp. 82–83.

31. This assessment is based on ibid., pp. 81–100, as corroborated by interviews in Sacramento. Fisher's suggestion that the shift in 1972 to roll call voting in committees and the recording of votes has increased partisanship was not corroborated in interviews. "What it has done is increase the flow of bad legislation: it's harder to say 'no' because there is always someone who wants every bill passed," grumbled one legislator.

32. Jewell and Olson, *American State Parties and Elections*, p. 289.

33. Ibid., p. 237.

34. Joseph P. Harris, *California Politics*, 3rd ed. (Stanford, Calif.: Standord University Press, 1961), pp. 11–20; Lee and Berg, eds. *Challenge of California*, p. 17. See also the analysis by Elizabeth La Macchia, "The Deceptive Contradictions of County Voting Patterns," *California Journal* 8 (October 1977): 351–52, in which she notes the tendency of many former southern Democrats now residing in California to vote conservatively on ballot propositions, as well as for Republican candidates on occasion.

35. See Ed Salzman, "How the State GOP Lost Its Well-Oiled Machinery," in Wilhelm, Hoeber, and Salzman, *California Annual*, pp. 51–52, for his comment, "The cult of personality that brought the party back together again also provided the seeds for its decentralization . . . the Republican Party in the state was allowed to erode" (p. 52).

36. "A Practical Guide to California Government and Politics," in ibid., p. 19.

37. Tom Ellick, vice-president of corporate relations for the Fluor Corporation, quoted in the Los Angeles *Times*, January 30, 1978, p. 3. See also "GOP Leaders Plan Talks to Rebuild Party," Los Angeles *Times*, February 24, 1977, p. 1; "State GOP Maps Revitalizing Strategy," Los Angeles *Times*, July 23, 1977, p. 1; and Ed Salzman, "The GOP Battle Plan to Capture the State Senate," *California Journal* 8 (July 1977): 246–47.

38. Tony Quinn, "The Rapid Disappearance of Safe Political Territory," *California Journal* 10 (May 1979): 165–68.

39. Bruce W. Sumner, "Happy 100th Birthday California Constitution," *California Journal* 10 (June 1979): 215.

40. See Jewell and Olson, *American State Parties and Elections*, pp. 97, 104, and 137 for the meaning of such endorsements.

41. Interviews with Dagmar Fulton, County Chairperson of Alameda County Republicans, July 3, 1979, and with Gary Myerscough, executive director of San Fransisco County Republicans, June 26, 1979.

42. Interview with Paul Haerle, former state chairperson of California Republican Party, July 11, 1979. The same point was made by Myerscough. Other Republican groups of note are the moderate California Republican League and the contentious Young Republicans (presently divided into two warring groups).

43. Assembly Bill no. 12, first introduced December 4, 1978, and a letter from Assembly Speaker Leo McCarthy, March 23, 1979.

44. By-laws of the Democratic State Central Committee of California, as amended and adopted on November 18, 1978. Incumbents are reduced from seven to five or six appointees; unsuccessful candidates from five to two or three.

45. Ibid., and interview with Mary Warren, County Chairperson of Alameda County Democrats, July 2, 1979.

46. Letter of December 8, 1978, from Bion M. Gregory, legislative counsel of California, to the Honorable Michael Gage.

47. A legislative consultant reports that the opinion was kept quiet and "hauled out to get votes for A.B. No. 12 only as necessary" (interview, July 9, 1979).

48. Warren interview.

49. Interview with Assemblyman Walter Ingalls, July 9, 1979. Assemblyman Ingalls stated he had no objection to being quoted, since "my constituents won't care about parties."

50. Interview with Professor Edmond Constantini, University of California at Davis, July 9, 1979. I am very much indebted to Professor Constantini for his careful explication of the current status of Democratic reforms and his generous help in suggesting avenues for further inquiry.

51. Interview with Michael Dieden, political director of California Campaign for Economic Democracy, July 7, 1979.

52. Interview with Joseph Close, Democratic party activist, July 2, 1979.

53. Warren interview.

54. This comments was made with the request the speaker not be identified.

55. Myerscough interview.

56. Senate Bill no. 1135 (the "Schmitz Bill") and interview with State Senator John Schmitz, July 9, 1979.

57. Schmitz interview.

58. Jewell and Olson, *American State Parties and Elections*, pp. 278–83.

59. Haerle interview.

60. The rapid rise of the new Republican lieutenant governor, Mike Curb, may prove to be a case in point. See "Mike Curb—the Reagan of Tomorrow?" in the Los Angeles *Times*, July 15, 1978, p. 1.

9

MINNESOTA: THE PARTY CAUCUS-CONVENTION SYSTEM

Thomas R. Marshall

*I*n decades past, the label of *political reform* belonged to the Progressives. To the Progressives, political parties were barriers between voters and candidates or officeholders. Parties meant bosses, machines, graft, smoke-filled rooms, and, inevitably, corruption. In the Progressives' view, strong party organizations were little valued.

The Progressives' antiparty sentiment struck a deep and responsive chord in U.S. politics. In state after state, the Progressives eliminated nomination through party convention and adopted the direct primary. In some states, the Progressives eliminated party registration and permitted crossover voting in primaries. In a few states, the Progressives even enacted a blanket primary.

Despite the Progressives' successes, their solution to political parties was not equally appealing to everyone. To others, party reform meant something quite different. Instead of weakening the political parties, a second group of reformers sought to strengthen the parties' role in elections and in organizing the government.

To these latter reformers—herein referred to as strong, or responsible, party reformers—parties play a vital, even necessary role in modern, electoral democracy.[1] To strong party reformers, parties should offer a

The author acknowledges the assistance of Bob Coursen and Steve Brandt, of the Minneapolis *Tribune*; Rick Scott, Claire Rumpel, and Joe Tessemer, of the Democratic-Farmer-Labor Party; Bill Morris and Evie Teegen, of the Independent Republican Party; and Michele Bock of the University of Texas at Arlington. This research was conducted under a grant from the Organized Research Fund of the University of Texas at Arlington.

forum for policy discussion and debate by the parties' loyalists. Parties should offer clear policy choices to the voters. A party's candidates should run on the party's platform and, once in office, should enact the party's promises. Parties should also actively recruit citizens into the party organization, thereby bringing citizens' demands into the party system for accommodation, compromise, and implementation. At a minimum, responsible party reformers urge that parties structure elections and organize the government. By linking party-labeled candidates to policy promises and performance in office, parties allow ordinary voters to exercise control over the government by penalizing errant incumbents and tagging responsibility for governing onto a party coalition.

These three goals—policy making, recruitment, and structuring elections and the government—dominate much of the responsible party literature. Unlike the earlier Progressive reformers, strong party reformers urge political parties to adopt ever-broader activities. Yet faced with the Progressives' legal obstacles to stronger, more effective parties, how can responsible party reformers reassert the parties' role?

PARTY REFORM IN MINNESOTA

Minnesota politics clearly bear the legacy of that state's Progressive heritage. Candidates for local and statewide office gain nomination through open primaries, not in party conventions. Minnesota requires no party registration, thereby permitting crossover voting in primaries.[2] Until the 1970s, candidates for local office and for the state legislature did not even run under party labels in the general election. Until very recently, the state legislators organized under a set of labels that were entirely different from the official parties' names.

Legally, then, Minnesota's two major parties resemble those in many other states: weak, decentralized, and formally impotent. As a result of the Progressives' earlier successes in "reforming" Minnesota politics, strong party advocates cannot rely on the parties' official or legal position to achieve their goals. How, then, could modern-day reformers influence policy, foster recruitment, or structure elections and the state government within these constraints?

In some states, strong party reformers supplemented the official party with extralegal party clubs; in Wisconsin, California, New York, and elsewhere, modern reformers organized party clubs. Elsewhere, as in Massachusetts or the national Democratic Party, strong party advocates wrote new charters, formed policy commissions, or held periodic conclaves to discuss party polities and goals.

Party clubs, commissions, and rules changes are by no means unknown in Minnesota either. Both the Democratic–Farmer–Labor (DFL) and the Independent Republican (IR) parties* often rely on these techniques.[3] Yet in Minnesota, responsible party advocates rely primarily on another institution: the caucus-convention system.

The Caucus-Convention System

First established in the 1800s, the caucus-convention system survived the Progressives' antiparty reforms, albeit in a legally regulated form. The system achieves several strong party reforms. Through the caucuses and conventions, party activists can organize before the primaries to settle on favored candidates, write party positions, and woo previously inactive adults into the party structure.

Minnesota's caucus-convention system begins with a precinct caucus, held separately by both parties in each of Minnesota's nearly 4,000 precincts. Since Minnesota precincts are relatively small in size, the precinct caucus is essentially a neighborhood meeting. By state law and party practice, the precinct caucuses are open to any party supporter who feels inclined to attend. State law specifies the time and place for the caucuses and even regulates their order of business.[4]

At the local precinct meetings, attenders elect the precinct's party officers for the next two years as well as voting on delegates to attend the district and state party conventions. At these later conventions, delegates may endorse but do not actually nominate the party's local and state candidates. At the presidential level, though, Minnesota does not hold a presidential primary but selects its national convention delegates directly from the parties' district and state conventions.

The caucus-convention system serves not only as the basis for the party's organization but, also, as a debate forum for the party faithful. At the precinct caucuses, attenders may introduce, discuss, and pass (or reject) policy resolutions. Later, at district or state conventions, these resolutions may be written into the platform.

Local precinct caucuses offer a convenient way for political newcomers to enter the party. As described later, many interest groups, civic organizations, newspapers, candidates, and the parties themselves actively encourage newcomers to attend local caucuses.

If the caucus-convention system, in theory, works to achieve responsible party goals, how successful has it actually been in practice? In particular, how well has the system achieved the first two major reform goals

---

*The Republican Party of Minnesota officially changed its name to the Independent Republican (IR) party at its 1975 State Convention. Unless the reference is to a period exclusively prior to 1975, the IR label is used.

described earlier, that is, policy making and recruitment? First, have the caucuses and conventions actually provided a forum for policy discussion? Has that system led to clear policy differences between Minnesota's two major parties? Has the system permitted grass-roots party activists to control the parties' candidates and officeholders? Second, has the caucus-convention system served to recruit adults into active political roles?

POLICY MAKING

Policy Discussion

State law, party rules, the media, civic organizations, and interest groups all encourage voters to attend precinct caucuses and to raise and debate issues. Attenders may introduce issue resolutions concerning international, national, state, or purely local issues. Whether grass-roots activists really do demonstrate a concern for issues, though, must be measured empirically. Samples of precinct caucus meetings in 1972 and 1974 were analyzed to test whether policy discussion and debate were common at the local meetings.[5]

Results presented in Table 9.1 indicate that grass-roots party activists show a considerable concern with issues. At the precinct caucuses, some 30,000 to 35,000 resolutions were offered each year in each party. As a result, most caucus attenders were exposed to some discussion and debate over issues. As Table 9.1 indicates, four-fifths of the local caucus meetings for both parties discussed at least one policy resolution. Two of every three meetings evidenced some controversy over the resolutions process, with some resolutions being defeated, withdrawn by sponsors, or passed only after debate.

Policy Clarity

Grass-roots caucus attenders in Minnesota are apparently quite concerned with issues, just as other accounts of party activists elsewhere have suggested.[6] Yet strong party reformers are not only concerned that the activists discuss issues but, also, that these discussions lead to clear and apparent policy differences between the parties. When the parties adopt clear and distinct issues, ordinary voters can choose between their alternative stands.

Policy clarity occurs when each party adopts a clear position on an issue and when one party's position clearly differs from the other's. Policy clarity may result either from resolutions at the grass-roots precinct caucuses or from higher-level conventions. Of course, it is possible that

TABLE 9.1:
Policy Discussion at Minnesota Precinct
Caucus Meetings, 1972 and 1974
(percent)

Number of Resolutions	1972		1974	
	DFL	GOP	DFL	GOP
No caucus meeting held	3	14	3	17
No resolutions offered	19	7	8	5
All resolutions passed routinely	18	17	20	14
One or two resolutions passed after debate, defeated, or withdrawn	21	26	20	23
Three or more resolutions passed after debate, defeated, or withdrawn	39	36	48	41
	100	100	99	100
Number of precincts in the sample	100	100	105	105

Source: Minneapolis *Tribune* News Research Department.

policy clarity may not occur from any level of the caucus-convention system.

At the precinct caucus level, attenders biennially discuss thousands of separate resolutions. However, in fact, issue clarity between parties seldom if ever occurs from neighborhood caucus meetings. In 1972 and 1974, DFL and IR precinct caucuses differed clearly only on the single issue of impeachment for then-president Nixon (in 1974). On none of the thousands of other local, state, or national policy questions discussed at precinct caucuses in 1972 or 1974 did clearly differing policy stands emerge from the local meetings.

Why do grass-roots caucuses, attended by issue-concerned activists, not offer distinct and opposing policy stands more often? Party officials and interest group leaders suggest several reasons. Several interest groups urge members to avoid arguing over issues and to concentrate instead on being selected a party officer or delegate. Some groups completely bypass the caucuses and focus their efforts on platform writing or on lobbying candidates or officeholders individually. Where a party is largely agreed on some issues (for example, labor issues for the DFL), few resolutions may be offered to belabor an obvious consensus. On some more controversial issues (for example, abortion), both advocates and opponents are likely to appear in both parties.

Apparently, open and accessible meetings at the grass-roots level do not automatically produce issue clarity between the parties. Instead, what happens is that the opportunity to offer and discuss issues expands the total number of issues raised but does not ensure that the same issues will be debated at most meetings or that the parties will adopt clearly differing stands.

If policy clarity does not result from the precinct caucuses, then perhaps the better-structured party conventions might provide it. In fact, within the last decade, both parties have experienced a strongly worded and well-publicized platform from its activists. However, both parties have since taken steps to deemphasize policy clarity in their platform writing. Even when policy clarity does occur in the party platform, it has not led to policy control by the activists.

In 1974, the Republican state delegates passed a resolution urging Minnesota to rescind its ratification of the Equal Rights Amendment (ERA). Shortly thereafter, the party's statewide candidates publicly disassociated themselves from that stand. Later, in 1976 and 1978, the party's managers tried to avoid controversial social issues and focus instead on more consensual issues. The party's managers offered the delegates a "straw vote" on divisive issues (such as abortion, gun control, and the ERA). Only more widely accepted issues—for example, tax limits, sunset legislation for state agencies, and incentives for businesses—were included in the platform.[7] On controversial issues, individual candidates were left completely free to fix their own positions, and no party stand was written.

Within the last decade, the DFL has also worked with a clear and well-publicized platform. In 1972, the party's state convention managed to pass only three positions before adjourning—urging the granting of amnesty, the decriminalizing of marijuana, and the enacting of gay rights. Many of the party's candidates, including the governor, disavowed the platform. More recently, the party's state convention has taken up issues between votes on endorsing candidates and choosing party officers. Since the party uses lengthy and time-consuming procedures to choose its delegates and officers and to endorse its candidates, few issues are often passed at the convention. More platform issues are adopted later, by the state party's Executive Committee. As a result, few issues gain much publicity.

Within both parties, then, recent practices have discouraged the adoption of many controversial issues in the platform. IR conventions now separate the most divisive issues from its official platform; the DFL usually manages to take up only a few issues at its state convention. As a result, average voters would understandably have some difficulty discerning many clear party differences. Neither party's managers believe that the average voter can see many issue differences between the two platforms or is very interested in that declaration.

Policy Control

The most rigorous party responsibility position holds that party-labeled candidates should run on party issues and, once in office, enact the party's platform. Yet, Minnesota's caucus-convention system shows little evidence of achieving policy control by the activists, either over candidates or officeholders.

Minnesota's statewide candidates have shown an unmistakeable reluctance to run on the party activists' issues. In both 1972 and 1974, the DFL, then the Republican Party's activists, passed a strong and controversial platform; in both years, statewide party candidates hurried to separate themselves from the platform. The evidence is clear: when the party's platform is most clear, different, uncompromising, and well-publicized, statewide candidates are *most* likely to disavow the activists. In Minnesota, as elsewhere, candidates usually prefer to run on their own issues, especially on their own (or their opponent's) performance in office, on name recognition, on popular or reformist issues, or on broad themes. Even candidates who win the party endorsement have freely disassociated themselves from the activists' platform and directed their own campaign efforts. Strongly worded controversial issues stands are, in the words of one party leader, seen by Minnesota candidates as "sure losers."

If party activists cannot force candidates to run on the platform, they have been even less successful in dominating the party's elected officeholders. In both houses of Minnesota's legislature, DFL and IR legislative caucuses adopt party caucus priorities. These positions, though, are only coincidentally the same as the party's platform stands. Legislative caucus issues are usually those that win near-unanimous support from party caucus members. These issues usually focus on "silent ideology" issues, involving party-identified groups (for example, labor regulation and tax burden policies) or ongoing state programs (for example, educational funding and Dutch elm disease control). Controversial and divisive social issues that so often concern party activists—such as abortion—seldom merit party caucus positions in the legislature.

Both legislative party caucuses have several incentives or rewards to offer party members: committee seats and chairpersonships and campaign funds. In distributing these benefits, though, party loyalty is seldom a controlling factor; in fact, party loyalty is usually thought to rank fairly low in distributing rewards or as a legislative norm in Minnesota.[8] Seniority, support for the caucus leader, and achieving a regional-urban balance are all more important than party loyalty per se. As well, in distributing the legislative caucuses' campaign funds, a candidates' ability to win the seat and the contest's closeness appear to be controlling factors. To be sure, party disloyalty may lead to a loss of prestige, support by other legislators, and even, in extreme cases, of a committee seat; such instances, however, appear to be uncommon in recent legislative sessions.*

Overall, then, what has been the impact of the caucus-convention system on policy making? The system does encourage a great deal of policy discussion. However, grass-roots resolutions seldom lead to policy clarity, either at the grass roots or at higher-level party conventions. On very few issues do the two party conventions take clearly differing well-publicized stands. Party activists have been even less successful in achieving policy control, either over endorsed candidates or over officeholders. Candidates and officeholders—even those who win party endorsement—prefer to run on their own issues and, once in office, to define their own priorities. Few statewide candidates or the legislative party caucuses apparently take the platform seriously as a program to enact.[9]

RECRUITMENT AND PARTICIPATION

Responsible party reformers often urge parties to recruit previously inactive adults into the party. Through involvement within the party, citizens learn political skills. At the same time, citizens transcend a narrow, single-issue focus by working within a broad-based, coalitional party structure. Within the party, citizens moderate their political demands and achieve their goals without destabilizing the entire party system. The party organization, too, benefits from its recruiting efforts when newly active citizens campaign for the party's candidates, contribute to party fund-raising drives, and share the day-to-day labors of the party headquarters.

Minnesota's open precinct caucuses appear to offer adults a convenient access to the parties. Precinct caucus meetings are located within the neighborhood (access is guaranteed both by state law and party rules), and the meetings are well publicized.

The caucus-convention system might succeed in the recruitment function to the extent that the caucuses involve large numbers of attenders, or the system might succeed in bringing in many persons without prior political experience, or the system might encourage attenders to become further involved in politics.

---

*As indicated above, one reason for the relatively slight importance of party loyalty may lie in the practice of legislative caucuses[1] taking stands only on those issues where nearly all the caucus members are already in agreement.

TABLE 9.2:
Attendance at Minnesota Party Caucuses
in Recent Years

Attendance	1972	1974	1976	1978
Attendance at DFL caucuses	71,000	54,000	58,000	75,000
Attendance at IR caucuses	30,900	25,000	60,000	60,000
Total attendance	101,900	79,000	118,000	135,000

Source: Data taken from official party records, projections by the parties, or surveys conducted by the Minneapolis *Tribune* News Research Department.

One test for recruitment in the caucus-convention system is to examine the total turnout or attendance at local caucus meetings. Table 9.2 indicates attendance at recent precinct caucuses in Minnesota. As data in Table 9.2 indicate, caucus going varies widely from year to year and from party to party. When party enthusiasm is high and a lively battle is underway, precinct caucus meetings are heavily attended, as in the 1972 Humphrey-McGovern struggle. When the party is dispirited or in off-years, attendance at caucuses falls off, as for the Republicans during the 1974 Watergate gloom.*

How does this turnout compare to the total electorate in Minnesota? In fact, only a relatively small fraction of all Minnesotans attend the caucuses. In recent years, from 6 percent (IR in 1974) to 11 percent (DFL in 1972) of all party identifiers attended a caucus meeting. By contrast, about a quarter to a third of all party identifiers normally vote in statewide primary elections.

By the turnout test, then, caucus-convention attendance is not particularly impressive. Far fewer Minnesotans attend caucus meetings than vote in primary or general elections. On the other hand, attending a caucus

---

*Caucus turnout before the 1968 McCarthy-Humphrey battle was evidently much smaller than recent attendance. Normal attendance before 1968 has been estimated at no more than 5,000 to 10,000 at each party's caucuses.

Although caucus turnout is smaller than equivalent primary participation, the *quality* of representation appears to be about the same. On several tests of policy-, candidate-, or party-related attitudes, caucus attenders appear to represent all party identifiers about as well as do equivalent primary voters. Where differences appear, DFL caucus attenders are (predictably) somewhat more liberal than party rank and file. On demographic items, though, caucus participants were typically better educated, not identified with a church, younger, and male. Again, however, differences were not much larger than for equivalent primaries. For a discussion, see Thomas R. Marshall, "Turnout and Representation: Caucuses Versus Primaries," *American Journal of Political Science* 22 (February 1978): 169–82.

meeting is a more demanding political act than simply voting in a primary election. Caucus going involves attending a meeting, participating in discussion and debate, choosing party officers and delegates, and meeting politically concerned neighbors.

If the level of caucus going is compared with the number of U.S. adults who are politically active beyond simply voting, then the picture changes markedly. As one recent account of political participation in the United States explained: "Activities that require . . . more than trivial amounts of time and energy . . . tend to be performed by no more than 10 to 15 percent of the citizens."[10] Caucus attending is also about as common as meeting going in Europe's supposedly "mass" political parties. Certainly a greater percentage of party identifiers attend Minnesota caucuses than attend party club meetings in other states.

The caucus-convention system also recruits adults to the extent that the politically inexperienced (or novices) attend. In recent years, a third to a half of precinct caucus attenders reported no prior involvement either in Minnesota's parties or interest groups. Large numbers of precinct caucus attenders are newcomers to Minnesota politics. In 1976, for example, a statewide sample of DFL caucus attenders were asked whether "including the last presidential campaign in 1972, had you done any work for the party or for any candidates of the party these last four years?" Just over half (51 percent) answered no, while 40 percent replied that they had worked for the party or its candidates.

Whenever lively political battles draw in larger-than-usual numbers of caucus attenders, then the number of novices also swells. In 1968, antiwar amateurs supporting McCarthy broke precedent by actively encouraging a large turnout at precinct caucuses. In that year, thousands of antiwar activists turned out, overwhelming the party regulars in most of the state's urban, suburban, and college districts. Afterwards, political novices once again turned out in large numbers at 1972 DFL caucuses, during 1976 in IR caucuses, and at both DFL and IR caucuses in 1978. In 1972, for example, just over half (54 percent) of DFL caucus attenders were newcomers. By contrast, in 1974, a low turnout year, the number of novices at DFL caucuses was only about a third (37 percent) of all attenders.

Attending a local caucus meeting also fosters adult political recruitment, by encouraging attenders to become more active within the party organization, during the upcoming elections, or through special interest groups. At the neighborhood meetings, about a quarter to a half of all caucus attenders are chosen to serve as local (precinct) party officers, as delegates or alternates to party conventions, or both. Delegates and alternates are often contacted and solicited by candidates seeking the party's endorsement. Both parties collect precinct sign-in sheets; later, party-endorsed candidates and the party organization itself use those lists to recruit volunteers and donors. Officials in the DFL and IR parties estimate that one-half to three-quarters of all attenders become active in the primaries or general elections following the caucuses.

Aside from the parties and party-endorsed candidates, several interest groups in Minnesota focus on the caucuses. Some interest groups actively encourage their members and supporters to attend and to be chosen delegates or party officers.* Usually, this encouragement comes through notices in newsletters or announcements at group meetings. Some groups, though, encourage caucus attendance by telephoning or by special mailings. Some groups also recontact their members and supporters who were chosen delegates or party officers for help in letter-writing campaigns or in lobbying. A few groups—mostly small, human rights organizations—even use the caucuses to identify and recruit potential members.

How successful is the caucus-convention system in recruiting adults to active political roles? To be sure, the system does not draw in a large total percentage of the state's electorate. Yet, it serves as a gateway for a steady influx of newcomers to enter the stable, ongoing world of political parties.

For those who do attend, the caucus-convention system provides ample opportunity for further involvement in campaigns, in the party itself, or in interest groups. Newcomers are introduced to other politically concerned neighbors. Attenders may volunteer—or even be drafted—to serve as a party officer or as a convention delegate or alternate. Attending a caucus may lead to requests for help later on by candidates, the parties, or interest groups.

Minnesota's caucus-convention system at least partially satisfies the demands of responsible party reformers that parties recruit adults into active political roles. Newcomers are easily involved in coalitional party politics, thereby transcending narrow interest group ties. In U.S. politics, where few opportunities exist to join stable, broad-based political groups, even the relatively small numbers involved in the caucuses and conventions cannot be ignored.

OTHER PARTY REFORMS

Partisan Elections

Political scientists often describe structuring the vote as a political party's minimal function. Yet from 1913 until the 1970s, Minnesota's state

---

*A survey in 1976 of interest groups and organizations in Minnesota found 41 groups who contacted their members about the caucuses and encouraged attendance.

legislature and its local officeholders were all chosen in nonpartisan elections. Ballot designation for state legislators was reinstated only in 1973, after the DFL regained control of the state legislature. In 1974, candidates for the state House ran with party labels, and in 1976, state Senate candidates ran with party designation. The mayors and councilpersons in Minneapolis, St. Paul, and Duluth now also run with party designation. Other local offices, however, such as school board and park board members, continue to be elected in nonpartisan elections.[11]

Legislative Party Caucuses

Until the last decade, candidates for state legislature not only ran in nonpartisan elections, but once elected, organized under Conservative and Liberal caucus labels. Although Republicans generally tended toward the Conservative caucus and DFLers usually moved into the Liberal caucus, exceptions to this pattern were common. In the late 1960s, the Liberal caucus publicly changed its name to the DFL caucus. A few years later, in the early 1970s, the Conservative caucus followed suit and organized under the Republican (later the IR) banner.[12]

Endorsements, Nominations, and Campaigning

Unlike most other states, Minnesota chooses its national convention delegates wholly through the caucus-convention system. Minnesota Progressives did enact a presidential primary in 1916, but it was abandoned thereafter except for one more trial in 1952 and 1956. Except for those three years, the state has always picked its national convention delegates and alternates from the parties' district and state conventions. For presidential nominations, then, if not for state and local nominations, the parties' activists retain their control.*

For state and local races, however, Minnesota candidates win their place on the general election ballot in direct and open primaries. Since party loyalists cannot directly control nominations, they organize before the primary to endorse candidates. Minnesota's caucuses are held in the winter (usually in February or March), with district and state conventions coming in the late spring and early summer. Party loyalists are thereby able to endorse a favored candidate and organize on that candidate's behalf before the fall (usually September) primary.

Although the party endorsement does not actually appear on the primary ballot, endorsement may still help a candidate defeat his or her

---

*Considerable sentiment for a presidential primary exists in Minnesota, but party officials, chiefly from the DFL, have thus far succeeded in blocking a primary.

opponent. Before the primaries, both parties circulate party endorsement cards to voters. In hotly contested primaries, the party organization itself may sponsor telephone banks and district walkathons to support party-endorsed candidates. Not infrequently, if the party endorsement is one-sided, a nonendorsed candidate will drop out before the primary. Since the DFL merger in 1944, DFL endorsed candidates have won the primary about four out of five times.*

After the primary, an endorsed candidate who also wins the nomination may have a wider variety of services from the party organization. In Minnesota, the DFL usually spends about $500,000 to staff its state office and provide a long list of services to its endorsed candidates.[13] These include bulk mailing assistance, information on campaign finance regulations, advice on fund raising, photographic and media-oriented services, voter-targeting advice, legislative research, party endorsement leaflets and pamphlets, and election eve telephone banks.†

The IR also provides a similar range of services, even in advance of the formal endorsement. In 1978, the IR also conducted a series of legislative district polls and provided several in-field campaign advisers to help the party target its priority districts in state legislative races. The advisers also supervised the campaigns of state legislative candidates and assisted candidates with their organization, budget, and media efforts. In addition, the IR funnels a great deal of campaign money through its state party office to selected candidates. In 1978, for example, the party collected nearly $1.5 million, most of which was returned directly to the party's state legislative candidates.

Party officials in both parties readily concede that many long-time incumbents and those from "safe" districts neither need nor often use the party's help. For first-time candidates and those from more marginal districts, though, the party endorsement and organization may bring badly needed resources and provide the margin between victory and defeat.

---

*A candidate who fails to win endorsement may still compete for the nomination in the primary. In recent years, several unendorsed candidates have gained the party label by winning the primary. This has occurred especially within the more diverse DFL. At least once within the last six years, a U.S. congressman, the state auditor, and (in 1978) the U.S. Senate nomination went to an unendorsed candidate. Also, several state legislators won nomination without a formal party endorsement. See also G. Theodore Mitau, *Politics in Minnesota* (Minneapolis: University of Minnesota Press, 1970), p. 70.

†Both parties raise funds to pay for these services from the typical sources—party fund raisers, special events, and so forth. Both, however, also solicit contributions from ordinary party members. The IR adopts a community chest approach in its Neighbor-to-Neighbor Drive, as volunteers go door-to-door to solicit small donations from prospective Republican donors. The DFL uses a DFL Sustaining Fund for donors, who can contribute on a monthly, quarterly, or semiannual basis. In a normal year, the IR may raise over $400,000 from its drive; the DFL usually raises $200,000 or more from its program.

SOURCES OF SUPPORT FOR PARTY RENEWAL

Within the last decade, Minnesotans have witnessed an unprecedented effort to revive that state's political parties. For the first time in half a century, candidates for the state legislature and in Minnesota's largest cities appear on the general election ballot with party labels. Party caucuses in the state's legislature now openly identify themselves as party affiliated. Party precinct caucuses and conventions are better attended than ever before; issue discussion is more common at the party's gatherings; and a small but steady stream of political newcomers are constantly funneled into party politics. Both party organizations provide more services to party-endorsed candidates than ever before.

What accounts for this sharp departure from Minnesota's antiparty heritage? The last decade of party reform may be seen as resulting from a combination of four factors: elite-level support, occasional political crises, the state's activist strata, and Minnesota's peculiar political culture.

At the elite level, many of Minnesota's major politicos during the last few decades have fostered stronger parties. Harold Stassen and other reform-minded Republican leaders encouraged Republicans to work within the party. In the 1940s, Humphrey and others helped engineer the fusion of the Democratic and the Farmer-Labor parties.[14] During the late 1960s, McCarthy's antiwar candidacy brought thousands of peace supporters into the parties. Also, former Minneapolis Congressman Donald Fraser (of the McGovern-Fraser Commission) worked tirelessly to build stronger, open, and policy focused parties. Unlike many other state politicians elsewhere, Minnesota's most charismatic politicians have typically been strongly party oriented.[15]

Several of the political reforms discussed earlier resulted directly or indirectly from political events or crises. In 1972 and 1974, the DFL won an unprecedented control of statewide offices and of the state legislature. As Watergate cut deeply into Republican popularity and as several Minnesota corporations and individuals were implicated in the Nixon campaign's funding scandals, DFL legislative majorities passed a comprehensive state-level campaign finance reform bill. The bill limited campaign spending, required more careful reporting, established a state-level tax checkoff to subsidize statewide and legislative candidates, and permitted the parties to make substantial contributions to individual candidates.* DFL legislative

---

*Minnesota's state campaign finance law is ambivalent about the parties' role in elections. Minnesotans can check off $1 on their state income tax for a public finance subsidy fund and may even designate whether their contribution shall go to the DFL, to the IR, to a minor party, or into a general fund. The tax checkoff does not increase a taxpayer's liability or reduce his or her refund, and up to 25 percent of the state's taxpayers check off the fund.

majorities also imposed party labels for state legislative candidates and for mayor-council elections in the state's largest cities.

Minnesota's issue activists have demonstrated a continuing interest in taking their issues to the political parties. Feminists; pro- and antiabortion advocates; educators; farmers; organized labor; racial, sexual preference, and ethnic minorities; and others have all organized into issue caucuses within one or both parties and have sought to elect their spokespersons to party posts and influence party policy making. Unlike interest groups in many states, Minnesota's special interest groups have not eschewed party ties; rather, they have frequently organized to influence party decisions within the party setting. As a result, party politics and interest group politics in Minnesota have never been as removed as in some states. When interest groups and parties are at least loosely tied, interest group officials are apparently less likely to oppose some strong party reforms.

Finally, Minnesota's popular culture has been supportive and tolerant of several, but by no means all, strong party goals. For the last two decades, Minnesotans have overwhelmingly favored party labels on the ballot.[16] Also, voters agreed that the governor and lieutenant governor should be elected as a team.[17] Although Minnesotans are unwilling to abandon primaries for party conventions in candidate nominations, they do agree that the party endorsements exert a good influence on the nominations process.[18] Overall, Minnesota's culture is typically described as issue-oriented, reformist, purposive, and moralistic.[19] In that setting, many strong party reforms are easily accepted by the voters.

If a candidate accepts public financing and accompanying spending limits, then that candidate receives a fixed amount from the fund. Major state officeholders are eligible for funding on a fixed basis (divided among five top statewide offices). In state legislative districts, candidates receive funds as dictated by that district's taxpayers. Candidates who refuse public funding are not limited in their overall spending, although they are limited in the size of contributions from different sources.

State law does allow the party some role in supporting its candidates. A party can directly transfer up to one-half a candidate's allowable expenditure. A party may also help candidates by organizing phone banks on behalf of three or more candidates or by printing sample ballots. Of course, party leaders can also informally direct contributors to deserving campaigns. Both parties also provide a number of services for endorsed candidates, such as polling, campaign strategy, fund-raising advice, and so forth.

Leaders in both parties seem, on balance, satisfied with the regulations, although complaints are still heard. DFLers recognize that state taxpayers have favored the DFL by preferring them in the checkoff by a ratio of two or three to one. DFLers, however, complain that candidates should be forced to stay within spending limits or that if one candidate does not accept public funding and spending limits, then the other candidate should also be allowed to exceed the state spending limit. IRs often turn down the public funding and spending limits in key races, preferring to raise and spend more money—which they can raise more easily than the DFL.

PRACTICAL LIMITS OF PARTY RENEWAL

Within the last decade, Minnesota's strong party advocates have taken substantial steps toward reasserting the parties' role in state politics. Among the greatest advances are those involving elections. Minnesota parties today provide more services, and sometimes funds, for its endorsed candidates than ever before. For the first time in half a century, candidates for the state legislature and in the largest cities compete under party labels. For the first time in decades, state legislators openly caucus under party banners.

Organizationally, both state parties rely on the quasi-public/quasi-private caucus-convention system. Although the caucus-convention system has long since been stripped of its legal control over nominations—except in choosing national convention delegates—it still fosters several strong party goals. Most noticeably, the system recruits adults into activist political roles and provides a convenient forum in which issue-oriented amateurs may organize. Over the last decade, the neighborhood caucuses have channeled waves of popular protest and the demands of interest groups into the party organization.

Minnesota's parties and their activists, however, have been markedly less successful in achieving the more ambitious of responsible party reforms. To date, party activists have enjoyed no more success in dictating policy measures to party candidates or officeholders than have party activists elsewhere.

Why have Minnesota's parties and their activists been successful in achieving some goals but not in realizing others? Minnesota's experiences in returning to stronger, more active parties suggests at least five conditions conducive to strong party reforms.

First, responsible party reformers are most likely to succeed when their efforts are seen as assisting, but not coercing, the voters. Ballot designation and party-labeled legislative caucuses all can be defended as helping voters make an intelligent electoral choice. In Minnesota's purposive and reformist political culture, these goals win continued popular support.

Second, responsible party reformers are likely to succeed if they can tap popular outrage over corruption or when their efforts may be passed as antiboss or antimachine. The state's extensive campaign finance reforms, passed during the Watergate scandals, and which at least in part encourage party support of its candidates, illustrate this situation.[20]

Third, when strong party reformers present their efforts as allowing free discussion of issues, they gain support more readily. Open and accessible caucuses that provide a forum for discussing controversies or which serve as a sounding board for voters carry considerable appeal to Minnesotans.

Fourth, when property goals coincide with a dominant party's interests, these reforms are more likely to win acceptance. Ballot designation and partisan elections, again, were viewed by DFLers as favoring that party's candidates. Well-attended caucuses, too, aid both parties by drawing in potential volunteers, donors, and campaigners. Both parties are fully aware of that potential and encourage widespread attendance. Finally, when responsible party reforms are seen as saving taxpayer dollars or as preventing undesirable, unethical, or dishonest election tactics, reforms are more easily accepted. Retaining Minnesota's caucus-convention system instead of a presidential primary is often justified in terms of saving taxpayer dollars, preventing crossovers or "raiding" by opposition party voters, and preventing the "marketing" of presidential candidates via the mass media.

As modern-day reformers try to move beyond these conditions, however, they quickly run up against the self-interest of voters, candidates, and officeholders. Predictably, strong party reformers have made little progress here. In dictating clear and controversial issue stands, party activists conflict with the interests of candidates, who find those stands at best unappealing as election issues. Candidates who win nomination without party endorsement predictably show little sympathy for strongly worded platforms. Yet even endorsed candidates apparently feel free to disregard such planks in favor of more popular votegetting appeals. To date, the party endorsement process has been no guarantee that the party's candidates will run on the activists' stands.

Also, when strong party measures run against the self-perceived interests of voters or officeholders, those changes are unlikely to win acceptance. To many Minnesotans, especially rural residents, party registration smacks of coercion and restricts a voter's freedom to pick and choose among candidates. Not surprisingly, strong party enthusiasts hold out little chance of realizing that goal very soon. Party legislators may now caucus under party labels, but they still readily disregard the activists' positions when those stands run counter to the legislators' district pressures or personal views.

Not all strong party reforms depend on success in the legislature or on official party policies. Some party reform goals depend either on the realignment of interest groups and factions or on the changing nature of the electorate and party activists.

When interest groups win a party consensus for their goals, then the party system approximates party responsibility even if the parties do not formally impose discipline on their nominees and officeholders. In both Minnesota parties, at least a few issues exist on which party activists and the leadership are largely in agreement. This silent ideology unifies each party on a few goals even if the party unity is not complete and even if one party does not always clearly oppose the other's stance.[21] For example,

among DFLers, a broad consensus exists among its activists and officeholders in support of family farms, prolabor issues, liberal stands on the ERA,
and tax burden policies favoring the working class and senior citizens. A
similar consensus exists among IRs on tax burden policies favorable to
business, major corporations, and the middle or upper middle classes and
on opposition to liberal stances on abortion.

Admittedly, in neither party does a complete agreement on all these
goals exist or on the means by which to implement them. Yet, in neither
party would a candidate at the state level be likely to win party endorsement
or backing if he or she clearly opposed these key party positions. When a
candidate who is out of sorts with the party positions wins the nomination,
that insurgent is likely to be abandoned by the party faithful.

The changing nature of the electorate and of the party activists has also
linked party fortunes with the popularity of the top party leadership. When
party leaders are widely unpopular and perceived as erring by the electorate, the entire party ticket is likely to suffer. As a result, Minnesota's party
system is "responsible" in that the party's fortune is closely tied to that of its
most visible leaders.

Within the last decade, each party in Minnesota suffered an electoral
disaster. In 1974 and 1976, the Watergate revelations brought the national
GOP leadership into disrepute and discouraged and alienated thousands of
Minnesota Republicans. The party's fund raising fell off; strong candidates
shied away from the ticket; and the party's volunteers failed to work for the
party. As a result, the party suffered two disastrous elections, as the
resurgent DFL swept all but the Republican strongholds.

Later, the DFL, too, suffered serious losses in 1978. When both
Senator Hubert Humphrey and Senator Walter Mondale's Senate seats
became vacant, then-governor Wendell Anderson resigned to accept
appointment to a Senate seat. In the 1978 primary, the DFL's other
endorsed candidate, U.S. Representative Fraser, was upset by a conservative businessman who had openly courted crossovers in the primary.
Anderson's appointment fueled charges that the DFL was "office swapping"
and had grown arrogant and unresponsive. Fraser's loss meant that liberal
and moderate DFLers sat out the election or openly worked for the IR
Senatorial candidate. In the fall election, the DFL lost the governorship and
lieutenant governorship, both U.S. Senate seats, and large numbers of state
House districts.*

At least in major "swing" elections, then, the unpopularity of key party

---

*Interestingly, neither party's leaders viewed the 1978 outcome as a repudiation of DFL-
enacted liberal policies by the state's voters. Both parties' officials cited, instead, a number of
other reasons: the inability of major DFL officeholders to campaign effectively, the improved
appeal of IR statewide candidates, widespread charges that the DFL had grown arrogant and
aloof in office, the failure of DFL activists and liberals to work for the ticket after Fraser lost the

candidates or leaders has spelled doom for scores of party-labeled hopefuls. The process is admittedly indirect. As a national or state party leader grows unpopular, public opinion polls plummet. The party faithful decline to canvass or turn out party voters, and the party's ticket, from top to bottom, fares poorly in the election. Sometimes, the resulting changes in the legislature or city halls may even change the political ground rules—for example, by reapportioning seats, enacting public financing, or placing party labels on the ballot.

Ironically, the party activists and its lesser candidates may have little or no control over the unpopular party leader's actions. Minnesota Republicans had little influence at the Nixon White House. DFL party activists were at best unenthusiastic about Anderson's move to the Senate and about Robert Short's upset win in the primary. In both cases, though, the party's fortunes waned with those of its top leadership.

Silent ideology issues as well as the tie-in between top party leaders' popularity and the party's electoral welfare both suggest that political realities have also encouraged party responsibility within Minnesota parties. As well as the various political reforms over the last decade, these two factors have fostered at least a mild version of party responsibility in the state's two-party system.

On balance, Minnesota's last decade has been one of considerable renewal and strengthening of the party system. Strong party reformers have achieved many, albeit not all, of their goals. In so doing, they have overcome many of the Progressives' strictures against the parties. Without doubt, the state's two major parties are more open, active, and vibrant organizations than at any other time within this century. Both the successes and the failures of responsible party reformers in Minnesota may suggest important limits on, and possibilities for, party renewal elsewhere.

NOTES

1. For an original statement of the responsible party position, see the American Political Science Association, *Toward a More Responsible Two Party System* (New York: Rinehart, 1950). A more recent discussion is found in John Saloma and Frederick Sontag, *Parties—The Real Opportunity for Effective Citizen Politics* (New York: Random House, 1972).

2. See Frank J. Sorauf, *Party Politics in America* (Boston: Little, Brown, 1976), pp. 214–16. Minnesota is one of only seven states that still permit crossovers in party primaries; two other states also hold blanket primaries.

3. The Democratic-Farmer-Labor Party resulted from the merger of the Farmer-Labor Party and the Democratic Party in the 1940s. For a discussion on Minnesota's party heritage see Millard Gieske, "Minnesota in Midpassage: A Century of Transition in Political Culture," in

---

fall primary, and the perceived failure of DFL state legislative majorities to deal effectively with such issues as the domed stadium, capitol mall project, and with legislative pay raises and pensions.

Perspectives On Minnesota Government and Politics, ed. Millard Gieske and Edward Brandt (Dubuque, Iowa: Kendall/Hunt, 1977).

4. See *Minnesota Election Laws*, 1974, S.202.25, "Caucus Business."

5. A more extended discussion of this section is found in Thomas R. Marshall, "Party Responsibility Revisited: A Case of Policy Discussion at the Grass Roots," *Western Political Quarterly* 32 (March 1979): 70–78.

6. See, for example, Francis Carney, *The Rise of the Democratic Clubs in California* (New York: Holt, Rinehart and Winston, 1958), and James Q. Wilson, *The Amateur Democrat* (Chicago: University of Chicago Press, 1966).

7. See the *Minneapolis Tribune*, issues of June 19, 1976, p. B06; June 15, 1978, p. B20; June 19, 1978, p. A01; June 6, 1978, p. A08; June 25, 1978, p. A10; June 26, 1978, p. A01; and the *Minneapolis Star*, issues of June 19, 1976, p. B06; June 14, 1978, p. A24. In 1978, however, IR convention delegates rejected their party leaders' advice and voted to reinsert several "social issue" planks.

8. See Donald Leavitt, "Changing Rules, Norms and Procedures in the Minnesota Legislature," in Gieske and Brandt, eds., *Perspectives*, pp. 185–201, and Edward Brandt, "Legislative Voting Behavior in Minnesota," in ibid., pp. 202–22. Interviews with party officials in the IR and DFL also suggested these results.

9. These conclusions also generally agree with descriptions elsewhere, namely, that party activists have been unable to assert policy control through party clubs or conferences. See Carney, *Rise of Democratic Clubs*, pp. 18–19; Wilson, *Amateur Democrat*, pp. 292–301; and Leon Epstein, *Political Parties in Western Democracies* (New York: Praeger, 1967). Several party leaders did acknowledge, however, that the platforms could have a long-term effect in influencing attitudes of officeholders, candidates, and party leaders.

10. Sidney Verba and Norman Nie, *Participation in America* (New York: Harper & Row, 1972), p. 32.

11. *Perspectives*, pp. 113–15.

12. For a description of party politics in Minnesota's officially nonpartisan legislature, see Steven Seitz and L. Earl Shaw, "Partisanship in a Nonpartisan Legislature: Minnesota," in Gieske and Brandt, eds., *Perspectives*, pp. 177–84.

13. For an earlier discussion of DFL services for endorsed candidates, see Robert Agranoff, "The Role of Political Parties in the New Campaigning," in *The New Style in Election Campaigns*, ed. Robert Agranoff, 2d ed. (Boston: Holbrook Press, 1976), pp. 123–41.

14. See Gieske and Brandt, eds., *Perspectives*, pp. 44, 24–27.

15. For a longer description of Minnesota party leaders, see William Hathaway and Millard Gieske, "Minnesota Political Parties and Politics," in Gieske and Brandt, eds., *Perspectives*, pp. 103–21.

16. See the Minnesota Polls, issues no. 201, 219, 232, 263, 283, 303, 308, and 321. Unpublished Polls from the Archives of the Minnesota State Historical Society, St. Paul, Minnesota.

17. See the Minnesota Polls, issues no. 254, 294, 305, and 308.

18. See the Minnesota Poll, issue no. 253, and the Minneapolis *Tribune* poll, released in June 1974.

19. See Daniel Elazar, *American Federalism: A View from the States* (New York: Crowell, 1966), pp. 84–126, and Donald Leavitt and Bruce Nord, "Minnesota's Changing Political Culture," in Gieske and Brandt, eds., *Perspectives*, pp. 31–54.

20. For a longer discussion, see Charles Backstrom, "Ballots and Election Procedure in Minnesota," in Gieske and Brandt, eds., *Perspectives*, pp. 149–59.

21. For a discussion of the concept of silent ideology, see Sorauf, *Party Politics in America*, pp. 387–92.

10

MASSACHUSETTS: THE DEMOCRATIC PARTY CHARTER MOVEMENT

Jerome M. Mileur

*I*n the federal system of the United States, party renewal requires action on the state level as much as within the national organizations. Massachusetts Democrats have taken a series of steps in this direction over the past three years, among them the development of a charter for the state party. Inspired by the national party charter adopted in 1974, Bay State Democrats have been working to restructure their state and local committees as part of a general effort to revitalize the party. These efforts continue as this volume goes to press.

The culmination of the charter movement was a state convention on May 19, 1979, called to act on a proposed party charter. Preceding the convention were nearly two years of groundwork by a special commission, a series of public hearings, preparation of a preliminary draft and its revision after broad public discussion, and the election of delegates. The state convention acted affirmatively on the first five of nine articles in the proposed charter and then recessed until the fall for want of a quorum. The Massachusetts experience illustrates both the opportunities and the difficulties of state party renewal.

ORIGINS OF THE CHARTER MOVEMENT

In the half century since the presidential candidacy of Al Smith in 1928, Massachusetts politics have been transformed from one-party Republicanism to one-party Democracy. By 1971, Democrats commanded two-thirds of the state's congressional delegation, better than two-thirds of both houses of the state legislature, and even greater majorities in the major cities of the commonwealth. Yet, the party had just lost the governorship for the fourth time in ten years, after a divisive primary in which the candidate endorsed by the party convention, State Senate President Maurice Donohue, was beaten by the candidate he had defeated in convention, Boston Mayor Kevin White. Democratic leaders in the state legislature, frustrated by the party's gubernatorial failures in the 1960s, fingered the endorsing convention as the culprit and, in 1972, overrode a Republican governor's veto to repeal statutory authorization for the convention.[1]

The charter movement arose against this backdrop, growing out of a more general initiative toward party revitalization that began in the late spring of 1976. The state committee had been moribund in the 1970s. Deeply in debt, it had no staff, no telephone, and provided no services to either candidates or local committees. Its offices were used for storage and little else. Local committees were also largely dormant, though pockets of activism could be found most often in the larger towns outside the major cities. With the elimination of the state convention, most local committees saw little reason for their existence.*

The initiative to revive the party came from two young, relatively liberal political activists, John Eller and Joseph Krzys, who had worked together on campaigns and come to agree on the need for a stronger party. Eller, administrative assistant to the speaker of the Massachusetts House for seven years, was frustrated by the lack of connection between the "party in convention" and the "way laws are written," which he felt fed popular suspicion of state government and contributed to the decline of public confidence in it. He believed that a different structure was necessary to give people more effective access to government and saw parties as the "only pot mixed up enough to represent the 'street'."[2] Krzys, who headed a small educational consulting firm and had been active in community organizations as well as political campaigns, believed in the virtues of a strong two-party system and was generally disgusted with the campaign dealing of candidates and special interests.[3]

Neither Eller nor Krzys had preconceived notions of what specifically should be done to revitalize the party, but they met with then-State Chairman Charles Flaherty to propose that meetings be called with local committee chairpersons around the state to ask what they wanted the party

---

*Massachusetts law provides for two levels of party organization: statewide (the state committee) and local (town and ward committees). Ward committees in a given municipality comprise the city committee, but the latter has no independent authority or jurisdiction. State law makes no provision for an intermediate level of party organization, but some counties, especially in western Massachusetts, have active party committees.

to be and how they wanted to be "plugged into" the policy process.[4] Flaherty was a state representative who aspired to higher office but who had gotten lost in the personality mazes of one-party politics. Moreover, his leadership of the party was being challenged by then-Governor Michael Dukakis, who was pressuring him to resign the chairmanship. For Flaherty, there was nothing to lose and possibly something to gain from agreeing to the proposal. He did, and on September 19, 1976, the first meeting was held at Mt. Holyoke College in western Massachusetts. Nine others followed by the end of November, covering all counties in the commonwealth.

The meetings evoked a good deal of anger from local Democrats, who decried and deplored the indifference to their interests of both the State Committee and the state political system. Complaints ranged from the meaninglessness of being a Democrat to the handling of patronage. The meetings, however, produced more than anger. They also yielded a 12-point state committee "action plan" for revitalizing the party and a call for a state issues convention in June 1977. The action plan covered a broad range of organizational issues: communications, leadership, discipline, finances, committee functions and responsibilities, intraparty relations, conventions, and more.[5] Local committees were asked to react to the plan at a second round of eight hearings held in the first two months of 1977. These generated many of the same complaints but less anger and more constructive suggestions for change.

The idea for an issues convention responded both to repeated complaints from local Democrats that abolition of the preprimary endorsing convention was the principal cause of "rot" in the party's grass roots and to the belief that, as a witness at one hearing put it, "people who are Democrats have the right to expect that they'll have something to say about what their party and its officials do."[6] In proposing the convention, Jerome Grossman, a Democratic national committeeman and a leader among the state's "new politics" liberals, argued that

> democrats need and want a vehicle whereby they can organize themselves around issues to make sure that candidates understand what the grass root Democrats are feeling and thinking. A platform convention would help Democrats to express themselves on the issues, would be a natural vehicle for the revival of activities at the local committee level, would bring together Democrats from all over the state, would help to unify the party, [and] would give direction to potential candidates for state-wide office.[7]

Plans for the convention called for delegates to act on ten issues selected by local party committees, with platform planks developed from resolutions adopted by local committees.

In late February 1977, the Democratic state committee formally approved both the action plan and the call for an issues convention. By this time, the committee was showing signs of a new vitality: it had employed a staff director and was publishing an occasional newsletter. Moreover, its chairman, Flaherty, was being mentioned regularly as a possible candidate for statewide office in 1978. In addition, the revitalization initiative had attracted a third activist, Patrick Halley, a legislative staffer and former employee of the State Committee, who saw the party as potentially a countervailing force against the media and special interest dominance of state politics.[8]

Two subcommittees of the state committee, both of which included local party members, were appointed to plan the issues convention, one to draft proposed platform planks and the other to develop resolutions on party structure. The latter, chaired by the state committee vice-chairman Richard Driscoll, called a third round of hearings with local Democrats, holding 11 meetings in a two-week period in late April and early May 1977. These were followed by a meeting in late May, at the University of Massachusetts in Amherst, to draft resolutions on party structure. The major problem was how to handle the question of an endorsing convention, which local Democrats generally wanted but about which the party's elected officials had reservations—the more so because 1978 was an election year for all of them.* A secondary problem was the large number of specific but relatively minor recommendations for structural change made by local Democrats, which could not be dismissed but were too numerous to handle as separate resolutions. The idea for a charter commission, similar to that at the national level, emerged at this meeting and won approval because it bought time on the convention question and permitted the assimilation of structural details into a larger reorganization plan. The subcommittee thereupon adopted an "eleventh issue" for presentation to the issues convention, calling for a commission to draft a party charter and directing the commission to address certain questions.[9]

The issues convention approved the proposal for a charter commission, the membership of which Flaherty named shortly before resigning as state party chairman in September 1977. The commission consisted of 25 persons—a man and woman from each of the state's mainland counties, plus a third from Suffolk (Boston). The eleventh had set the size of the commission and also required that its membership have

> appropriate geographical representation, affirmative action representa-
> tion, labor representation, State, City, Ward and Town committee

---

*Every state and national officeholder in Massachusetts, executive and legislative, except U.S. Senator Edward Kennedy, was up for reelection in 1978.

representation and limited representation from elected officials with no more than three members being salaried, selected officials.[10]

Members of the commission, for the most part, were local party activists, who represented no particular interests or constituencies within the state or party. One-fourth of them had been members of the state committee's Subcommittee on Party Structure, including the commission chairman Richard Driscoll, who had chaired the subcommittee and brought determined leadership to the commission.* Members differed in philosophy but were united in the desire for a more effective party. The draft charter reflects the local and strong party orientations of the commissioners.

THE DRAFT CHARTER

The organizational meetings of the Charter Commission set the tenor and direction of its work. First, the commission defined its job broadly as that of drawing a charter for the state party similar in conception to that of the national party. The mandate given the commission directed it to consider certain specific questions, but this was not construed as a limitation on its assignment. The commission also agreed that significant changes were required to achieve a truly effective party structure and that the goal should be to frame the best charter possible, unconstrained by existing state statutes and party by-laws. Political "realities" dogged this decision but never overwhelmed it.

These decisions, combined with the local and strong party values of commission members, guided the writing of the charter. They focused commission attention on three general and related goals: a more open and representative party, a more active and purposeful party, and a more effective and accountable party. The means to these ends were generally seen as broadening participation in party affairs, trying the state committee organizationally to the local committees, and reestablishing a party role on issues and in nominations.

Party Conventions

The charter restored the preprimary endorsing convention that was

---

*Driscoll assembled a staff of 15 volunteers, about half of whom had been members of the subcommittee on party structure, including the staff director, Joseph Krzys, who, with John Eller, had originally urged Flaherty to take the revitalization initiative. The staff provided strong support in planning agenda and organizing materials for commission meetings, in recording and summarizing testimony at hearings and feedback on drafts of the charter, and in advising the commission on the legal and political implications of its decisions. They also reinforced the local and strong party orientation of commission members.

abolished in 1972 by a Democrat-controlled state legislature. Local Democrats repeatedly attributed the deterioration of town and ward committees to the elimination of state conventions. An architect of that action, former Speaker of the state House of Representatives David Bartley, called it "a mistake."[11] The commission vote to restore the endorsing convention was nearly unanimous, but commissioners did not want simply to reinstate the old convention system, because there had been problems with it and because it was tainted with failure and rejection. A return to an endorsing convention required statutory changes in primary election laws. A fresh analysis and a new system seemed politically more practicable.

The commission was not opposed to primaries, which were generally regarded as a wholesome check on the party. But it was agreed that the party should have control over—or at least a voice in—who ran for office in its name, that is, over who had access to the primary ballot. A survey of state laws and party practices led commissioners to support a "challenge primary" system modeled after that of Connecticut. The charter requires a candidate to obtain a majority vote of the state convention to win endorsement for office and provides that any candidate who receives at least 20 percent of the convention vote on any ballot for a particular office may challenge the endorsee in the state primary. No one may obtain access to the party's primary ballot in any other way. Unlike Connecticut, but like the earlier Massachusetts system, the preprimary convention would be concerned only with statewide executive offices and U.S. senator.

In addition to the endorsing convention, the charter provides for an issues convention to be held biennially in odd-numbered years (endorsing conventions would meet in even-numbered years). The issues convention was intended to serve two closely related purposes: to maintain activity in town and ward committees between endorsing conventions and to give rank-and-file Democrats a voice in the public policy directions of their party. Following the precedent of the 1977 state issues convention, the charter requires that the development of resolutions for the convention begin with caucuses of local Democrats. It also directs the convention to adopt an "agenda" for action rather than a platform, because commissioners felt that conventions could better give direction as to priorities than on the substance of public policy.

The charter also requires that the delegate allocation formula for both endorsing and issues conventions be based on the one-Democrat, one-vote principle, which is a departure from earlier practices. Commissioners were persuaded that earlier allocation formulas, which generally underrepresented the more populous and active suburban communities and overrepresented small and ordinarily Republican towns, were a major factor in the party's gubernatorial frustrations in the 1960s. The charter further requires that the delegate allocation formula give equal weight to party registration and average vote in the last general election for the party's presidential and gubernatorial candidates. This provision sought to treat both city and suburban areas fairly: the former tend to have high Democratic registration and low turnout and the latter the reverse. Finally, the charter sets standards for openness, outreach, and publicity in the process for selection of convention delegates.

Party Committees

By law, members of local and state committees are presently elected for four-year terms at the state's presidential primary. Local committees consist of from three to 35 members, depending on local option, who run as a slate. The state committee consists of 80 popularly elected members and ten affirmative action members, who run as individuals. Almost every aspect of party organization was faulted at party hearings both before and after the Charter Commission was created. The state committee was indicted as unrepresentative, unresponsive, and unable to muster a quorum for most of its meetings. Local committees were charged with being full of "deadwood" and inactive in most places most of the time. An unsuccessful candidate for Congress put it more strongly, telling the commission that there is "almost no real Democratic Party organization in this state at the local level."[12]

Five of the seven substantive articles in the proposed charter deal exclusively with party committees and address almost all of the complaints heard by the commission. The charter shortens the term of office for state committee members from four to two years, changes the basis of their selection, and enlarges the committee from 80 to 160 elected members.* It also shortens the terms for officers of local committees from four to two years and outlaws slate voting; however, it does not alter the time and term of local committee election. Finally, it provides for the removal of state and local committee members for specific cause, with causes specified that range from nonattendance at meetings through public disloyalty to party candidates to conviction for a crime.

For the commission, the critical organizational decision—and one it regarded as among the two or three most important features of the proposed charter—was a change in the basis of state committee selection. The election of both state and local committees at the presidential primary has resulted in the two levels of party organization being politically inde-

---

*In addition to the 160 elected members, the charter provides for a number of ex-officio members (Democrats holding state executive office, party legislative leaders, members of Congress, and national committee delegates) and also for affirmative action members not to exceed 10 percent of the total membership.

pendent of one another. There has been no internal political dependency and, thus, no internal party accountability. The charter provides that members of the state committee will be elected directly by members of town and ward committees.

The commission, with one abstention, was unanimous in its support for this change, but it encountered problems with two related operational questions. The first was the district from which to elect state committee members. They are presently chosen from state Senate districts, and initially, this was not changed. However, technical problems arose from the fact that some state Senate districts in cities follow precinct lines, while the smallest unit of party organization is the ward, and ward committees may not have members from all precincts within their jurisdictions. The commission shifted briefly to election from counties and, then, to congressional districts. But local committees objected to the later, and in the end, the commission returned to the state Senate district as the best choice, voting that each of the 40 should elect two men and two women to the state committee.

The other operational question involved how local committees would vote for state committee members. Two values collided: a belief in the one-Democrat, one-vote principle and a desire to involve all town and ward committee members in the selection of state committee members. A weighted vote seemed the solution, but doubts arose about a fair count if town and ward committees voted individually. In some Senate districts, moreover, assembling all local committee members in one place meant a caucus larger than a state convention. In the end, the commission approved language that left this operational question to the state committee.

Participation

The question of participation in party affairs caused the commission more difficulty than any other. There was general agreement on the need for a more active and broadly based party but disagreement on how best to achieve it. The sharpest division occurred with respect to who should vote at the local level for delegates to state conventions and members of the state committee. One group of commissioners pressed for an open caucus system, in which all enrolled Democrats would be eligible to participate, arguing that frequent and extensive involvement of party identifiers would create greater interest in the party and make it more responsive to general rank-and-file interests. Another group urged a closed committee system, in which only elected members of local party committees would be eligible to vote for both convention delegates and state committee members, arguing that this would give greater meaning to membership on town and ward committees and, thereby, strengthen the party at that level. There were some ideological overtones to this division, as liberals tended more toward the first position and conservatives toward the second.

In the end, a compromise was achieved that gave each side part of what it regarded as an essential principle in revitalizing the party. It was agreed to use the caucus method to elect delegates to both the issues and endorsing conventions, and the committee method to elect members of the state committee. Four arguments won approval for the caucus system: (1) it promised to correct abuses that had occurred in delegate selections to earlier party conventions when the committee method had been used; (2) it would create greater interest in the party to open delegate selection to all local Democrats; (3) it encouraged members of town and ward committees to stay active and abreast of local concerns to avoid insurgency; and (4) it gave local committees power to call and conduct the caucuses and, thus, a certain advantage in the process. Two arguments carried the committee system: it gave local committees an important function and, therefore, a reason for being; and accountability within the party should be between permanent *units* of party organization—between state and local committees—and not between the state committee and a momentary local electorate.

This compromise, which came relatively early in commission deliberations, had positive effects on subsequent debates. It submerged ideological differences between members, created a "win some, lose some" atmosphere in which no one lost face, and kept attention focused on the ultimate goal of strengthening the party. This spirit pervaded all aspects of the commission's work except the drafting of an affirmative action article.

The commission devoted more time to affirmative action than to any other aspect of the charter. Unlike other questions, lines of difference on this issue were vague. There was general agreement on the need for affirmative action, but disagreement as to the proper approach. Some members believed a strong outreach program that encouraged broader participation in the party was sufficient; others wanted specific target group representation on party committees at all levels. The latter also desired performance tests, goals rather than quotas, but the commission decision to abolish slate making in the election of local committees made enforcement of any tests problematical at best. An article was eventually drawn that identified target groups and required both state and local committees to establish affirmative action committees and procedures to encourage a representative diversity of membership.

Some local committees objected that this "solution" in fact mandated quotas, which were specifically disavowed in the national charter and, therefore, they argued, impermissible or at least inadvisable in a state charter. The commission reacted to the criticism by adopting language, parallel to that in the national charter, disclaiming that anything in the affirmative action article implied quotas. This prompted one member of the commission to resign—a black woman—whose primary interest was in the affirmative action aspect of the charter and who would not compromise on the issue.

THE POLITICS OF PASSAGE

The strategy for charter adoption followed logically from the origins of the movement and the orientations of commission members. Commissioners agreed early that, politically, their success depended on support from the party's grass roots. The movement had gotten its impetus there; the constituency for change was there; and the hope for ratification lay in organizing and mobilizing a procharter constituency among town and ward committee members across the state. The decision to begin commission work with a series of six hearings spread geographically around the commonwealth reflected this strategy, for it was aimed in part at involving local Democrats with the commission. Moreover, commission deliberations were colored continually by the desire to ensure the support of local Democrats for the charter.

Democrats in elective office—state legislators, executive officers, and members of Congress—seemed an unlikely constituency for party revival. Many were on record as opposing an endorsing convention. All, of course, knew how to win in a weak-party system, so any change posed a potential threat to their tenure. At the very least, a delicate logic was required to persuade successful politicians of the urgent need for sweeping change in a system that had worked well enough to produce *them.** Commission strategy aimed at not offending unnecessarily the "party-in-government," especially state legislative leaders, whose support would be instrumental in winning the statutory changes needed to implement major provisions of the charter. No systematic effort was made to enlist active support for the charter among Democrats in state and national offices, and for the most part, they were indifferent to the movement.†

The Democratic State Committee was expected to be cool toward the charter, which made basic changes in its nature and composition. Many state committee members did object to these changes, especially that which altered the method of their election. Commissioners generally discounted

---

*The same was not true for Democrats in local elective office, who could see themselves as beneficiaries of change and, in general, were part of the grass-roots support cultivated by the commission.

†As an afterthought, the commission scheduled a seventh hearing at the start of its work for the state House so that state legislators and executive officers might give testimony. No one came, though several submitted written statements.

these objections because members of the state committee, like themselves, represented no real constituencies within the party and, unlike themselves, were not likely to cultivate rank-and-file support for their position. At the same time, the commission did not ignore these objections, because the state committee had the power to call (or not call) the convention to act on the charter. Members of the commission therefore met regularly with the state committee to discuss charter provisions, but the general aim was to neutralize objections through fair play rather than accommodation. Few changes in the charter resulted from these meetings.* Moreover, support for the charter by key members of the state committee, principally its chairman, Chester Atkins, who had replaced Flaherty, reinforced commission strategy.

In its call for a convention, the state committee did affect charter ratification in a way and for reasons not anticipated by the commission. It adopted a two-thirds rule for ratification of each article of the charter and, also, for ratification of the full charter, which, in effect, meant that each article had to be voted twice and both times obtain a supramajority. In addition, state committee rules for the convention defined a quorum as a minimum of 700 delegates or 50 percent of those registering for the convention, whichever figure was higher. The explanation for these rules was that since implementation of major charter provisions required legislative action, it was politically desirable to approach the legislature with a document that had been approved by a substantial proportion of convention delegates and not merely a simple majority.

Members of the commission saw these rules as a serious threat to ratification of the charter, imposing a kind of double jeopardy played in the presence of a time bomb. First and foremost, commissioners feared that those who lost on one article would unite with those who lost on other articles to muster the one-third plus one vote against final passage of the charter (which would defeat as a whole that which they could not defeat separately). Second, commissioners feared that delegates would depart the convention as the session wore on, leaving it without the quorum to act— even though possibly all of the individual articles had been adopted and two-thirds of those remaining in favor of final passage. At the convention, members of the commission worked to change the state committee rules from two-thirds to a majority requirement for ratification of the charter, but failed—getting 55 percent of the vote, falling 161 votes short of the necessary two-thirds.[13]

---

*The commission did drop a provision for an executive committee of the state committee as a direct result of these meetings and also lowered plans to enlarge the size of the state committee from 250 to 160 (instead of the present 80 elected members), in part to accommodate state committee objections but more to accommodate those of local Democrats.

In addition to divisions between local and state committee Democrats and between the party's rank and file and its elected officials, there was a division based on geography. During the several rounds of hearings that preceded the charter convention, both the party revitalization initiative and the charter movement seemed to evoke strongest support in areas most removed from the city of Boston.[14] This division materialized dramatically at the convention, as delegates from the six westernmost state Senate districts cast 93 percent of their votes in favor of one key charter provision, while 71 percent of the delegates from the five Boston Senate districts voted in opposition.[15]

The geographic distribution of charter support also reflected the places of residence of the most active commission members. Eight of the 25 commissioners came from western Massachusetts, the area of strongest support, and all were regular participants in its work. The area south of Boston, the second most supportive of the charter, had four commission members, three of whom were very active, including the chairman, while that to the north of Boston, the third most supportive area, had two commissioners, both active. On the other hand, Boston had three commissioners, one of whom resigned and another who rarely attended meetings. The state's central area, which was next least supportive of the charter, had two commission members, one of whom was active for a time and then dropped out.

Finally, the distribution of charter support was affected by a mix of ideology and events. Following the compromise on the role of local committees in selecting state committee and state convention delegates, liberalism and conservatism played little part in drafting the charter. Commissioners were agreed on the need for a stronger party, drew a charter to that end, and anticipated support and opposition in those terms. But the 1978 state elections intervened to cause many liberals to oppose what they called a "loyalty oath" in the charter. The provision in question required members of party committees at all levels not to oppose party nominees publicly and gave those committees the power to discipline members who did. Many party liberals had opposed the Democratic nominee for governor in 1978, Edward King, who had defeated incumbent Michael Dukakis for the nomination. Some liberals organized committees of Democrats to support King's Republican opponent. Many of them also had supported the Republican candidate for the U.S. Senate, Edward Brooke, though seemingly more for coalitional than ideological reasons.

These liberals formed a "progressive caucus" to fight the loyalty oath in the name of individuality, freedom of conscience, and maintaining diversity within the party.[16] They argued that the charter bound members of party committees to accept party nominees but did not bind nominees to accept the party platform. Members of the commission and other proponents of the discipline provision argued that it did not require committee members to *support* a party nominee, only to refrain from public opposition, and that the decision to discipline was left with individual committees where it required a two-thirds vote. The progressive caucus challenged the provision early, failed to overturn it, but got 45 percent of the convention vote in their losing effort, which, while not enough to amend the article containing the loyalty oath provision, was enough to defeat the article on final passage.

The article, however, was not lost but, rather, was adopted by a three-fourths vote of the convention. More than 150 delegates who opposed the loyalty oath provision switched to support adoption of the article as a whole.[17] The vote was interpreted by many commissioners as evidence that the great majority of delegates would support the goal of a stronger party despite objections to particular provisions in the charter, but the convention recessed before the theory could be put to the tough test of reinstating the preprimary endorsing convention.

CONCLUSION

Newspaper assessments of the convention were generally favorable. One columnist observed that a "start was made" toward a more definable Democratic Party, adding:

> For one thing, the convention adopted more than half of the articles on its agenda. . . . For another thing, the delegates were serious about codifying their party's structure and goals. They may have been divided between old-liners and liberals, but a vast majority was there . . . to come up with a party charter.[18]

The Boston *Globe*, editorializing on the loyalty oath issue and the defeat of the progressive caucus, noted that ideologically, "Party discipline works both ways," and added:

> If the major political parties are to halt their organizational decline and become coherent entities, which they are not at present in Massachusetts, they need a structure for maintaining some kind of internal discipline. In Springfield, the Democrats went about as far as they could go.[19]

At the time of recess, the convention had approved all of the charter articles pertaining to the organization of party committees. Fifty-two amendments to the proposed charter had been considered and 27 of them adopted, but none made a major change in commission recommendations. For the most part, the changes reflected the dominance of town and ward committee interests at the convention. Delegates restored powers to local committees, rejecting a provision to abolish slate making, and weakened those of the state committee, denying it the powers to establish and enforce minimum by-laws for local committees and to monitor the activities of local committees with respect to support for the party's nominees and platform. At the same time, they strengthened significantly the powers of a proposed state party judicial council, authorizing it to "take whatever action necessary" against "anybody or officer of the Party" to enforce the charter.[20]

The commission's grass-roots approach appears to have worked, and therein lies several lessons. First, there is no natural constituency for party renewal. Elected officials have little incentive to change the rules by which they have succeeded. Democratic reformers are usually more attracted to the devices of direct citizen participation than to the building of parties and political infrastructure. Journalists tend to equate parties with politics, not democracy, and to treat them as institutions of self-interest rather than of the public good. Among voters, even the strongly partisan, party renewal must compete for attention and interest with many other issues and with candidate loyalties. A constituency for change must therefore be created, and it must be built of the conventional materials of politics: principle, self-interest, opportunity, and will. But, typically, it lacks one of those materials: power—for as the state party chairman Chester Atkins warned the commission, "Nobody's going to get beaten on this issue."

Second, there is no one best strategy for party renewal. Strategies must be suited to particular situations. Commission strategy was shaped by the circumstances, personalities, and structure of politics and parties in Massachusetts at a particular point in time, as well as by the political history and culture of the state. Moreover, strategies are defined primarily by weakness, not strength. The commission turned to itself and to local Democrats not because either had power but because they were the only resources available to support basic changes in party structure. Finally, the best strategy is that which requires no major adjustments over time. Commission strategy had the advantage that from the inception of the party revitalization initiative through the charter convention, appeals were made to the same constituency—town and ward committees—in the interest of the same goal—strengthening the party.

That the commission approach has worked so far does not mean it will succeed in the end. The two-thirds rule continues to imperil passage of the charter. The five articles adopted in the first session of the convention must of course be voted on again at the next session. The convention recessed before acting on the question of a preprimary endorsing convention, which was expected to be the most controversial provision in the charter. It did, however, take one vote on the question, rejecting an amendment to delete charter language empowering the state convention to make endorsements.

The division seemed much the same as that on the loyalty oath question—the vote splitting the same, 55 to 45 percent, and the coalitions being similar, with the progressive caucus again in the minority. But fewer than half the delegates voted, and the issue may be of such importance and intensity that few opponents will switch, as they did on the loyalty oath, to support a convention article that provides for preprimary endorsement.

Beyond the convention lies the state legislature, where the commission's grass-roots effort may fail amid the congestion of many other issues. The final lesson, and perhaps the most important one, is that the legal context for party renewal at the state level is far more complex than at the national, because almost all party and election law is state law. There were no statutory impediments at the federal level to implementation of the national party charter: it went into effect upon approval by the charter convention. State party charter commissions, however, if successful in convention, will almost certainly be faced with the need for statutory change to implement their plans. The commission in Massachusetts has taken a "one step at a time" attitude toward this reality, concerning itself first with convention ratification. But that, however, one commissioner observed, "only gets us in the front door."

ADDENDUM

Massachusetts Democrats adopted their first state party charter on November 17, 1979, when the Charter Convention, adjourned in May, was reconvened at Holy Cross College in Worcester. The major fight, as expected, came on the question of a pre-primary endorsing convention. Convention opponents reminded delegates that a Democratic legislature had abolished an earlier convention system because it had divided the party and been beneficial only to Republicans. They argued also that a convention system was less democratic than a direct primary because it narrowed participation in party affairs and gave greater power to elites.

Proponents insisted that the Charter called for a significantly different, more open convention system than that previously used and that prior experience was therefore no guide. They argued that the proposed system would strengthen the party role in the nominating process and that a stronger party was needed to blunt the growing political influence of public relations firms and single-interest groups. They contended too that a convention system would produce more representative government, more effective government, and therefore better government.

The convention article barely achieved the two-thirds margin required for adoption, passing 562–270. A switch of eight votes would have reversed the outcome. The three remaining articles of the charter were adopted without controversy, and final ratification of the entire charter was by a surprisingly easy five-to-one margin, 609–123.

Approval of the endorsing convention and of the charter itself was facilitated by a compromise reached between the Charter Commission and leaders of the "Progressive Caucus" prior to the resumption of the convention. The commission agreed to an amendment of the so-called loyalty oath that tied candidates to the party platform and to a reduction from 20 to 15 percent in the convention vote required for a primary challenge of the party-endorsed candidate. In return, a number of caucus leaders agreed to support both the convention article and the charter. Not all caucus leaders agreed to the compromise, but it effectively split their ranks and was probably decisive in passage of the convention article.

Ratification of the charter shifts the movement for party reform to the state legislature, which must re-write a number of state election laws if charter provisions are to be fully implemented. The pre-primary endorsing convention is again likely to be the most controversial issue. State Representative Barney Frank, a leader of the Progressive Caucus who was not a party to the compromise with the commission, foresees legislative failure for the convention proposal, saying it will "never pass" because the "leadership is against it." But Senate Majority Leader Daniel Foley disagrees, saying that he would support it and that "the convention's vote on this issue will have some very strong influence on the legislative vote."[21] The commission itself, though its mandate expired with the Charter Convention, plans to file legislation to implement the charter and may try to reconstitute and broaden its membership to become a lobby for the charter and other election reforms aimed at strengthening the state's political parties.

NOTES

1. For a general history of Massachusetts politics, see Alec Barbrook, *God Save the Commonwealth* (Amherst: University of Massachusetts Press, 1973). For accounts of Democratic Party frustrations in the 1960s, see Edgar Litt, *The Political Cultures of Massachusetts* (Cambridge, Mass.: MIT Press, 1965), and David B. Mayhew, "Massachusetts: Split-Level Bipartyism," *Party Politics in the New England States*, ed. George Goodwin, Jr., and Victoria Schuck (Durham, N.H.: New England Center for Continuing Education, 1968).

2. Interview with John Eller, August 3, 1979.

3. Interview with Joseph Krzys, August 3, 1979.

4. Interview with John Eller, May 19, 1979.

5. *The Massachusetts Democrat* (January/February 1977): 1, 2.

6. Minutes of Public Hearings, 1977, Massachusetts Democratic State Committee, Boston (in the files of the committee).

7. Memorandum from Jerome Grossman to members of the Democratic State Committee, November 15, 1976 (in the files of the state committee).

8. Interview with Patrick Halley, August 3, 1979. Halley was administrative assistant to State Senator Chester Atkins, who was to succeed Flaherty as state party chairperson.

9. *The Massachusetts Democrat* vol. 2, no. 2 (June/July 1977): 1, 3.

10. Minutes of the State Issues Convention, Massachusetts Democratic State Committee, Boston, June 11, 1977 (in the files of the committee).

11. Notes, Massachusetts Democratic State Committee Meeting, Northampton, March 1977.

12. Minutes of Public Hearing, Massachusetts Democratic Charter Commission, Northampton, November 12, 1977 (in the files of the commission). The candidate noted that only 14 of the 88 town and city committees in his district gave any financial help and that only ten others met with and endorsed him.

13. Minutes of the Charter Convention, Massachusetts Democratic State Committee, Boston, May 19, 1979 (in the files of the committee).

14. Interview with Krzys, August 3, 1976.

15. The key vote was on passage of Article II of the charter, which was vigorously contested. Minutes of the Charter Convention, Massachusetts Democratic State Committee, Boston, May 19, 1979.

16. Boston *Globe*, May 17, 1979, p. 27.

17. Minutes of the Charter Convention, Massachusetts Democratic State Committee, Boston, May 19, 1979.

18. Glenn A. Briere, Springfield *Morning Union*, May 23, 1979, p. 17.

19. Boston *Globe*, May 23, 1979, p. 18.

20. Minutes of the Charter Convention, Massachusetts Democratic State Committee, Boston, May 19, 1979.

21. Boston *Sunday Globe*, November 18, 1979, page 33.

11

THE PRESIDENCY AND THE PARTIES

Thomas E. Cronin

*I*t is frequently said that the president is the leader of his political party. In fact, however, a president has no formal position in the party structure. In theory, the supreme authority in our parties is the national presidential convention. More directly in charge of the national party, at least on paper, is the national committee (and each national committee has a national chairperson).

In practice, successful presidents usually control their national committees and, often, their national conventions as well. Although the national committee picks the national party chairman, a president almost always lets the committee know whom he wants. Modern presidents hire and fire national party staff almost at will. Several of our recent presidents have ignored their national party committees. Some have treated them with contempt.

Political parties once were a prime source of influence for a president. It used to be said, for example, that our most effective presidents were effective in large part because they had made use of party support and took seriously their party leadership responsibilities. But as our parties have declined in organizational importance, there has been more of an incentive for presidents to "rise above" party.

Today, the presidential-party relationship is strained. National party chairpersons come and go with embarrassing regularity and regular embarrassment. Between 1967 and 1978, for example, there were a total of eight Democratic and six Republican national chairpersons. Few party chairpersons of the president's party have enjoyed much influence. Many were regarded at the White House as little more than clerks.

The central concern in this chapter is the awkward alliance between presidents and their parties. Both president and party need each other. Yet both often become frustrated and even annoyed with the other. What has been the role of the president as party leader? What of the presidents' use of party as an appeal to Congress for support of their programs? Why the apparent growing divorce between presidents and their parties? What are the limits on presidents as party leaders and the limits of the party as a check on presidents? Could something be done to encourage more cohesion between presidents and parties? These are the questions under consideration.

PRESIDENTS AS PARTY LEADER?

Our earliest presidents vigorously opposed the development of political parties. They viewed them as factions and divisive—something to be dreaded as the greatest political evil. By 1800, however, the contest for the presidency had become a battle between political parties. The Jefferson-led Republicans took on and defeated the John Adams-led Federalists. But even Jefferson, sometimes called the founder of what later became the Democratic Party, had doubts about party contests for the presidency. He disliked the Federalist Party and their narrow, elitist constituency. He hoped the Federalist Party would shrivel and collapse, thus allowing the more representative Republicans to remain in permanent control. Jefferson's party was in fact dominant for two generations.

Parties just naturally arose. Out-of-power interests coalesced to put their own candidates in contention for the presidency. Party clashes became routine. The evolution of political parties had much to do with the successful functioning of both the presidency and the Constitution. They solved in part the problem of presidential recruitment. They served also as a means of checking presidents, of keeping them responsive to concerned grass-roots citizens, for to remain in office a president would have to win renomination from his political party.

As they evolved, parties helped narrow down the number of candidates, prepared platforms, and creatively mediated among the diverse interests that were pressing claims and pushing ideological views on future officeholders. Parties usually were able to find the common middle ground among more or less hostile groups so that agreement could be reached on general principles.

Moreover, the parties enabled officeholders to overcome some of the limitations of our formal constitutional arrangements. Political parties facilitated coordination among the branches. President Jackson especially used his resources to promote partisan control of government. Jackson's achievements as party leader transformed the office, so much so that he is often called the "first modern president."

> The President became both the head of the executive branch and leader of the party. The first six Presidents usually acted in a manner that accorded Congress an equality of power. However, starting with Andrew Jackson the President began more and more to assert his role not simply as head of the executive branch but as leader of the government. By the skillful use of his position as head of the party he persuaded Congress to follow his lead, thereby allowing him to assume greater control of the government and to direct and dominate public affairs.[1]

Many historians and political scientists hold that the effective presidents have been those who have, like Jackson, strengthened their position by becoming strong party leaders. Cooperation and achievement could be achieved through party alliances. "Since the office did not come equipped with the necessary powers under the Constitution, they had to be added through a historical process by the forceful action of vigorous Presidents whose position was strengthened by the rise and development of political parties."[2]

Few presidents have been able to duplicate Jackson's success. Most have found it exceedingly difficult to serve as an activist party builder and party leader while trying to serve also as chief of state and national unifier. President William Taft lamented that the longer he was president, "the less of a party man I seem to become."[3] President William Howard McKinley said he could no longer be president of a party for "I am now President of the whole people."[4] Others complain that they cannot simultaneously be faithful party leaders and serve the nation impartially.

What, at least in theory, are the obligations of a president as a party leader? These of course differ, depending on one's conception of the presidency and the party system. The textbook model has generally held that the president should promote party platforms, reward party loyalists, punish party mavericks, run proudly with the party ticket, and heed the interests and advice of party leaders. The president—at least in theory—should be a party builder and strengthen the party ranks by communicating the party's purposes and positions. Presidents, it is believed, should be as much the product of their parties as their leader. It should be a two-way street, with parties serving to check ambition and to ensure accountable leadership. A president would be expected to consult regularly with local, state, and national party committee officials.

Presidential practice is distinctly different. Few of our recent presidents have spent much time working with party officials save as it was absolutely necessary for their renomination. Most presidents of late have mistreated their national party committees. David Broder wrote, for example, that Lyndon Johnson acted as though party obligations and partisanship was the enemy, not the servant, of responsible government.

> He [Johnson] did not see political parties as necessary vehicles for communicating the often inchoate preferences of the voters to those in power. Nor did he see the parties as instruments for disciplining the whims of the elected leaders and holding them accountable for their actions. Instead, he saw them as unwanted intruders on the process of consensus government.[5]

The Nixon presidency in many ways was the ultimate in presidential hostility toward its own party. Nixon dumped Republican Party Chairman Ray Bliss, who was widely acknowledged as a brilliant party builder. Nixon time and again sought to divorce himself from the Republican label and from supporting Republican candidates. Nixon regularly ignored Republican Party officials and set a similar tone for his White House staff. Once, when National Chairman Robert Dole had been trying for some time to see the president, a White House aide is alleged to have said to Dole in an obvious put-down: "If you still want to see the President, turn on your television set tonight at 7:00. The President will be on then." Nixon yearned to be above partisan responsibilities. He yearned to be a bipartisan foreign policy leader. Accordingly, Nixon's definition of presidential leadership was that a president is there to make global decisions that no one else can make. He also felt that party officials do not know enough to clarify foreign policy issues, not to mention to make foreign policy decisions. Thus, Nixon would be the peacemaker, the statesman, the globe-trotting diplomat.

But when a president strives to be above party, critics say, what often results is that he and his aides grow dependent on more secretive and covert political operations. The campaign abuses of 1972 are the result. A president who divorces himself from his party does so at the risk of becoming a prisoner of his own whims. A partyless presidency is potentially an arbitrary one, one which may be too much in the business of self-promotion at the expense of party and public interests. Walter Mondale said it well when he wrote:

> A President out of touch with party politics is a President who feels no accountability to the men and women who are close to the realities of political life. Such a President has severed one more essential link in maintaining the sense of perspective vital for the effective functioning of the Presidential office and the achievement of restraint on arbitrary Presidential action.[6]

LIMITS ON PRESIDENTIAL PARTY LEADERSHIP

Once in office, presidents often bend over backward in an attempt to minimize the partisan appearance of their actions. This is so in part because the public yearns for a "statesman" in the White House, for a president who is above politics. A president is not supposed to act with his eye on the next election; he is not supposed to favor any particular group or party.

Herein lies one of the major paradoxes of the presidency.[7] On the one hand, a president is expected to be a pure and neutral public servant, avoiding political and party considerations. On the other hand, he is supposed to lead his party, help cooperative members of Congress get reelected, and work closely with party leaders. Also, he must build political coalitions and drum up support, including party support, for what he feels need to be done.

To take the president out of partisan politics, however, is to assume incorrectly that a president will be so generally right and the leaders and rank and file of his party so generally wrong that a president must be protected from the push and shove of political pressures. But what president has always been right? Having a president constrained and informed by party platforms and party leaders is what was intended when our party system developed.[8] How often this was actually done is difficult to estimate.

If past is prologue, future presidents will more often than not shun the image of party leader. In an era of weaker party identification and rising independents, it is inevitable that presidents will strive to be impartial officeholders. This may be why so many of our recent presidents have appointed a few cabinet members from the opposition party. John Kennedy appointed Republicans Robert McNamara and Douglas Dillon to two vital cabinet posts (defense and treasury). Johnson chose John W. Gardner to head up the Department of Health, Education and Welfare, the cornerstone agency for his Great Society. Presidents of both the major parties relied on Henry Kissinger, James Schlesinger, Elliot Richardson, and Daniel P. Moynihan.

Another profound influence which limits the modern president as party leader is the fact that he must now communicate to citizens by television. Television is the main source of information for the citizen. Television is also a major weapon in the arsenal of presidential leadership. But it is also one that apparently forces a president to bypass party structures. The nonpartisan direct television appeal has replaced the party rally. As a result, the party has lost one of its main functions—namely, being a source of information and communication between citizens and their government.

Presidents know that appeals to party on television addresses are not politically wise. Presidents are instructed by their pollsters and marketing managers to rely on popular appeal and encourage popular leadership rather than party leadership. Party organization thereby becomes subordinate. Time and again, a personalized entrepreneurial politics emphasizing the president triumphs over a politics emphasizing party purposes and party issues.

Television has also provided a means for third-party and extraparty interests to communicate their views to the public and bypass traditional party structures. George Wallace, John Lindsay, and Independent James Longley of Maine all were beneficiaries of the availability of television time. News coverage of the Ralph Naders has helped to promote yet other alternatives to the party process.

Another more subtle factor in lessening the role presidents play in party activities lies in the fact that for at least a generation now, ours has been a candidate-financed election system, not a party-financed system. A few states are an exception to this pattern—states such as Wisconsin. Most of the time, most candidates raise their own funds and organize their own staffs and campaign committees. Generally speaking, the ablest organizers, campaigners, and media consultants have worked for candidates— candidates for the presidency, candidates for Congress, and so on. As the parties have grown weaker and as candidate-based organizations have become the routine, people who have remained as workers with party organizations are often less talented—or so at least is the perception of many people now involved in elective politics. The most talented campaign people now are usually in the White House or in Congress, either in office or in staff positions. So much is this the case that elected officeholders and their staffs often do not take "the party people" very seriously.

Such a view has generally been present in the White House. Take the Carter presidency. The Democratic National Committee staff is controlled by the White House staff. They take their instructions from Hamilton Jordan and Tim Kraft, two of the people who masterminded the Jimmy Carter primary victories in 1976. Neither Jordan or Kraft were party professionals or party leaders. On the contrary, they were candidate loyalists who proved themselves and won their reputations as candidate promoters.

Not surprisingly, these candidate-oriented professionals look down on party officials and, especially, party staffers. What have they ever won? This may not be as it should be, but it is the way attitudes get formed in the world of the practioners.

Every recent White House has had an aide—usually a senior aide— assigned the function of liaison with the national committee staff of the president's party. Such persons (Kenneth O'Donnell for Kennedy, Marvin Watson for Johnson, and Tim Kraft for Carter) meet with the chairperson of the national committee, arrange for an occasional presidential visit to state and national party fund-raising functions, and host visits from visiting party delegations. Sometimes, for example, a state party chairperson or even a state party committee will be invited to the White House for staff briefings and perhaps even a lunch with the president. This liaison aide will also oversee sensitive party patronage decisions and handle suggestions and complaints coming from national committee members and state chairpersons.

But the work of this White House aide has been overshadowed by the gradual development in the contemporary White House of an office of interest group liaison. With a notable institutionalization in the Nixon White House, this staff (sometimes numbering as high as 15 or more staffers) has sought an outreach to ethnic, professional, labor, business, religious, and every conceivable citizen interest organization. Aides such as William Baroody, Jr. (Nixon and Ford) and Midge Costanza and Anne Wexler (Carter) have pioneered this effort of working directly with groups that once enjoyed their access to politics primarily through the political parties. These aides bring delegations of these interest group leaders to the White House for briefings. They provide an opportunity for these interest groups to bring their views and grievances directly to top White House aides. In addition, these White House aides try to provide information and inside know-how to these group leaders, with the hope they will back the president's programs in Congress and try to get their organization to support the president. It is estimated that the Carter interest group liaison operation worked with as many as 800 groups and organizations by 1979. Groups and officials that once may have worked through party leaders (or bosses) now are organized on a national scale and often as not have a lobbying office in Washington ready and willing to deal directly with White House aides and cabinet officials. Mayors, governors, county executives, labor leaders, ethnic group advocates, and so on—they no longer need or want to go through the party bosses to be heard. Plainly, this direct access and direct consultation operation has removed yet another function that party officials often believed was theirs.

Presidents in recent years have also believed, rightly or wrongly, that many of the toughest problems they face are policy controversies that defy party clarification or traditional party problem-solving approaches. These presidents develop the view that many of the great issues of the day require study by blue ribbon bipartisan presidential advisory commissions or by White House task forces. In order to get a prominent elder statesman or top professional of some standing to accept the chairpersonship of such a commission, a president usually has to promise that partisanship will play no role in the selection of personnel for such commissions. Time and again, the reliance on these presidential advisory system mechanisms have further minimized the role that party organizations have played as agenda setters and problem definers, not to mention as problem solvers.[9] A similar problem faces a president when he tries to recruit significant well-known individuals to serve as cabinet officers. One of the first things such persons often ask is: "Can I have a free hand in selecting my deputies and top aides in this department?" It is as if they are saying the concerns of this department have outgrown party definition. They will often say as well that if they take the job, they will be seeking nonpartisan answers and will need nonpartisan or bipartisan support. In effect, they are also saying: Don't visit on me any party hacks or former campaign advance men or defeated party officeholders!

In sum, these are several, but by no means all, of the limits that make it difficult for a president to aggressively serve as a party leader. I have not bothered to elaborate on the well-worn observation that our parties become truly national only for the purposes of electing a president and organizing the national legislative. Although the national committees and the national government now enjoy greater influence in the conduct of presidential primaries, they still have exceedingly little influence over our decentralized party structure between elections.[10] Hence, a president's practical influence over his party is sharply limited. His power as party leader comes to end when he needs it most. He is virtually unable to recruit party candidates for Congress or other offices and has little or no influence in the selection of state and local party officials. His once vast influence over patronage appointments is now considerably circumscribed. Presidents and cabinet members must weigh patronage claims of the party against their own need for expertise and talented assistance. Patronage has its limits. President after president is amazed at the ingratitude of those who have been on the receiving end (and, of course, for every one person who wins a position, or a lucrative contract, or some other presidential favor, there are several more who felt they should have won it instead).

PRESIDENTS AND USE OF PARTY APPEAL IN CONGRESS

Presidential control of party supporters in Congress has seldom been great. "Party indiscipline" writes Schlesinger, "far from being a novelty of our fallen times, is one of the conditions that American democracy has endured from the start."[11] Of course, the situation varies from time to time. But President Carter assuredly experienced a lack of party discipline or party cohesion among the Democrats in Congress. In the late 1970s, he found members of his own party were strong-minded and independent. Many of the Democrats who were elected in the 1972 and 1974 elections came from previously Republican districts, and they acted, not surprisingly, as if they owed the primary allegiance to the views of the district or state constituencies rather than to party platforms or to the White House.

Carter found that appeals to party were of marginal benefit, as he increasingly found he needed Republican votes as well to secure most of his victories. Cater said it well several years ago when he noted that "a President, Democrat or Republican, finds himself measuring Congress in terms of the coalitions for him and against him on specific issues. His task of building a winning coalition provides a constant temptation to devise means of persuasion other than appeals to party loyalty.[12] This was a pre-Vietnam, pre-Watergate observation that would appear to be even more valid today. One effect of Vietnam and Watergate has been an enhanced public cynicism toward our presidents. Johnson, Nixon, Ford, and Carter have been unpopular presidents, widely distrusted and often lacking public approval of their performances—especially as their terms have worn on.

When presidents such as the recent ones fall in the polls, their ability as party leaders in the Washington community withers. A sag in the president's popularity worries members of Congress of his party, for they fear his standing may make them more vulnerable to opposition attacks back home. A senior political aide to Carter put the matter in useful perspective:

> When the President is low in public opinion polls, the Members of Congress see little hazard in bucking him. . . . After all, very few Congressmen examine an issue solely on its merits; they are politicians and they think politically. I'm not saying they make only politically expedient choices. But they read the polls and from that they feel secure in turning their back on the President with political impunity. Unquestionably, the success of the President's policies bear a tremendous relationship to his popularity in the polls.[13]

Presidential attempts to unseat or purge disloyal members of Congress in his own party have not worked. Roosevelt's celebrated "purge" of nonsupportive Democrats in the congressional elections of 1938 was mainly in vain. Anti–New Deal Democrats won reelection or election for the first time in most of the places where he tried to wield his influence.

Presidential coattails, once thought to be a significant factor in helping to elect members of a president's party to Congress, have had little effect in recent years. Recent research studies indicate that there are fewer competitive congressional districts. Members get reelected because of the quality of their constituency services and the fact that they can take advantage of incumbency—not on whether or not they have worked cooperatively with the White House. Congressional races are not notably affected by national issues or national trends anymore. Time and again, presidents have found in midterm congressional elections that they can do little to help members of their own party who are in trouble. Ford campaigned vigorously in 1974 for dozens of members of Congress only to see most of them defeated. Carter experienced similar disappointments in 1978, especially in Senate races.

Presidents today have little retaliatory leverage to apply against un-cooperative legislators. Members of Congress, as a result of various congressional reforms, have more and more resources (trips home, larger staffs, more research facilities, more home offices and office staffs in their districts, and so forth) to help themselves win reelection. With the dramatic growth of government programs and governmental regulation, members of Congress are in a good position to make themselves nearly indispensable to local officials and local businessmen, who need to have a Washington "friend" to cut through the red tape and expedite government contracts or short circuit some federal regulation. These kinds of developments have enhanced reelection chances for most members while, at the same time, making them less dependent on the White House and less fearful of any penalty for ignoring presidential party appeals: Fiorina, a student of congressional elections, sums up these developments as follows:

> As late as 1958, congressional votes could be characterized as over-whelmingly party-line votes. Consequently, they were broadly reflective of the general policy differences which divided the parties. As the federal role has expanded, however, and federal programs have come to touch the lives of countless citizens, the relationship of a congressman to his constituency has changed. Increasingly, congressmen are elected as individuals, not as members of a party, and increasingly they are elected as nonpartisan, nonideological providers of constituency services.[14]

Note too that many members in Congress today are the product of "movement" or "new politics" experiences. Many of them had to buck local party establishments to win election in the first place. In this age of television and direct mail campaigns, candidates for Congress have often run virtually as independents or as outsiders. Their loyalty to party is thin to begin with. Their base back home is much more tied to professional, business, new politics, or consumer interest groups than to old-line political party opera-tives. Moreover, they have often built their own personal organization rather than tried to infuse new life into local party organizations. Often, the local party apparatus is moribund anyway.

From the president's vantage point, it is seldom helpful to punish party mavericks. In this reformed Congress, with power more dispersed and decentralized and where nearly everyone has a piece of the action, there is just too much risk for a president to single out a few party "disloyalists" for retribution. White House congressional relations aides know all too well that it is best to abide by the motto of "no permanent allies, no permanent enemies." You may lose someone on a vote today, but his or her vote may be crucial on some other measure next week. Then, too, a president has fewer patronage plums or perquisites these days with which to persuade a wavering member of Congress. More and more patronage jobs of the past are now civil service positions or are selected on the basis of merit. More and more governmental contracts or so-called pork barrel expenditures come under close congressional or press scrutiny or are subject to some funding formula.

In short, a president's appeal to his fellow party members in Congress is effective only some of the time. It sometimes will help, but this kind of appeal is more unpredictable today than in the past. Party caucuses may be a bit stronger in Congress, but legislators know that neither the White House nor fellow members in Congress will penalize them if they can claim that "district necessities" forced them to differ with the party on a certain vote—even a key vote. Regional differences in Congress these days are sharper than they have been in the recent past, and these, too, have increased party fragmentation. Presidents doubtless will contrive to encourage party cohesion, but just as clearly, party support will vary on the kinds of measures the president is asking them to support and on whether or not parties continue to lose importance in national political life.

PROPOSALS TO INCREASE COHESION
BETWEEN PRESIDENT AND PARTY

Thus it is claimed our national parties are fast becoming an endangered species. With this development have come proposals that might revitalize the parties and might help them recapture some of their historic mediating and moderating influence in U.S. political life.

Readers should be warned that most Americans could not care less. As earlier chapters have explained, most Americans are indifferent—at best—to the purposes of our parties. Moreover, even some informed observers say they do not know whether there is much realism in trying to resuscitate the parties. Critics of party renewal efforts sometimes contend there is too much nostalgia for a romanticized two-party system that seldom or never really was.

Still, rethinking public policy toward the parties is much needed. In the campaign to revive and protect them, the following are the measures, at least bearing upon the presidency, one hears most often. I will now examine some of the pro's and con's.

Many proponents of party renewal (including some contributors to this volume) propose that federal funding of presidential elections should be abolished or at least significant portions of this public financing should be channeled through the parties. They say federal funding bypasses parties too much and encourages autonomous, entreprenurial political adventurers who are unaccountable to anyone. Campaign funds, these proponents argue, should go to the party organization. Party regulars or party establishments would then have some control and, thereby, more of a function. Candidates would have to demonstrate their loyalty and their willingness to run with the ticket and on the platform as a quid pro quo of getting adequate financial help. This would presumably tie a candidate, and perhaps later the officeholder, to a closer relationship to the national committee. Moreover, it is pointed out by veteran observers that the two national committees already have experienced accounting offices and these staffs could help reduce the staff work, start-up costs, and probable errors of a newly formed candidate organization. Campaign financing legislation encourages separate candidate committees to be set up to receive and account for public funds, at least in primary elections.[15] If candidates trusted their national committees and national committee staffs, the funds could—at least in theory— come through these party officers to the candidates (this could be done at both the primary and general election stage).

However, the fact is that the abuses of our previous system of private financing to candidates had to be remedied. The system we have had for a long time has been predominantly a candidate-financed system, vividly illustrated by this description from the late U.S. Senator Hubert Humphrey:

> Campaign financing [talking about the pre-1974 system] is a curse. It's the most disgusting, demeaning, disenchanting, debilitating experience of a politican's life. It's stinky, it's lousy. I just can't tell you how much I hate it. I've had to break off in the middle of trying to make a decent, honorable campaign and go up to somebody's parlor or to a room and say, "gentlemen, and ladies, I'm desperate. You've got to help me." . . .
>
> And you see people there—a lot of them you don't want to see. And they look at you, and you sit there and you talk to them and tell them what you're for and you need help and, out of the twenty-five who have gathered, four will contribute. And most likely one of them is in trouble and is somebody you shouldn't have had a contribution from.[16]

In response to these kinds of situations and the Watergate revelations, Congress passed the Campaign Reform Act of 1974. This is not the place to outline that act. But it is true that it reaffirmed a primarily candidate-oriented public finance system. It substituted in effect a publicly financed candidate system for a privately financed candidate system. National party committees receive some public funds ($2 million each in 1976, about $3 billion in 1980) for running the quadrennial national conventions.

Why did this campaign finance reform ignore and bypass the parties? Most members of Congress apparently just did not want to strengthen party committees. Members of Congress have little interest in giving party officials more power over who gets money in national elections. Congress obviously was thinking of itself as well. If public financing is extended to congressional campaigns, a likely development at some future point, the last thing a member wants is to have to submit to local and state party officials for campaign funds. As things stand now, the candidate raises his or her own funds. It is a highly individualistic arrangement, and few members of Congress will entrust so important a career lifeblood factor to party bosses. Especially is this the case with officeholders who had to buck the party to get elected merely a few years ago. Further, in their weakened state, party machinery sometimes get taken over by extremist factions. Take the Massachusetts Republican Committee. Its officers in recent years have been rightish issue-oriented extremists. Yet the Republican officeholders (Edward Brooke, Silvio Conte, Margaret Heckler, and so forth) have been moderates. Why would these officials support funds to be given to the party state committee? For similar reasons Senator Robert Kennedy helped lead a fight against public funds going to the national committees in 1967. He hardly wanted a Johnson-dominated Democratic National Committee to control funds for the 1968 elections.

If public funds are made available to the national committees, it will probably be done through indirect side payments of some kind or another. Thus, Congress in 1979 approved a lower postal rate for parties to use in fund-raising efforts. Another subsidy, which would make sense, is the provision of free television time to national party committees to present their views and purposes to the American people. Modest assistance of this kind may help to prop up the major parties. Too much funding of the parties, however, might cement into permanence the present parties at the expense of some future party that would be deserving of a chance to catch on.

A second general proposal to enhance cohesion between presidents and their parties calls for giving more power to party regulars. One variation calls for holding fewer direct primaries on the grounds that party conventions or party caucuses would allow party loyalists to have more of a say in the presidential nominating process. (I remain unconvinced, however, that a return to the smoke-filled room technique for candidate nominations will measurably strengthen our parties.) Another variation of this proposal urges an automatic seating of state party chairpersons and elected party officeholders—such as governors and U.S. senators—at the national convention. The reasoning here is that these kinds of persons have long-standing commitments to the preservation of the party and have a stake in the future of the party—not just in who the candidate will be this time. It is felt that these party professionals know better how to bring desperate factions together and how to compromise on explosive issues that might divide the party.

Yet another proposal calls for regular party midterm conventions. Actually, this is not all that new an idea. Both parties have experimented with policy councils and midterm conferences of one kind or another for several decades. However, these are usually favored by the out-of-office party. Issue-oriented party participants not now holding office favor these as occasions when the party can take stock of how it is doing on its old agenda of issues. It can also provide, they claim, a forum to adopt new positions and reaffirm the party platform commitments of two years earlier.

Critics of these miniconventions, as they are sometimes called, say they invite too much party divisiveness in full public view. The Democrats in recent years have held two formal midterm conference—one in Kansas City in late 1974 and a second in Memphis in late 1978. At the simplest level, these conferences strike many people as public entertainments—part sporting events and part theater. Will the liberals condemn the moderates? Will a Ted Kennedy upstage the president? To what extent can a president turn it into a party and personal rally? Media attention focuses, predictably, on who wins and who loses, as well as upon mavericks, who often get more attention than they probably deserve. Still, an incumbent president who comes to listen and learn as he meets for a few days with several thousand party regulars and activists is a president who avoids that great temptation for presidents—to become isolated. Further, he gets a chance to see and hear the intensity of concern over contemporary issues. He must hear also about whether or not he is handling the job of president in an appropriate manner. There is much to be said for this midterm party audit—an audit of the president, as well of party policy positions. These party midterm conferences are to be encouraged. They deserve to be continued and refined.

Be aware, however, that members of Congress (and many state legislators and statewide officeholders) often view these midterm gatherings with a lukewarm to opposed stance. There are two reasons for this. First, it can complicate congressional elections (especially if the conventions are held before early November), by raising issues that a legislator would rather not run on or have to take a side on. Second, the platform or policy clarification role to some extent competes with, and even threatens, the responsibilities of the congressional party caucuses. Members of Congress, moreover, believe they are in a much better position—as elected officeholders and as members of congressional committees with extensive staffs—to formulate policy positions than are party delegates to the party's midterm convention.[17]

PROSPECTS

One of the many reasons politicians rely on the media rather than the party organization is that the media route is easier. Keeping a party organization intact or rebuilding a political party in a community is an exacting undertaking. We need to have a better understanding of why this is and why there appear to be patterns of party organization and practices of local parties that apparently ensure decay. Could it be otherwise? Might different practices or different incentives help overcome the ruts and the rot?

There have been some healthy signs in the 1970s. The party caucuses and party conferences in Congress have shown more signs of life. Indeed, the Democratic Party caucus in the House of Representatives in the mid-1970s was instrumental in revitalizing that institution.[18] Party caucuses were the instrument used to help modernize and democratize the House of Representatives. The party caucus was also a place, at least for awhile, to discuss party commitments and adapt old commitments to new policy problems.

Then, too, there is a growing appreciation that parties need to be preserved: they need to be made constructive and a vital part of the political process. Those who are aware of the chaos and paralysis produced by thousands of new interest groups, each having an impact directly on the government in narrow public policy areas, long for almost any instrument that might prevent direct parochial impact and encourage intermediary processes of trade-off, mediation, and so forth. Stronger parties would obviously help here.

Party organizations may simply be no longer effective in many of those traditional functions, but parties are definitely worth saving. They help to give the electorate reasonable choices at the election booth. They can provide a forum for candidates of somewhat common perspectives to agree on broad purposes. They certainly will continue to be important in organizing the legislative branch. Perhaps, too, they sometimes will formulate strategies that can help us overcome some of our toughest economic policy questions.

Perhaps most important to the preservation of parties is a commitment to avoid further weakening of them. Direct popular election of the president (as a substitute for the Electoral College) ought not to be considered. Fortunately, a move to do this was defeated in the U.S. Senate in midsummer 1979. To move to the direct election plan would encourage splinter and single-issue parties and further weaken our major parties.[19] Similarly, a national primary might be a severe blow to our party system. Political scientist Austin Ranney views the national primary proposal with alarm, saying it not only would greatly weaken state parties but it would mean "a virtual end to the national parties as anything more than passive arenas for contests between entrepreneurial candidate organizations."[20]

Can parties as institutions be made to serve as a more effective check on presidents? This might be desirable, but again, the weakened condition of the parties and the history of party fragmentation and lack of discipline suggests that the prospects are not inviting. One should not overlook, however, the role that party officials and party stalwarts have played in checking and balancing presidents of their party. Johnson was forced to quit his 1968 bid less by Eugene McCarthy's insurgency than when Robert Kennedy and party regulars in Wisconsin and elsewhere made it clear he was unacceptable to broad segments within the Democratic Party. So, also, Nixon was forced to resign when it was clear the stalwarts in his own party—men like Goldwater, Hugh Scott, and others—could no longer support him. Carter sometimes found himself checked by party regulars who viewed him as less responsive to their party platform than they were willing to accept.

Parties need to be protected and preserved even if they are not likely to be much strengthened. Presidents in the future, as in the past, will find party leadership a necessary yet exacting task. The incentive is to ignore the party. A six-year nonrenewable presidential term would encourage that tendency and for that reason should not be approved. The four-year term with the necessity of renomination at least ensures that most presidents in the first term will recognize the importance of the party to their political survival. A political party should retain the threat of dumping a president who has turned his back on his party's pledges or has ignored the party platform. We shall have some presidents in the tradition of the Jacksons, Wilsons, and Roosevelts who will serve as party leaders—but just as likely, we will have presidents in the Eisenhower mold, who eschew party responsibilities.

We really have not had a president in recent decades who has gone the extra mile and tried to be a party leader. The incentive system may seem stacked against it, but the counterintuitive strategy might just pay some surprising dividends. Thus, former cabinet member and citizens movement leader John W. Gardner can say:

> As a mobilizer of some experience, I can't help but wonder whether a President strong enough and imaginative enough to rebuild his party aggressively might not get an interesting payoff. Someone spoke the other day of "the fashionable wave of grassroots participation," as though it would pass rather quickly. I don't see it that way. There was a wave in the 1960s, followed by a wholly different wave in the 70s—and I anticipate others to come. The feeling for grassroots participation will be, I think, a dependable part of our future. If I were a President looking for a means of moving a nation in disarray—and wondering, as every modern President must wonder, whether it is even possible—I would not neglect the possibility of turning my party into an instrument of mobilization. I know all the realities that make it an impossible dream—but I'd sure as hell try it.[21]

That is a pretty supportive statement from a widely respected *nonpartisan* leader—and that is the turnaround sentiment that will have to spread as a precondition for taking parties seriously. Parties will doubtless endure, but in the future as in the past, they will serve us in direct proportion to our taking them seriously and our willingness to make them work.

NOTES

1. Robert V. Remini, "The Emergence of Political Parties and Their Effect on the Presidency" in *Power and The Presidency*, ed. Philip C. Dolce and George H. Skau (New York: Scribners, 1976), p. 32.

2. Ibid., p. 33. See also Robert Remini, *Martin Van Buren and the Democratic Party* (New York: Columbia University Press, 1959).

3. Quoted in Arthur B. Tourtellot, *The Presidents on the Presidency* (New York: Doubleday, 1964), p. 387.

4. Ibid., p. 5.

5. David Broder, *The Party's Over* (New York: Harper & Row, 1977), pp. 76–77. Related evidence of presidential manipulation and failure to engage in party-building or even party-heeding activity is found in Donald Allen Robinson, "Presidents and Party Leadership: An Analysis of Relations Between Presidents, Presidential Candidates, and Their Parties' National Committee Headquarters since 1952" (Paper delivered at the Annual Meeting of the American Political Science Association, Chicago, Illinois, September 1974). The reader may also want to consult the now dated but historically useful study of national party committees and their functions: Cornelius P. Cotter and Bernard C. Hennessy, *Politics Without Power: The National Party Committees* (New York: Atherton Press, 1964).

6. Walter F. Mondale, "The President and the Parties: In Need of Revival," *Democratic Review* (October/November 1975): 93. See also, Walter F. Mondale, *The Accountability of Power* (New York: McKay, 1975).

7. I have discussed the paradoxes of the presidency at length in my *The State of the Presidency*, 2d ed. (Boston: Little, Brown, 1980), pp. 322.

8. See James W. Ceasar, *Presidential Selection: Theory and Practice* (Princeton, N.J.: Princeton University Press, 1979).

9. A description of the rise of presidential advisory groups is provided in Thomas E. Cronin and Sanford Greenberg, eds., *The Presidential Advisory System* (New York: Harper & Row, 1969).

10. On this nationalizing trend, see Austin Ranney, *The Federalization of Presidential Primaries* (Washington, D.C.: American Enterprise Institute, 1978).

11. Arthur Schlesinger, Jr., "Crisis of the Party System, I," *Wall Street Journal* May 10, 1979, editorial page.

12. Douglass Cater, *Power In Washington* (New York: Vintage, 1964) p. 192.

13. Quoted in Dom Bonafede, "The Strained Relationship," *National Journal* (May 19, 1979): 830.

14. Morris P. Fiorina, "The Incumbency Factor," in *Public Opinion* (September/October 1978): 42. See also Morris P. Fiorina, *Congress: Keystone of the Washington Establishment* (New Haven, Conn.: Yale University Press, 1977).

15. See Gerald Ford's response to this problem in his memoir, *A Time to Heal* (New York: Harper & Row/Reader's Digest, 1979), p. 295.

16. Quoted in "How It Was for Mr. Humphrey," New York *Times*, October 13, 1974, p. E18.

17. I want to thank political scientist John Kessel for reminding me about this reality.

18. See Norman J. Ornstein, "The Democrats Reform Power in the House of Representatives, 1969–75," in *America in the Seventies*, ed. Allan P. Sindler (Boston: Little, Brown, 1977), pp. 1–48.

19. For a more modest reform of the electoral college that blends the best of these two plans, see Thomas E. Cronin, "Choosing A President," *The Center Magazine* xi:5 (September/ October 1978), and Thomas E. Cronin, "The Direct Vote and The Case for Meshing Things Up!" *Presidential Studies Quarterly* ix:2 (Spring 1979): 144–62.

20. Austin Ranney, *The Federalization of Presidential Primaries* (Washington, D.C.: American Enterprise Institute, 1978), p. 39.

21. John W. Gardner in personal communication to author, August 1, 1979.

12

PARTY RENEWAL: THE NEED FOR INTELLECTUAL LEADERSHIP

James MacGregor Burns

*F*or a century and a half, Americans have lived under two constitutions. One is the Constitution of the United States—the constitution that sits under glass in the National Archives, adorns the appendices of textbooks in American government, and serves as the court of last appeal for oratorical gladiators in the Senate and jurisprudential gladiators before the High Bench. The other—a collection of party rules and traditions, legislative enactments, popular practices, and understandings—has no name. It cannot be found in the National Archives or any other central place. It is rarely the subject of lofty oratory or final appeal. But both the formal and the informal charters are constitutions in that they define authority, allot power, regulate political behavior, regularize procedures, and affect public policy.

Contrasts between the two constitutions are sharp and vivid. The formal Constitution, struck off in a few months in one place by a few dozen men, was soon ratified in a dozen states by state conventions meeting for a few weeks. The party constitution was worked out by many thousands of men (and, lamentably, few women) in many scores of states, counties, and localities over a period of about 50 years. The first was deeply rooted in centuries of intense moral, political, and legal thought in Europe and America; the second had impoverished intellectual roots. One represented a central, strategic idea—an idea with the intellectual credentials of a Locke, a Montesquieu, and countless other philosophical giants—carefully applied to the needs and aspirations of a young republic. The other was shaped, without central plan or purpose, in a series of local, state, and national political situations, often for limited, parochial objectives. The Constitution was conceived and dedicated by the most illustrious and respectable leaders—men like Washington and Madison within the Philadelphia Convention, Adams and Jefferson outside of it. The party charter was spawned outside the law, never became quite respectable, (as McWilliams suggests, and hence, as a constitution, was born a bastard and grew up an orphan.

The formal Constitution was accepted from the start, and, indeed, became a symbol of unity and soon a mechanism of national unification. The party charter not only was largely unaccepted but was sharply opposed by the established leadership of the new republic, as Pomper and Crotty note. It was significant enough that Washington, Madison, and others simply opposed parties as factious, selfish, turbulent, and divisive. But most of the early leaders opposed or misconceived the essential theory of parties—the theory of majority rule, party rotation in office, party authority, party opposition, party structure, and party distribution of power, in short, of party *system*—that made the party constitution in fact a *constitution*.

As time passed, the formal Constitution and the party constitution melded into each other to some degree. The former broadened out into a cluster of laws, regulations, usages, and understandings; the latter took on some legal authority, legislative authority, and, on occasion, even some respectability. But the central strategies of the two charters remained different, and quite opposed to each other. The strategy of the Constitution was to tame power by granting necessary authority to national officers responsible to conflicting constitutencies and to reserve authority to state and local officers, who also had conflicting constituencies—all with an eye to taming power by fragmenting it. The strategy of the party constitution was to tame power by granting authority to popular majorities, who would be opposed by active minority parties, and subject to popular confirmation or repudiation in regular, open, and fairly conducted elections.

The Constitution had no easy time of it in an industrializing, urbanizing nation wracked by sectionalism and regionalism in a time of heightening feeling over a transcending moral issue. But its intellectual plight was nothing compared with that of the party charter. Once launched on its illegitimate career, the idea of party was attacked not only by the founders, not only by consensual politicians like Monroe, not only by military heroes like Jackson, but even by the most powerful intellectual gun in the U.S. armory, John Calhoun. Half a century later, the most brilliant leadership of the Progressives devised both the theoretical justification and the practical means of demolishing strong parties. More recently, as earlier pages remind us, the media politics of personality further challenged the role and rationale of party.

Yet through most of these years, for at least a century, ordinary men and women, facing the ordinary needs and tasks of a self-governing people, meeting in ordinary places, in noisy taverns and quiet church halls, sometimes in crowded garrets or smoke-filled basements, day after day, year after year, called the meetings, conducted the debates, adopted the party rules, elected the delegates, canvassed the houses, put out the party propaganda, argued the issues, framed the platforms, fought the diabolic party enemy, and put their candidates into mayors' offices, county court-houses, state legislatures and executive offices, the U.S. Senate, House of Representatives, and the presidency. But if the 1787 charter was the product of a "first cadre" of political luminaries, and if that constitution was made to work by a "second cadre," comprised of a host of members of Congress, federal and state judges, state officials, and nationally known publicists, then the job of shaping and establishing the party charter fell to a "third cadre," comprised of grass-roots activists, part-time politicians, and interest group leaders. The names of most of these party builders are as unsung as the framers of the Constitution are celebrated: precinct men like Aaron Burr (celebrated for a very different reason), working out campaign methods in Manhattan in 1800; local politicos, inspired by the ideals of Jefferson's republicanism, helping to develop the first genuinely nationwide political movement; working men's leaders hardly known today outside the pages of the *Dictionary of American Biography*; radical leaders like Frances Wright and Thomas Skidmore; and countless more.

So well did these "unsung and unnamed" activists build their parties that stages were reached—in the 1830s and 1840s, again in the 1880s and 1890s, and perhaps in the 1930s and 1940s—when the party constitution acted as a worthy rival to the formal Constitution, when the party politics of building group and governmental coalitions served as a counterpoise to the constitutional system of separation of powers and checks and balances—when, in short, the party strategy of uniting and dividing people along horizontal lines was balancing the constitutional strategy of dividing them through the separated and competing organs of government. But these periods were relatively brief. And the past half century has been a period of ominous party decline.

It is unnecessary here to recapitulate the nature and symptoms of that decline, so well surveyed in earlier pages. But certain weaknesses stand out. One is psychological and attitudinal—the ebbing of party membership and party identification. Not only does this mean that "quantitatively" the parties lack the opinion and voting support necessary to elect their candidates, yielding place to the politics of media and personality, but that "qualitatively," the parties have ceased to be "home" or "family" or "neighborhood" for millions of voters. They have ceased, as McWilliams points out to foster the emotional and personal bonds, the sense of trust, that link private feeling and community life and sustain public spirit and civic virtue. The much maligned city machines, with their precinct bosses and wardheelers, hardly redistributed income as massively as legend relates;

certainly, they did not hand out *all* those coal sacks and Christmas baskets. However, they provided a sense of home, a feeling of political and community place, to Americans—especially immigrants—who desperately needed it. What politically can substitute for that kind of party in providing this sense of connectedness except temporarily and synthetically joining the followers of some apocalyptic leader?

A second major weakness of the parties is of course organizational, as so many pages of this work attest. Organized and disorganized followings of candidates and officeholders have filled part of the void left by party shrinkage. The portrait Cronin presents of presidents who absolutely dominate the national leadership corps of their parties, hiring and firing national chairpersons at will, is merely the most important example of a phenomenon that exists at every level of party. Bypassing the party organization, candidates campaign on their own, raise their own money, issue their own pronouncements, build their own constituency—and in legislatures and executive offices, go their own way. The whole strategy of the party constitution—the strategy of uniting government—is inverted, as individualistic political organization becomes a means of enhancing fragmentation of authority rather than of unifying it.

But the main weakness of the party constitution, I think, is intellectual. In part, this problem is conceptual, or at least definitional. At times, in describing parties, writers resemble not merely blind men feeling different parts of an elephant but feeling completely different animals. One notes how often the idea of "party reform" is confused with the idea of "party renewal"; as Casey's knowledgeable study of Democratic party reform suggests reform may have great importance in itself without necessarily strengthening party organization or impact. Often, indeed, reform is the enemy of renewal. Then, too, it is hard to agree on the fundamental essence of parties in a democracy, as Robinson contends, when would-be reformers—and one could add, all of us—disagree on the nature of democracy. But beyond this, our intellectual effort in the study of parties is inadequate. By a modest estimate, probably a hundred times more work has been done (including the work of writers for law journals) in analysis and explication of the formal Constitution than in examining and theorizing about the party system. Despite the excellent work of Austin Ranney, David Broder, and many others, including a number of contributors to this volume, we do not have the big, definitive, powerfully theoretical study of the party constitution that we need. We do not have an intellectual bible for party renewal.

What of the future? Happily, the contributors to this volume are not traumatized by their typically gloomy findings on the state of the parties. For one thing, there is flux and innovation in the superstructure of the national and some state parties, whatever the stagnation at the base. The vitality (relatively, at least) of the Minnesota caucus system (described by

Marshall, the bold and comprehensive effort of the Massachusetts Democracy to pull itself up by its own bootstraps, as interpreted by Massachusetts Charter Commission member Jerome Mileur; the recent faltering steps toward revitalizing California parties, as reported by Lawson, after decades of Progressive-inspired party moralization and demoralization; the significant efforts at party renewal in the national organizations the Democrats' commissions and charter building, for example, or the national Republicans' of local party efforts, as depicted by Longley and Bibby, these and other developments suggest that major opportunities for party renewal are opening up even as others are closed.

Whether our parties can be truly revitalized will probably turn on whether renewal can be extended to the typically torpid, poorly led, badly organized, and underfunded state and local sectors of the parties. Clearly, a gargantuan effort would be necessary in both parties. But here, I think, an exciting opportunity opens up—the intensive development of a grass-roots caucus system at the base of the party system.

Such a caucus system must be open enough, participatory enough, and potentially influential enough to satisfy party "reformers." It must be organized well enough, financed amply enough, and structured powerfully enough into the base of the party system as to satisfy both Robinson's *revisionists* and his *neoclassicists*. The task would not be easy, if only because tokenism would meet the needs for neither democratic participation nor organizational efficiency. Thus, an open caucus must not be merely a ritualistic meeting that partisans may attend if they insist but must be a regular set of meetings to which party members are invited, urged, and politely pressured to attend—meetings in which women, elderly persons, blacks, young people, recent immigrants, and poor persons are made especially welcome—meetings in which major controversial issues are debated, positions taken by majority vote, and resolutions passed for transmission to higher party levels and to the press. Similarly, they must be caucuses that send not only resolutions but delegates to higher party conclaves, that supply leadership to the party at every level, that establish a sound and democratic financial base at the grass roots of the party, and that elect and "unelect" members of the next higher echelon of ward, precinct, and town committees.

The caucus system must be the party's answer—indeed, it is the only feasible answer—to that great institutional enemy of parties, the primary system for choosing party nominees. If caucuses will not involve such numbers of voters as primaries tend to do, qualitatively, the caucuses can mobilize sizable numbers of party activists, who would offer a far more informed, thoughtful, and responsible contribution to candidate selecting than is made by the primary voter in a visit of a few minutes to a polling place. If primaries appear to bring a measure of intraparty democracy to nomination politics, the caucuses could supply a far superior kind to democracy, measured by intensive voter participation, thorough canvassing of candidates and issues and careful consideration of the present and potential link between a would-be nominee and the party. If the primaries "opened up" parties (to the point, indeed, of creating a void), the caucus system could help restore a sense of place, of home, of neighborhood, within the parties; could help restore a world of small publics and local polities; could help realize, perhaps, Jefferson's splendid vision of a ward system that, in McWilliams's words, could combine the warm if parochial patriotism of local communities with the broader, more enlightened perspectives of central regimes.

Is such a reform-and-renewal possible? The chances are not good, considering the extent of present party decline and decay, the enormous role of party primaries combined with the electronic politics of personality, and the intellectual confusion that besets the study of politics. Thoughtful students of U.S. parties, whether academics or practitioners, can do little about the main obstacles to party renewal. But they can get on with their main responsibility of trying to bring the qualities of clear definition, historical evidence, comparative analysis, institutional insight, and creative imagination to the study of party possibilities. To that task, the earlier chapters, I believe, make a significant contribution.

INDEX

Adams, John, 177, 195
AFL-CIO, 43, 89–90
aggregation of interests by parties, 5–8, 10, 25–27; by Minnesota caucuses, 141–42
Alger, Horatio, 11
Allswang, John M., 33
American Independent Party, 127
American Political Science Association, Committee on Political Parties, 15, 35–38, 40
Anderson, Wendell, 156–57
Aristotle, 9
Arterton, F. Christopher, 72–73
Atkins, Chester, 169, 172

Bailey, Stephen, 34
Bancroft, George, 58
Baroody, William, Jr., 182
Bartley, David, 164
Baxter, Leone, 122
Beer, Samuel, 20, 21, 25
Bentham, Jeremy, 26, 28
Bibby, John F., 47, 102–14, 198
Bliss, Ray, 107, 179
Bottomore, T. B., 20, 23–24, 26
Brock, Bill, 106, 107–8, 110, 111–12
Broder, David, 179, 197
Brooke, Edward, 170, 188
Brown, Edmund G., Sr., 123
Burr, Aaron, 8, 196
Bush, George, 104

Calhoun, John, 195
California, 116–36, 140; Democratic Council of, 123–24, 131; Democratic Party reforms, 130–33; party renewal in, 128–36; Progressives' reforms in, 117–21;

Republican Assembly, 129; Republicans' County Chairs Associations, 129–30; Republican reforms, 133–36
Campaign for Economic Democracy, 127, 132
Campbell, Tim, 52
Carter, Jimmy, 2, 4, 46, 47, 52, 79, 82, 83, 95, 181–82, 183–84
Casey, Carol F., 14, 197
caucus-convention system of Minnesota, 15, 141–49, 154, 155, 197–98; suggestion for expansion, 198–99
centralization vs. decentralization of parties, 35–36, 38–39, 45–48, 70–85, 114
Chesterton, G. K., 53
Churchill, Winston, 20
civil rights movement, 69–70, 87
class issues, 14–15, 22–23, 26
Coffey, Bert, 131
Common Cause, 27
community aspect of parties, 7–10, 51–65, 148–49, 196–97, 198–99
Connally, John, 134
Constitution of the US, 1–2, 7, 51, 83, 177, 194–96
conventions: affirmative action in delegate selection, 42, 83, 91–94, 96; Democratic, of 1964, 87; of 1968, 41–42, 71, 73, 87–89, 90; of 1972, 72, 74, 87, 89, 91, 92–95; of 1976, 72–73, 87, 93–94, 94–95; of 1980, 89, 94; midterm conventions, 16; 37, 47, 80–81, 82–83, 188–89; proportional representation at, 41–42, 94–96; Republican, of 1968, 73; of 1976, 105; of 1980, 106

Costanza, Midge, 182
Cronin, Thomas E., 197
Crotty, William J., 14, 195

Dahl, Robert, 20
Daley, Richard, 73–74, 91
democracy, role of parties in, 4–15,
    18–28, 194–97; within parties,
    23–24, 39–40, 63, 85, 131–32,
    198–99
Democratic Farmer-Labor Party of
    Minnesota, 141–57
Democratic National Committee, 70–72,
    76–78, 79–80, 87–88, 92, 94, 95,
    103–7, 113–14, 181
Democratic Party Charter, of national
    party, 81–83; in Massachusetts,
    159–74; and affirmative action, 167
demography of parties, 76–78
Dillon, Douglas, 180
Dole, Robert, 179
Donohue, Maurice, 160
Driscoll, Richard, 162, 163, 175
Dukakis, Michael, 161, 170
Dutton, Frederick, 94

Eisenhower, Dwight D., 191
Eldersveld, Samuel, 9, 39
elections, party role in, 7–8, 43, 56–59,
    109–13; in California, 124, 126–28;
    in Minnesota, 149–50
Eller, John, 160
endorsement conventions, 163–65
European parties, 34–35

Fair Political Practices Commission of
    California, 127
Federation of Republican Women, 129
Federalist papers, 1, 32; Party, 1, 4,
    56–57, 177
financing, of parties, 14–15, 37, 79–81,
    108–9, 151, 181, 186–87; of
    Republican National Committee,
    113
Fiorina, Morris P., 185
Flaherty, Charles, 160, 162, 169

Foley, Daniel, 174
Ford, Gerald, 6, 182, 186
Ford, Henry Jones, 34
Frank, Barney, 174
Fraser, Donald, 71, 152, 156

Gardner, John W., 180, 191
Goldwater, Barry, 133, 191
Grossman, Jerome, 161

Halley, Patrick, 162
Hamilton, Alexander, 2, 12
Hayden, Tom, 20, 27, 127, 135
Heckler, Margaret, 188
Herring, E. Pendelton, 25
Hobbes, Thomas, 58
Hofstader, Richard, 56
House Judiciary Committee, 117
Hughes Commission, 88, 92
Hughes, Harold, 88
Humphrey, Hubert, 41–42, 79, 147, 152,
    156, 187

idealist view of parties, 34–38
Independent Republican Party of
    Minnesota, 141–57

Jackson, Andrew, 3, 61, 177–78, 191,
    195
Janda, Kenneth, 35
Jarvis-Gann property tax initiative, 127
Jefferson, Thomas, 2, 4, 8, 55–56, 59, 61,
    64–65, 177, 195, 196, 199
Jewell, Malcolm E., 39
John Birch Society, 133
Johnson, Hiram, 118, 132
Johnson, Lyndon, 4, 8, 90, 97, 179,
    181–82, 184, 188, 191
Jordan, Hamilton, 181

Kariel, Henry, 20, 26
Kennedy, Edward, 189; Kennedy, John
    F., 4, 180, 181; Kennedy, Robert F.,
    41, 79, 188, 191
Key, V. O., Jr., 8, 38
King, Edward, 170
Kissinger, Henry, 180

Kraft, Tim, 181–82
Krzys, Joseph, 160

Lawson, Kay, 198
Libertarian Party, 127
Lincoln, Abraham, 4
Lindsay, John, 181
Local Elections Campaign Division of
    Republican Party, 110–11, 113
local party organization, 22–23, 27,
    41–44, 51, 107–10, 122–23, 130–31;
    in California, 120–21; in
    Massachusetts, 165–68, 198–99; in
    Minnesota, 139–57
Locke, John, 63, 194
Longley, Charles H., 198
Longley, James, 181

Machiavelli, 95
Macpherson, C. B., 20, 23, 26
Madison, James, 1, 5, 8, 12, 32, 55, 58,
    195
Mannheim, Karl, 20
Marshall, Thomas R., 198
Massachusetts, Charter Commission of,
    159–74; Republican Committee,
    188; State Convention of 1979, 15,
    159–74
McCarthy, Eugene, 41–42, 88, 90, 148,
    152, 191
McCarthy, Leo, 131
McGovern, George, 92, 94, 147
McGovern-Fraser Commission, 22, 40,
    42, 45, 71–72, 74, 81, 83, 88–91, 93,
    94, 96–100, 104, 106, 152
McKinley, William, 178
McNamara, Robert, 180
McWilliams, W. Carey, 9, 195, 196, 199
Meany, George, 43
media and politics, 61, 64, 180–81, 189;
    in California, 124
Michels, Robert, 20, 27, 39
Michigan, parties in, 72
Mikulski, Barbara, 72, 89, 91, 93, 95,
    96–97, 98
Mileur, Jerome M., 198
Mill, James, 26

Mill, John Stuart, 22, 26, 28
Minnesota parties and reform, 53,
    139–57
Mississippi Freedom Democratic Party,
    87–89
Mondale, Walter, 156, 179
Monroe, James, 57, 195
Montesquieu, Baron Charles de, 194
Mosca, Gaetano, 20
Moynihan, Daniel P., 180

Nader, Ralph, 181
national party organizations, 69–85;
    demography of, 76–78
New Deal, 36–37, 40
New York parties, 140
nihilist view of parties, 32–34
Nixon, Richard, 4, 8, 79, 81, 105–6, 143,
    152, 157, 179, 184, 191
nominations, party role in, 19, 43, 141,
    150–51, 156

O'Brien, Lawrence F., 92
O'Donnell, Kenneth, 181
O'Hara Commission, 81
Olson, David M., 39
Ostrogorski, M., 26, 33

Pareto, Vilfredo, 20
participation through parties, 9–10,
    21–28, 52–61, 82–84, 98, 122–23,
    142–44, 146–49, 166–68, 198–99
Pateman, Carole, 20, 23, 24
Peace and Freedom Party, 127
Plato, 53, 54, 59
Plunkitt, George Washington, 5, 9,
    60–61
policy, party influence on, 6, 43–44,
    58–61; in California, 126; in
    Minnesota, 145–46
Political Action Committees, 125
Pomper, Gerald M., 32, 84, 195
president, advisors of, and parties,
    182–83; cohesion with parties,
    176–80; influence on elections, 184;
    role in party leadership, 177–83; use
    of party appeal in Congress, 183–86

primaries, 15, 62–64, 118; cross-filing for, in California, 119–20; endorsement for, in Minnesota, 150–51; national primary proposal, 190
Progressive Party, 13
proportional representation, 94–98

radical Republicans, 8
Ranney, Austin, 20, 103, 190, 197
Reagan, Ronald, 124, 127, 134, 135
recruitment by parties, 146–49, 154
reform of parties, in California, 116–36, 140; Jeffersonian reforms, 2, 32–33, 55–61; in Massachusetts, 140, 159–74; in Minnesota, 139–57; modern Democratic Party reforms, 18–19, 40–48, 69–75, 80–83, 87–100; modern Republican reforms, 18–19, 73, 102–14, 133–36; Progressive reforms, 3, 13, 33–34, 61–62, 117–21, 139–41; proposals for renewal, 15–16, 69–85, 107–14, 128–33, 152–53, 189–90, 197–99; renewal's limits, 27, 154–57
Republican Governors' Association, 112
Republican National Committee, 70–71, 77–81, 84, 86, 103–14
Richardson, Elliot, 180
Ripon Society, 75
Robinson, Donald A., 12, 39, 197, 198
Roosevelt, Franklin, 4–5, 20, 184
Rousseau, Jean Jacques, 20
Rule 29 Committee, 104–6

Schattschneider, E. E., 24, 31–32, 34, 35, 38, 63, 64
Schlesinger, Arthur, Jr., 183
Schlesinger, James, 180
Schmitz, John, 134, 135
Schumpeter, Joseph, 20, 22, 28

Shakespeare, William, 9
Sinclair, Upton, 122
Skidmore, Thomas, 196
Smith, Alfred E., 159
Smylie, Robert, 112
Solzynitzhen, Alexander, 6
Soviet Union, Communist Party of, 7
Stassen, Harold, 152
Steiger, William A., 104–5
Stevenson, Adlai, 123, 131
Stokes, Donald, 20
Students for a Democratic Society, 22

Taft, William H., 178
theory and party reform, 18–40, 170–71, 178, 197
Tocqueville, Alexis de, 10, 12, 16, 59

Urban Machine, 8–9, 11, 60–61, 145, 197

values of the US, 3–5, 10–14, 22, 32–34, 51–65, 139–40, 194–96
Van Buren, Martin, 5, 56–61, 65
Vietnam, 8, 37, 41, 69, 87, 123–24, 184

Walker, Jack, 20, 26
Wallace, George, 15, 181
Warren, Earl, 123–24
Washington, George, 1, 4, 32, 194
Watergate, effects on parties, 14, 16, 37, 126, 152, 154, 156, 184
Watson, Marvin, 181
Wexler, Anna, 182
Whitaker, Clem, 122
White, Joseph, 160
Wilson, James Q., 20, 25, 26
Wilson, Woodrow, 34, 191
Winograd, Morley, 72–73, 83, 89, 91, 93–94, 96, 97–99
Wisconsin parties, 140
Wright, Frances, 196

ABOUT THE EDITOR
AND CONTRIBUTORS

GERALD M. POMPER is Chairman and Professor of Political Science at Rutgers University, author most recently of *The Election of 1976* and *Elections in America*, and Director of the Center on Political Parties at the Eagleton Institute of Politics.

JOHN F. BIBBY is Professor of Political Science at the University of Wisconsin–Milwaukee, author of *On Capitol Hill*, and a principal investigator of a National Science Foundation study of state political parties.

JAMES MacGREGOR BURNS is Woodrow Wilson Professor of Government at Williams College, winner of the National Book Award and Pulitzer Prize for his biographies of Franklin D. Roosevelt, and author most recently of *Leadership*.

CAROL F. CASEY is Head of the Political Institutions and Process Section of the Congressional Research Service, U.S. Library of Congress, and former researcher for the Mikulski and McGovern-Fraser commissions of the Democratic Party.

THOMAS E. CRONIN is Professor of Political Science at the University of Delaware, author of *The State of the Presidency*, and member of the Twentieth Century Fund's task force on electoral reform.

WILLIAM J. CROTTY is Professor of Political Science at Northwestern University and author, most recently, of *Political Reform and The American Experiment* and *Decision for the Democrats*.

KAY LAWSON is Professor of Political Science at San Francisco State University and author of *Political Parties and Democracy in the United States* and *The Comparative Study of Political Parties*.

CHARLES H. LONGLEY is Associate Professor of Political Science at Bucknell University, a former candidate for national convention delegate, and author of chapters in *Paths to Political Reform* and *The Party Symbol*.

THOMAS R. MARSHALL is Assistant Professor of Political Science at the University of Texas–Arlington and author of articles in *Politics in Minnesota* and the *American Journal of Political Science*.

WILSON CAREY McWILLIAMS is Distinguished Professor of Political Science at Rutgers University, author of *The Idea of Fraternity in America*, and recipient of a grant on religion and politics from The National Endowment for the Humanities.

JEROME M. MILEUR is Associate Professor of Political Science at the

University of Massachusetts–Amherst, author of *Campaigning for the Massachusetts Senate* and *Liberal Tradition in Crisis*, and a member of the state Democratic Party's Charter Commission.

DONALD A. ROBINSON is Professor of Government and Director of American Studies at Smith College, author of *Slavery in the Structure of American Politics*, and Chairman of the Northampton (Massachusetts) Democratic City Committee.